VIETNAM SHADOWS

WITHDRAWN

THE AMERICAN MOMENT
Stanley I. Kutler, Series Editor

Arnold R. Isaacs

VIETNAM SHADOWS

*The War, Its Ghosts,
and Its Legacy*

THE JOHNS HOPKINS UNIVERSITY PRESS
Baltimore & London

Johns Hopkins Paperbacks edition, 2000
9 8 7 6 5 4 3 2 1

The Johns Hopkins University Press
2715 North Charles Street
Baltimore, Maryland 21218-4363
www.press.jhu.edu

Library of Congress Cataloging-in-Publication Data will be found at the end of this
book.
A catalog record for this book is available from the British Library.

ISBN 0-8018-6344-9

For Kathy

CONTENTS

PREFACE

It has been over for a generation, and the Cold War world that shaped U.S. policy has itself passed into history, but the Vietnam War still casts long shadows over American life. It lingers in the national memory, hovering over our politics, our culture, and our long, unfinished debate over who we are and what we believe. This book attempts to describe the aftermath of the war and its lingering legacies in various areas of American life, politics, and society. It focuses, in turn, on the veterans; on the social, cultural, and political rifts in what is called the "Vietnam generation"; on the war's remarkably long-lasting impact on U.S. foreign and military policy; on the metaphorical myth of the missing-in-action (we lost something in Vietnam, and we want it back!); on the difficulties of explaining the war (and the profoundly different America of that time) to the one-third of Americans who were young children or not yet born when it ended; on the experience of the million Indochinese immigrants who have reached the United States since the war; and finally, on how Americans—one at a time and as a nation—have sought to make peace with their enemy and themselves. This last chapter also attempts to give some glimpses into Vietnam's struggle with *its* memories and the many ironies of its evolution since the Vietnamese Communists' extraordinary victory in 1975.

My connection with Vietnam and its legacy is more than academic. As a correspondent for the *Baltimore Sun*, I reported on the war for nearly three years, from June 1972 to April 1975. The last months of that assignment were also the last months of the war, when the sudden, disastrous collapse of South Vietnam's army spawned terror and suffering on a scale that eclipsed even the years of tragedy that had gone before. This book does not touch directly on that history, nor, except in a few brief passages, does it present any personal recollections at all. But the sorrow and anger that remain with me from witnessing those events is reflected, I am sure, in much of what I have written here.

That background, as I have realized anew while writing these reflections, places me at the intersection of several different angles of vision on the subject. I was an observer, but close enough to events that I shared to an extent the experience of participants; I was a civilian, but from time to time saw the war from the same ground (if not with the same role or obligations) as the soldiers. It did not occur to me until I had nearly finished this book, but age, as well as occupation, also puts me on a kind of dividing line with respect to the war. Born in 1941, I am only a few years older than those commonly considered to belong to the Vietnam era. But those particular years represent a huge difference in experience, memory, and outlook. Indeed, I have sometimes felt that our memories make Americans my age a kind of last survivors—like children in a flood, led away from our native village just as the waters poured over to drown it forever. The America of my youth, following its righteous victory in World War II, basked in material comfort, worldwide economic and military supremacy, and limitless belief in a benign future. It was a calm, complacent, orderly place, soon to disappear so completely that those born just a few years later would never know what it was truly like. Yet if the great success of World War II and the immediate postwar era shaped the political and cultural landscape where I grew up, the Vietnam disaster dominated the world of my early adulthood, teaching me very different lessons about life and my country than my parents and their contemporaries had learned. And so, in my mid-fifties, looking back on events of my twenties and early thirties, it seems to me that here, too, I see them from some middle ground, on the fault line between those Americans whose generation is named for the national triumph of World War II and those who grew up into the frustrations and divisions and moral confusion of Vietnam.

Whether this dividing-line perspective leads to greater clarity or greater confusion is something my readers will have to decide for themselves. I can only assure them that I have been mindful of the great complexity and ambiguities surrounding the issues discussed in this book and have tried to avoid facile or careless judgments. I have tried to avoid, also, the partisan mythologies that continue to distort both sides of our unfinished national argument on Vietnam. It is even plainer to me now than it was at the time that neither side in that debate had a monopoly on the truth, or on morality. In these pages, to the best of my ability, I have attempted to state the facts accurately and fairly, without selectively stressing those that support one ideological viewpoint or another. My conclusions are, of course, fallible, and I am sure many readers will disagree with some or all of them. I only hope they will perceive my effort to draw those conclusions from a careful, honest, and fair examination of the facts.

In the soldiers' slang of the Vietnam War, home was commonly called "the World." It's a telling phrase, expressing their sense that they had been sent to someplace so distant and strange it felt like another planet. They were not the only soldiers to feel that way (in the Civil War, I have read, men who had experienced battle spoke of "seeing the elephant," another way of saying they had been somewhere foreign and weird). But for many reasons, those who fought in Vietnam were left feeling particularly shut off from the country whose uniform they wore. Many continued to feel isolated long after leaving Vietnam. In my effort to understand that experience, I received invaluable help from Robert Young Sr., Ron and Kathy Ferrizzi, and especially Randy Russin, all of whom answered my questions patiently and with candor and eloquence and illuminated for me just how far Vietnam veterans have had to travel to truly come home. I owe thanks and admiration as well to Ron Zaczek, Gordon Livingston, and Mark Treanor, for teaching me much that I would otherwise not have known about the veterans' experience. In that connection I am also more grateful than I can easily express to Bill Ehrhart, who is in many ways the conscience for all of us who write about Vietnam.

Not surprisingly, these individuals have reached various conclusions on the war and the meaning of their experience. On many issues they would sharply disagree with each other, and I imagine they will find things to disagree with in what I have written, too. I hope they will see, though, that I have tried to write with the full measure of respect that they and their fellow veterans earned but were too long denied.

Among the other people who helped with this book, I owe particular thanks to Lydia Trang, who represents the best of what our country has gained from the million or so new citizens who are also part of our Vietnam legacy. My other acknowledgements are, first, to Stanley Kutler, who commissioned the article that was the origin of this book and then found the way for the book itself to be written. I am grateful for his enthusiasm and support, as I am to Henry Tom and Barbara Lamb at the Johns Hopkins University Press.

For help in writing the chapter on our long, strange obsession with the imaginary missing-in-action, I owe thanks to Alan Ptak and Gen. John W. Vessey Jr. (Ret.) for sharing their perspectives on the issue. I also benefited greatly from the comments of H. Bruce Franklin, whose own work on debunking the MIA fantasy has been a valiant contribution to historical accuracy, and from a useful file of correspondence made available by Chuck Searcy. Maj. Dana Lindsley of the Defense Department's Office of Force Management Policy, Brian Sullivan of the Harvard University Archives, and Dave Sutherland of the Dundalk High School Alumni Association provided useful information for my chapter on the Vietnam generation. Jonathan D. Canter sent me the fascinating 25th reunion survey of 1970 Harvard graduates, and Dana Eure of the Iredell County Public Library in Statesville, North Carolina, kindly dug out and sent me newspaper clippings on the anti-amnesty demonstration held there in February 1977. Lastly, I thank Larry Rottmann for permission to reprint the poem that appears at the end of Chapter 8 and Bill Ehrhart (again) for the poem printed at the end of the bibliographic essay. No one named here is responsible for the judgments or conclusions stated in the book; the blame for any errors of fact or interpretation is entirely mine.

My remaining acknowledgements are, first, to my parents, Harold R. Isaacs (1910–1986) and Viola R. Isaacs (1910–1995). I miss them both. I am also grateful every day of my life to Jenny, Katy, and Robert, now our adult friends as well as our children. It gives me more pleasure than words can express to add to this list my sons-in-law, Matt and Steve, and my grandchildren, Amelia, Susannah, and Rachel. My final and greatest thanks are to my wife, Kathy, who took me for better and for worse thirty-four years ago and is still there, and whom I admire more than anyone else on earth. I dedicate this book to her.

A.R.I.

VIETNAM SHADOWS

1

THE WALL

"Dear Michael: Your name is here but you are not. I made a rubbing of it, thinking that if I rubbed hard enough I would rub your name off the wall and you would come back to me. I miss you so."

No one leaves notes or offerings at the rest of Washington's many monuments. But the Vietnam Veterans Memorial is different. From the moment of its dedication, the wall, with its 58,219 names inscribed on slabs of polished black granite, has seemed to give physical form to a whole nation's feelings of pain and loss. The names unify, while other words about the war continue to divide. "It doesn't say whether the war was right or wrong," a man whose son was wounded in Vietnam, but survived, said about the wall. "It just says, 'Here is the price we paid.'"

The memorial's emotional power is easier to describe than to explain. In part it comes from the names, which make the war's loss personal and concrete and immediate instead of distant and abstract. In part it comes from the reflecting surface, where those looking at the wall can also see the sky and trees and their own faces mirrored in the black stone behind the names of the dead.

There is a kind of mystery in those reflected images. It is as if the stone surface really became what its creator, Maya Ying Lin, imagined: a meeting place "between the sunny world and the quiet dark world beyond, that we can't enter." That sense of closeness between the dead and the living may explain why visitors so often do not just look, but touch, as if they can send their messages of sorrow and love through their fingertips. At the memorial, communication with the dark world seems possible. Thus, along with tears and touching, the wall of names became a place for tokens of remembrance: not only letters but also photographs, old dog tags and decorations, flags, religious medals, birthday and Christmas cards, faded scraps of uniforms and military equipment, souvenirs of war and high school and childhood.

These offerings expressed love and grief for the dead and often something more: a laying down of burdens, a release from the past. People came there to make peace with their memories—like a former marine sergeant named Frederick Garten, who left a ring and a note: "This wedding ring belonged to a young Viet Cong fighter. He was killed by a Marine unit in the Phu Loc province of South Vietnam in May of 1968. I wish I knew more about this young man. I have carried this ring for eighteen years and it's time for me to lay it down. This boy is not my enemy any longer."

Lin's design, selected when she was only twenty-one years old and studying architecture at Yale University, was at first bitterly denounced by those favoring a more conventionally patriotic monument. Opponents didn't like her design and some of them didn't like her, either: a young Chinese American woman who had only been in her early teens when the war ended, had no connection with it, hadn't even known anyone who had served in it.

When the U.S. Fine Arts Commission met to give final approval to the plan, Tom Carhart, a twice-wounded West Point graduate who had been one of the original fund-raisers for the memorial, arrived wearing his two Purple Hearts pinned on his suit jacket to tell the commissioners his reaction: "A black gash of shame and sorrow. . . . Black walls, the universal color of sorrow and dishonor. Hidden in a hole, as if in shame." (Later, Carhart told a television interviewer: "We want something that will make us feel a part of America.") If Carhart and many like him were outraged because the memorial wasn't heroic enough, a few others were bitter for exactly the opposite reason. "I didn't want a monument," wrote the poet Bill Ehrhart, who also came home from Vietnam with a Purple Heart, "not even one as sober as that / Vast black wall of broken lives. . . . / What I wanted / Was an end to monuments."

Eventually, in an attempt to make the memorial less "antiheroic," as Tom Carhart called it, Lin's austere plan was modified by adding a U.S. flag and a statue, sculpted by Frederick Hart, naturalistically representing three GIs and carrying the inscription: "Our nation honors the courage, sacrifice and devotion to duty and country of its Vietnam veterans."* Not all critics were reconciled, even then. But by the time Hart's statue was completed, two years after the wall was dedicated, the initial criticisms of the memorial had long since been overwhelmed by the public's reaction. The controversy over the design, which had attracted a good deal of coverage before the memorial's dedication, quickly faded from view, to be replaced by images of veterans, children, parents, and other visitors shedding healing tears and finding solace in the sight and touch of the names. The wall quickly became one of the most-visited of all Washington's attractions, and certainly the most emotionally compelling. Some veterans still wouldn't go, but others found themselves returning again and again. "It is exactly the right memorial," said a retired three-star general, "for that war."

Powerful as it was, though, the wall did not close the book on America's confusion and pain about Vietnam. The war and its ghosts continued to hover over the national life and spirit. Rather than becoming a historical event that would automatically recede into the past, Vietnam lingered as a symbol, a metaphor for everything that troubled Americans in the closing years of what had once been called the American Century.

It was the war that "cleaves us still," as George Bush once said. Presumably, Bush was referring to the obvious divisions: between those who supported the policy and those who opposed it, between those who served and those who didn't, between those who denounced the United States and its symbols and those who put flag pins in their lapels and bumper stickers on their cars proclaiming "America—Love it or Leave it."

But the country's division over Vietnam could also be something more elusive and profound. I think, for example, of the only time I had a serious discussion about our respective wars with my father, who was a war correspondent in the China-Burma-India theater in World War II— and had, as a young man a decade earlier, also seen the early stages of Japan's brutal war in China. (He was also in Vietnam shortly after the Japanese surrender in 1945, at the very start of the Viet Minh uprising against French rule. It is a curious bit of family history that my father, who reported on some of the first skirmishes of that long conflict, lived to see his son cover the end, three decades later.)

From childhood, I knew that my father accepted none of the sen-

*In 1993, a second sculpture was erected, honoring women veterans.

timental myths of war. He saw, as clearly as anyone I have known, the waste and degradation and cruelty. Probably that is why I assumed for years that he had come out of his war, in some fundamental way, with the same vision that I took from mine: that war, at its dark, bloody heart, is insanity. In Vietnam, from time to time during the nearly three years I spent reporting there, I would feel myself waking up, as if from a dream, thinking, *Who's the lunatic who invented this? Who figured out that this is how we decide what color bit of cloth will be fluttering in the morning over this village or that crossroads?* And whoever it was, I wondered, why wasn't he in an asylum, where he belonged?

That feeling came only intermittently, in what I came to think of as lucid moments. The truth is that the landscape of war was so completely familiar to my generation, the children of World War II, that most of the time it didn't seem crazy at all, but quite normal and sane. When I first arrived in Vietnam, in fact, one of the surprises was how much of the scenery and sensations felt familiar and well known: not everything, but a lot. But there was a kind of clarity in those moments of seeing the war as insane. I couldn't make the feeling last—it was like catching a fish with your bare hands and then having it slip away. Yet it was in those fleeting intervals that I thought I had grasped the truth of what I was experiencing. It had never occurred to me that my father didn't feel the same way. But that evening when we talked about it, the year before he died, ten years after my war ended and forty years after his, I learned—to my amazement—that I was wrong. His war was ugly and degrading, even tragic, but not absurd. It was necessary. The Japanese had to be beaten, and there wasn't any other way to do it. With all its cruelty and waste, it was still sane.

I was so surprised by that realization that I don't remember much of what we actually said to each other. I do remember thinking that I now understood in a new way just how profoundly, and in how many different ways, Vietnam had split this country apart. My father and I had no serious disagreements on Vietnam itself. But our generations' different experiences divided us on a much deeper level than that. Vietnam taught me (and, I think, most Americans who were there) that the world is, ultimately, absurd. World War II taught my father and his generation that the world may contain vast terror and evil—but also rationality and, even, a rough and approximate kind of justice. Between those two visions lay a gulf that was, and remains, almost impossible to cross.

The abyss between Americans whose lives were shaped by the great crusade of World War II and their children who grew up in the Vietnam era emerged clearly in a major survey of the baby boom generation conducted in 1986. Reporting on the survey, the writer William Greider wrote:

> The victory in World War II was not only a glorious triumph for the nation, but it taught deeper lessons about what one could expect in life. The United States could stand up for just causes, and if everyone pulled together, it could win. . . . The Sixties experience taught the opposite, . . . that the structure itself was corrupt, that individuals must follow their own moral compass and that they could not expect much moral leadership from above. The nation's framework, the sense of larger purpose and possibilities inherited from their parents' era, collapsed for this generation. It no longer seemed believable. And nothing has happened since to restore it.

It did not occur to me until many years after that conversation with my father that it didn't just have to do with America after Vietnam. It revealed something about our history during Vietnam, too. The men who made the choices that got the United States into the war, and who decided how to fight it, were also my father's age, sharing his experiences if not his particular knowledge or views about Vietnam. It was a generation whose vision of the world was shaped largely by the experience of World War II and the great triumph achieved by American resources and technological skill in that war. "A generation of men who believed that the world makes sense," one journalist wrote in an article about former Defense Secretary Robert S. McNamara. "That human events could be mastered. That if enough planes drop enough bombs on a backward Asian country, victory must follow."

The same article, whose subject was McNamara's long-delayed apologia for the war in his 1995 book *In Retrospect*, quoted one of its "lessons" from Vietnam: "We failed to recognize," McNamara acknowledged, "that in international affairs, as in other aspects of life, there may be problems for which there are no immediate solutions. For one whose life has been dedicated to the belief and practice of problem solving, this is particularly hard to admit. But at times, we may have to live with an imperfect, untidy world."

To which the reporter added a one-word comment: "May?"

The Vietnam War was not the only thing that changed America. It was probably not even the most important. A vast windstorm of changes in technology, in economic and family life, in racial and ethnic relations, and—possibly most profound of all—in matters of gender and sexual identity, gathered strength and speed during the last third of the twentieth century, swirling away old certainties, making everyone's world a more confusing, unstable, and uncertain place. Looking back, it's possible to trace the beginnings of the storm back far before Vietnam: taking shape in the huge turbulence of World War II, like a tropical storm forming in unseen air currents far out at sea; gently ruffling the seemingly placid air of the 1950s before reaching gale force in the following decades.

Even if the United States had never gone to war in Vietnam, the old system of racial segregation would still have been challenged, and fallen, and new racial tensions would have arisen. Women would still have assumed new roles, inside and outside the home, and men would still have felt troubled and threatened by challenges to old, deeply rooted concepts of masculinity. Suburbs would have provided unprecedented green comfort for millions while also dividing Americans ever more sharply by income and class. Tides of immigrants would still have arrived, making this a much more varied, multicolored society, with correspondingly more jostling and conflict as different groups vied for a place in their new country. Global business trends and technology would have wiped out traditional industrial jobs, transforming the occupational landscape and stranding millions of less-skilled, less-educated workers in poorly paid, unsatisfying, and impermanent jobs. Television would still have transformed the ways in which Americans saw themselves, and revolutionized the political process and the way we debate and decide national policies. And with all of these changes, old rules and traditions and standards of taste and conduct would have weakened; more people would have experimented with more freedoms, and, inevitably, more would also feel deeply threatened and anguished by the pace and wrenching nature of change.

Erase Vietnam from our history and one can reasonably speculate that America in the 1990s would still probably look much the same as it does: fragmented, self-doubting, cynical about its leaders, uncertain of its future, confused about its standards and beliefs. But, of course, Vietnam did happen, and it became the era's most powerful symbol of damaged ideals and the loss of trust, unity, shared myths, and common values. Like a magnet, which draws steel shavings scattered on a sheet of paper into a particular form and pattern, Vietnam gave visible shape to the great cultural changes sweeping over American society, defining, more than any other event, the era and its pains.

Perhaps because it was such an exact reverse image of America's epic victory in World War II, Vietnam—the "bad war"—had an extraordinarily shattering effect on the national spirit. World War II ("the last good war," American officers in Vietnam often called it, in tones ranging from sour to sardonic to wistful) had become in many ways the culminating myth of the American experience and national character. It was "such a triumph of American resources, technology, and industrial and military genius," as the author Neil Sheehan put it, that during the next twenty years of unprecedented prosperity at home and military and economic dominance abroad, Americans came to think the success of their society was guaranteed.

Following World War II, the country's military and political leaders and "the greater part of the political, academic, and business leadership" as well, Sheehan wrote, took their supremacy for granted: "the elite of America had become stupefied by too much money, too many material resources, too much power, and too much success." The country that marched into Vietnam in the mid-1960s, two decades after the great crusade against Germany and Japan, had forgotten that it could fail. America's generals of the sixties "assumed that they would prevail in Vietnam simply because of who they were," Sheehan wrote. The same could have been said of American society as a whole.

There had been the ambiguous Korean War, of course. But as the nation gradually stepped up its effort in Vietnam, the towering triumph in World War II was still the dominant image in the imagination of most Americans—and their soldiers, as well. The great majority of men who fought in Vietnam were born between 1945 and 1953, growing up in the sunlit, high noon of postwar prosperity and national self-confidence. A large number were certainly the sons of World War II veterans. Virtually everything in their culture—novels, movies, family stories, childhood games, schoolbooks, the traditional patriotic rhetoric of Veterans Day speeches and graduations and political campaigns—conditioned young men entering military service in the mid-1960s to think of Vietnam as their generation's turn to be, as one veteran said, "the good guys against the bad guys."

If their war was on a smaller scale, they still imagined it—at least in the first few years—as essentially the same experience as World War II, the memory of which was now softened and sentimentalized by twenty years of heroic legends. And when Vietnam turned out to be such a different and disappointing war, the contrast with their fathers' experience made the disillusionment even sharper. One veteran, in a poem that may not have been great literature but achieved a kind of eloquence in its sadness, closed with these lines: "I want to say out loud, had we been in your war, dad, we would have made you proud."

Perhaps because it struck at such powerful myths, Vietnam acquired a mythical nature of its own. The word became a synonym for all kinds of national failure or frustration, as when the mayor of one crime-ridden city referred to the failed war on drugs as "a domestic Vietnam." The country seemed unable to shake its memories of the war or the cultural and political divisions associated with it.

The moral confusion of the war was mirrored in the postwar debate over how to remember it. "We want to give ourselves absolution," one journalist wrote, "although we remain deeply divided—as individuals and as a people—over what it is we need to absolve (whether it is what we did fighting the war in Indochina or what we did protesting it at home)." In fact, the more one examines it, the more one comes to feel the issue lingered so long because it wasn't really about how we fought or protested the war, after all, but something much more profound. America's continuing divisions about Vietnam reflected, more than anything else, an unfinished argument about who we are—about just who it is, when we look at our reflected selves in the black granite of the wall of names, that we really see.

2

THE VETERANS

I want it to have been worth something, and I can't
make myself believe that it was.
—Bill Ehrhart

The strangest thing. I started thinking, "Maybe I wasn't
really there. Maybe I am imagining it."
—Diane Carlson Evans

I

"You don't go to war, come home, and not talk about it," Bobby Muller said from his wheelchair. But America's soldiers returning from Vietnam came back to a silence that, for years, silenced them as well.

"We lost the war in Vietnam, and that's why we don't talk about it," said a man in the audience the night Bobby Muller spoke. It was early 1979, nearly four years before the Vietnam Veterans Memorial dedication, almost ten years after Muller took a bullet in the spine near a place called Con Thien in the Republic of Vietnam.

He had wept with pride at the Marine Corps hymn after he enlisted, Muller recalled that night in Baltimore; had gone willingly to the war that crippled him, and then discovered that in his own country, no-

body seemed to care. "Goddamn it, no one feels responsible," he said. "Everyone thinks, hey, it wasn't my war! I didn't do it. It all got delegated to a couple of schmucks out there in that country, and when they come back—hey, man, it's your bad luck."

In the discussion that evening, people tried, with evident difficulty, to grapple with the troubled silence that seemed to surround Vietnam and its veterans. One man, of an age to have been in World War II or maybe in Korea, put his finger on one cause: No one knew what to say about this more recent war; not the people at home, not the soldiers themselves. The national experience in Vietnam never rested on any foundation of understanding, and so the men who fought there "were not standing on anything," he said. "There was no solid ground under them. Those of us in previous wars had solid ground, we knew where we came from, knew who we were and why we were there."

A woman wanted to know "how does all this relate to the violence that sort of has come out of Vietnam?" She didn't mean the war itself; she meant riots and snipers and shootings and store holdups in Baltimore and elsewhere in America. Others pointed out that American society and moral codes changed for many more reasons than just the Vietnam war, but she shook her head, unconvinced. Somehow she knew the war did it, and nothing anyone said could change her mind.

People spoke of the My Lai massacre and Lt. William Calley, of the destruction of Dresden, the firebombing of Japan, the Germans. "The horrible thing is that we were the ones," said a young woman, in obvious confusion and with many long pauses. "Maybe we weren't exactly like Hitler, we can't compare ourselves to that—but I don't think we can compare this war to World War II at all . . ." No one was suggesting—quite—that American soldiers in general were murderers or war criminals. But the words were spoken: "Calley," "Dresden," "Nazis," "body count." And they had an evil sound. It was painful to imagine how they might sound to Bobby Muller in his wheelchair on the stage or to the other veterans sitting with him or in the audience. Yet in its very incoherence and fragmented quality, the discussion that evening in a way explained the moral fog Vietnam had left in American minds: a confusion so deep that for many years, Americans found no way to speak about it to themselves and, consequently, no way to speak to their own returning soldiers, either.

The folklore that grew up around that homecoming, telling of soldiers routinely being cursed or spit on, was almost certainly exaggerated.

But the sense of being silenced, which *felt* a good deal like being shunned, was part of almost every soldier's experience. And the hurt was deep. "I want to go back to Vietnam and make it different," wrote a former Army nurse named Kathy Gunson some years after her return. "I want to come home to a marching band and a red carpet. I want to hear a 'thank you.' I want to hear 'I'm sorry.'" Another veteran, Jamie Bryant, remembered: "It was the spookiest thing. . . . In over ten years, there has really never been anybody who has asked me: 'What happened to you over there? What was it like?' It's like having a whole year of your life that didn't exist. When you first get back, you don't think about it much. Then you begin to wonder why no one asks the questions. Then you begin to feel like maybe it really isn't something you should talk about."

Many never did. Not infrequently, veterans reentered civilian life and told nobody, not even wives or girlfriends, that they had served in Vietnam. The absence of words meant more than an absence of gratitude or sympathy or respect. Unable to speak about the war, many veterans also had no way to find a reason or purpose in what they had lived through, no way to complete their experience by telling about it and thus coming to understand it.

The great majority were able to find some pride in their own conduct. If you asked, they would tell you they went, did their job, conquered their fear, didn't let down their friends. Like soldiers in any war, they had learned something about endurance and comradeship and about their own inner resources. But if their discoveries gave some purely personal meaning to their experience, it was not the same as finding an explanation, a worthwhile *reason*. Thus the war remained "like a piece of buried shrapnel," as one of them wrote, in a hidden and tender place within them. And like bearers of some terrible secret that could never be told, the returning soldiers felt themselves strangers in their own society. When he came home, the writer Larry Heinemann recalled years afterward, "I had the distinct feeling (common among returning veterans, I think) that this was not my country, not my time."

It was that sense of alienation that separated the Vietnam veterans from those of earlier conflicts. The difference was not so much in the wars themselves, since the tension and boredom and petty restrictions and stupidities of military life and the terrors and exhaustion of combat don't vary much from one war to another. ("When somebody is shooting at you and you are shooting back," the veteran and novelist Jack Fuller once wrote, "all wars are pretty much the same.") What made Vietnam and America's other wars so different was how they were assimilated afterward into the veterans' and the nation's experience.

Men who fought in World War II or Korea might be just as haunted by what they had personally seen and done in combat. But they did not come home, as the Vietnam vets did, to a country torn and full of doubt about why those wars were fought and whether they had been worthwhile. Nor did they return as symbols of a great national failure. Whatever troubling private memories they brought back with them, those earlier veterans did not have to grope for an explanation of what their experience had meant and what its purpose was. Their country—its political and intellectual leaders, its journalists and educators, its movies and popular novels—gave them the answer. They had been heroes in a necessary cause, they were told, and eventually most of them came to believe it was true. But those who fought in Vietnam were told . . . nothing. Even several decades later, Americans reached no common understanding, no comforting myth that could give sense or logic to that war, or absolve soldiers who had trouble coming to terms with the violence they had participated in.

"In past wars," Jack Smith, a psychologist and Marine Corps veteran, told the author Myra MacPherson, "through cleansing acts, society *shared* the blame and responsibility" with those who had done the fighting. "Victory banners, medals, and parades were ways of recognizing the tasks they did in the country's name," Smith added, but the country refused to give its name to Vietnam. "The responsibility and blame was left on the heads of the guys who fought it. They were left to sort out who was responsible for what." Another psychologist, John Wilson, explained to a *Los Angeles Times* reporter: "All cultures recognize that when we send someone to battle, it's difficult psychologically. . . . After the battle, most cultures also have a ritualized way of welcoming back the warrior and giving him a new identity and a new status in society. But we didn't do it for Vietnam veterans. . . . Many men felt isolated after Vietnam. They had to create meaning and make sense of what they did in Vietnam—and they had to do it alone."

If parades and medals were rituals of reconciliation, perhaps it was inevitable that an unreconciled war like Vietnam sometimes turned those rituals inside out, as on an April afternoon in Washington in 1971 when hundreds of veterans marched past the U.S. Capitol and, instead of receiving medals from a grateful government, threw away their decorations to protest the war. The reverse imagery was complete, down to the eight-foot-high temporary security fence below the Capitol's west front physically keeping apart the veterans and the government whose uniform they had worn.

At the head of the procession were parents of three men who had died. Gail Olson, a high-school band teacher from Russell, Pennsylvania, wore his son's fatigue jacket and carried a bugle. After blowing taps, he stepped to a microphone that had been set up next to the barricade so the demonstrators could stop, if they wanted to, and say something. Olson said into the mike: "My son's name was Sergeant William Olson. We're playing taps for all the dead—Vietnamese, Laotian, Cambodian, all our wonderful sons. Let us pray there will be no more, no more." Next was Evelyn Carrasquillo of Miami, who carried a U.S. flag and her son's medals mounted in a frame. "I will not turn my back on this country . . . but we've done our best for the Vietnamese," she said. "It's time to get out. Let's stop the war now." Unlike the veterans, she kept the medals—"all I have left of Alberto." The third Gold Star parent was Anna Pine, of Trenton, New Jersey, who carried her son's medals up to the microphone and then stepped away, weeping, with the medals still in her hand. Later she returned and threw them over the fence with the others.

Then, for two hours, the veterans filed by and tossed away their medals. Some simply dropped them over the fence. Others hurled them as hard as they could, as if aiming at the Capitol dome far overhead. Some men walked on crutches; a few were pushed in wheelchairs. Some of those who stopped to speak into the microphone sounded angry, some just sounded sad. "I'm turning in all the shit that wasn't issued and I had to buy it," one man said. Another said: "This is for all the dudes in Third Battalion, Charlie Company, Ninth Marines, who didn't make it." Another said: "Here's a Vietnamese Cross of Gallantry, which God knows I didn't earn until just now."

One of the men who marched that day was a tall, lean former Air Cavalry trooper with lank black hair named Ron Ferrizzi, who threw away a Purple Heart and a Silver Star he'd been awarded for pulling another soldier out of a burning helicopter. "My wife wanted me to keep these medals so my son would be proud of me," Ferrizzi told me. "But I'm not proud of them. It's all garbage. It doesn't mean a thing." He turned and walked away into the crowd. I watched him go, thinking with a pang that if Ron Ferrizzi had joined the fire department, say, instead of the Army, and if he'd been decorated for saving someone from a fire in his hometown in Pennsylvania instead of in Vietnam, he'd have kept that decoration, no doubt, and his son would be proud of him when he got old enough to understand, and he would be right to be proud. I thought about going after Ferrizzi to tell him that. But I didn't.

The next time I saw Ron Ferrizzi, twenty-three years later in the framing shop he and his wife Kathy owned in North Philadelphia, I mentioned that long-ago impulse. Ferrizzi shook his head. Nobody could take away what he'd done to earn those medals, he said, and throwing away the actual decorations was a necessary part of rejecting a war he passionately believed was wrong. "I was so relieved. It was like the seas parted for me. It was like physically striking back," he said. And there was another powerful reason: his two sons. "I never wanted my kids to come up to me and say, when am I going to get a chance to get my medals?"

Kathy Ferrizzi didn't disagree. But she still sounded a little sad when she remembered her own feelings at the time: "I was brought up, if you had medals you were proud of them, your children were proud of them, and they were handed down. And here he was throwing them all over the wall. I wasn't that thrilled. I didn't think that was the right thing to do.

"I never thought he was wrong" about the war, she added. "I just asked him not to give back his medals."

The veterans' march in 1971 was one of the last major antiwar protests, but it was not the last time Vietnam veterans would discard their medals. Nearly six years later, furious at President Jimmy Carter's amnesty for draft evaders, a former marine sergeant in North Carolina named Dale Wilson called on other outraged veterans to turn in their decorations to protest Carter's action. Wilson, whose grievous wounds in Vietnam had cost him both legs and his right arm, had not been bitter when he returned home, he wrote in a letter to his local newspaper, the *Statesville Record & Landmark*. He had enlisted in the Marine Corps "feeling that it was my patriotic duty to serve my country," he wrote, and even after being wounded, only days before he was due to rotate home, felt lucky that he had survived to see his country again.

But Carter's amnesty, Wilson felt, defiled his sacrifice and the service of every soldier who had fought in the war: "Now I am faced with the fact that those who ran when our country called can come back and take the jobs and positions in the community of those who deserve them: the United States veteran." Like Ron Ferrizzi, Wilson had a young son, and like Ferrizzi he felt his decorations were too tarnished to pass on. He would have kept them for his son, he wrote, "but as the war has been recognized as a mistake, I feel there is no honor in medals obtained through dishonorable conflict." A week after his letter was published, Wilson and other angry veterans, some from as far away as Pennsylvania and Ohio, gathered on a parking lot next to a Statesville grocery store. There, they nailed their decorations, and for good measure, an artificial limb, to the wall of an out-house they had brought to the site—"a symbol," Wilson declared, "of the universal political platform which promises relief and ends up with ----." When all the decorations had been hung on the wall, Doris Miller, whose son had been killed in Vietnam, touched a match to the outhouse, which had been soaked in kerosene, and with Wilson and the others, watched it burn to ashes.

The fact that men with such different opinions on the war as Dale Wilson and Ron Ferrizzi both ended up making the identical gesture of rage spoke volumes about how deeply Vietnam had torn the national spirit. Whether they were flung away by veterans at the Capitol protesting the war or by veterans on a North Carolina parking lot protesting the amnesty program, those discarded medals represented personal courage and sacrifice that deserved to be honored whether the war was justified or not. Tainting that honor for so many veterans might not have been the worst thing Americans did to themselves in Vietnam. But it was no small crime, either.

Robert L. Young Sr. didn't throw away his Vietnam medals. He was proud of them, or wanted to be. But because no one else cared, it was hard to sustain his pride. During his year as radioman in a mortar squad in the Twenty-fifth Infantry Division, Young earned a Bronze Star, Army Commendation Medal, and Combat Infantryman's Badge, among other decorations. But even while he was still in the Army after coming back from Vietnam, he never wore his ribbons off base. "The medals were like—how can I explain?—like you were a killer. It just seemed no one cared about that war. . . . No one was interested in the Vietnam veteran at all."

More than twenty years later, Young, now a postal worker in Baltimore, still sounded wistful and a little bitter. The medals "didn't mean anything to me any more," he said. "Like I was proud to have them, but who wanted to see them? When I got the Bronze Star over there, I was really proud. But over here, who cared if I got the Bronze Star?" As a kid, he'd seen homes where veterans had their medals mounted in cabinets on the wall. He sometimes thought about mounting his, but hadn't done it. "Who cares?" he said again, sounding not at all like someone whose medals didn't mean anything any more. "You'd like to show your kids someday, but you just get that feeling that no one cared."

Like many other African American veterans, Young came back from

Vietnam to family, friends, and neighbors who were, often, even more skeptical about the war than white Americans had become. People who didn't know he'd been in the service spoke disparagingly about black soldiers in Vietnam. "They would say . . . those dummies over there, most of them come back crazy. Black people would say," Young went on, "there was no reason for a black man to be there. It's not his war. His war is here at home." Thinking about it long afterward, in the neatly kept living room of the house his veteran's benefits had helped him buy, Young still sounded troubled and hurt, unsure if he'd been right to go to Vietnam, or wrong. "You're supposed to be a United States citizen, but you still have your people make you feel, why should you go over there and fight? I felt like, are they right?" Like many other black soldiers, he had originally thought of military service as a pathway to a better career than he might have found in civilian life. "I was proud to be in the service when I went in," he said. "I was proud. I went in thinking to make a career out of the service." But not after Vietnam, and the indifference or hostility he encountered when he came home. "After that, I was glad my time was up. I wasn't proud any longer. I lost all that pride of being a soldier. I just lost it."

To a listener, Young sounded like a man with such painfully mixed feelings that he wasn't sure exactly what they were. One could guess that his soldier's pride wasn't actually lost, but buried somewhere very deep within himself because he didn't know whether he should be proud or not.

It was hardly surprising if Vietnam left black soldiers, and other black Americans, even more troubled, disillusioned, angry, and confused than the rest of the country. The war coincided, almost exactly, with events that transformed the American racial landscape. America's gradual march into Vietnam—first with advisers, then with air power, then with ground combat forces—coincided exactly with the great wave of sit-ins and freedom rides in the early 1960s and the toppling of legal segregation with the 1964 Civil Rights Act and the 1965 Voting Rights Act. In the years that followed, the war and the civil rights struggle moved with a kind of ironic symmetry, as if each had become a metaphor for the other. While hopes for an easy military success faded away in the dense green jungles of Vietnam, hopes for a rapid, total victory over historic racial injustice foundered in the equally tangled terrain of race, class, and economic relations at home.

In Vietnam, as the U.S. ground war began, African Americans were overrepresented in the enlisted ranks of the armed services, where many blacks felt they had more economic security and better career opportunities than in civilian society. Briefly, the war was seen as a positive event, in the context of American race relations. A number of commentators, both black and white, hailed it as America's first truly integrated war. Black soldiers fighting alongside whites on a genuinely equal basis, the story went, would send—to their own country and the world—an inspiring message of interracial patriotism, unity, and common efforts in the nation's service. It soon became apparent, however, that black soldiers were not just carrying their fair share but were suffering disproportionate casualties, compared with white troops. In 1965 and early 1966, nearly 25 percent of U.S. troops killed in action were black, more than twice the percentage of blacks in the population as a whole. The Defense Department rather quickly acted to even out the racial balance in combat units, and the disparity in casualties dropped sharply—though not before creating an enduring impression that African Americans took unduly high losses throughout the conflict.

While the war bogged down in an increasingly frustrating stalemate, black rage at home broke out in fiery riots in Los Angeles, Newark, Detroit, and other cities. The crusade that brought down traditional segregation in the American South was less unified and less effective against the problems of poverty, poor education, lack of jobs, high rates of illegitimacy and drug use, and a deep anger and alienation that was often transformed into domestic violence or street crime. From both the streets and black intellectuals came a chorus of new, angry voices, challenging the traditional civil rights agenda of racial integration and alliance and preaching separatism or revolution instead. Black support for the war eroded rapidly. Opinion polls showed a majority of blacks opposing the war by 1969; two years later, according to one survey, more than four-fifths of African Americans felt the war was a mistake.

Support evaporated among prominent black leaders, too. For a time, some hesitated to criticize the war publicly, not wanting to burn their bridges to President Lyndon Johnson, their ally on civil rights and social programs. By early 1967, though, the Rev. Martin Luther King Jr. and others were arguing that the war had become the enemy of social and economic justice at home. The war, King declared, was not only killing young men in Vietnam but "devastating the hopes of the poor" in the United States. (Privately, Johnson may have agreed, at least afterward. Talking to his biographer Doris Kearns Goodwin after he retired, Johnson acknowledged that from the start, he knew that "that bitch of a war on the other side of the world" would destroy his vision of creating a Great Society in America. "I would lose everything. . . . All my programs. All my hopes to feed the hungry and shelter the homeless. All my dreams to provide education and medical care to the browns and the blacks and the lame and the poor." But LBJ felt he had no choice: letting the Communists take over South Vietnam would brand him as a coward and the United States as an appeaser, he told Goodwin, "and we would both find it impossible to accomplish anything for anybody anywhere on the entire globe.")

King's declarations against the war resonated among millions of African Americans. So did the earthier words of boxing champion Muhammad Ali, who refused induction into the Army and (at a time when many white athletes were easily getting draft deferments or reserve assignments) stood trial for draft evasion. "No Viet Cong," Ali declared, "ever called me nigger." The country's divisions over the war and over race deepened in tandem, especially in 1968, the year of the Tet Offensive, King's murder, racial violence, and a presidential campaign that in many ways established the cultural and thinly coded racial politics that would mark American political life for the next three decades. Reflecting increasing anger and polarization at home, racial tension simmered in the armed services, too. By most accounts, conflict was relatively rare among soldiers in the field, where men had to depend on each other for mutual survival in combat. But in rear areas, black and white soldiers in many units split into wary, hostile groups.

African American soldiers returning from Vietnam could not escape the raw racial nerves and the social and economic problems affecting black society in general. And, even more than white veterans, they could not escape painful doubts about just what their service meant: had they gone to Vietnam as part of assuming full citizenship in a society that aspired, at least, to true racial democracy? Or had they gone as expendable cannon fodder for a government and society that still denied basic justice to black citizens at home?

Many black veterans, like Robert Young, were still torn by those questions long after the war. More than twenty years after he came home, Young still could not find a good reason for the war. But he sounded as if he wished it could have been different. "It was all unnecessary. It didn't make sense. You were supposed to be helping the Vietnamese people, but they didn't want you. . . . I thought we were fighting to help those people to have a democratic society, that's what I thought. Then you find out they really don't want you. And you've got a whole year over there, you think maybe you'll find someone who appreciates your being there. Nope. . . . You say well, I did a good job. But you never accomplished anything. The only thing you accomplished was to go over to that country for a year and get shot at."

Young also sounded as if he had spent a very long time hoping for someone to tell him he wasn't dumb to go to Vietnam, or disloyal to the struggle for justice at home. "If they would have recognized the Vietnam veterans the same way they recognized the guys that did Desert Storm, the Korean War, whatever, it would have made it a little different," he said wistfully. But he didn't sound very hopeful that anything would change. "After twenty years, people say, are you still thinking about that dumb stuff? It's dumb to them now, it was dumb to them then. What are you going to do? . . . You might have a lot of hurt and pain within yourself, but you just let it ride. Nobody wants to hear about that."

II

It was certainly the moral and emotional confusion of *remembering* Vietnam, not just the confusion of being there, that produced the characteristic formlessness and the disillusioned, cynical tone in so many of the novels and memoirs written by returning soldiers—a literature that in turn helped shape a national memory of the war as not just tragic, but empty of meaning. The typical Vietnam book, the writer C.D.B. Bryan once observed, "charts the gradual deterioration of order, the disintegration of idealism, the breakdown of character, the alienation from those at home, and, finally, the loss of all sensibility save the will to survive."

The war produced some fine fiction, but it was striking that the most successful works often seemed to be those that viewed the war from an oblique angle: Tim O'Brien's stories in *The Things They Carried*, for example. The more traditionally realistic novels, with rare exceptions, ended up re-creating the war just as most soldiers had experienced it, without narrative or logical structure. In the "Generic Vietnam War Narrative," as Bryan called it, events do not flow from what has already happened, or explain what will happen next. Instead, there is only a succession of episodes, varying very little from one book to another: the hero's arrival (always by himself) at his unit, the first firefight, the first death of a friend. "There is the atrocity scene. . . . There are dope scenes: guys stoned at night lying out on the bunker roof, tripping on the light show of gunships and arc flares." And so on, Bryan continued: the helicopter assault, the R&R leave with its hurried, loveless sex, and at the end the scene where the hero "flies back to the

World and at the airport a pretty young woman spits on him and calls him a baby-killer."

For the novels and memoirs that came out of World War II, the event itself provided a kind of structure. In that war's generic narratives, groups of soldiers meet in training, wait for combat together (instead of arriving at the war alone), have their baptism of fire, and then fight in campaigns that lead them across Europe or the Pacific toward the eventual victory that will conclude both the war and, typically, the book. The Vietnam War had no such structure. It appears in virtually all the books (and movies and television shows) simply as a setting, an unchanging environment into which a soldier comes, spends his one-year tour, and leaves. At the end, the hero may have changed, but the war has not. There is no victory or defeat, not even any discernible progress toward one or the other. No battle is connected to any other battle; nothing happens to *explain* the war, which instead just *is*, like a jungle or a river. And thus nothing ever explains or vindicates the soldier's experience, either.

The Vietnam combat narratives that "wander through the war from day to day as aimlessly as the infantry soldiers whose travail they record" represent a kind of realism, wrote Jack Fuller, but, he added, "it is a primitive realism. It does not do the work of fiction, which is to give experience a sense of coherence." Moreover, the "cynical landscape of Vietnam," as another critic called it, turned the conventional rite-of-passage into something darker than in the literature of earlier wars. Instead of arriving at growth or understanding, these stories lead only to a kind of moral and emotional dead end—like the war itself, which, novelist Robert Stone remembered,

> carried with it the most awful sense of absurdity and futility. . . . To realize that the whole thing was absolutely cockeyed, that it was an enormous, breathtaking mistake, was alarming to begin with, and then you realized there was nothing much you could do about it—except to try to exist within it. Everyone was passing the buck. Everyone was putting everybody else on—kidding themselves and lying to one another. . . . The moral slipperiness and double-crossing in Vietnam bent everybody's head out of shape. It gave you the sense that everything was scrambled. And this kind of stoned despair created its own idiom, its own language. There was a distinctly "in-country" way of talking, an "in-country" sense of humor—like you were on another planet. It was a very spacey way of talking, a profoundly cynical attitude toward everything.

In most Vietnam novels, a soldier's aimless wandering doesn't end even when he leaves the war zone. The typical hero is no less lost and aimless after he comes home—burned out and emotionally damaged, seeming to himself, as a fictional veteran in Susan Fromberg Shaeffer's *Buffalo Afternoon* put it, like "a pane of glass, still whole, but with a crack down the middle."

If the chief quality of Vietnam literature was its lack of coherence, clearly this mirrored the incoherence of the actual experience, for the soldiers and for the country they came home to, too. "In war you lose your sense of the definite, hence your sense of the truth itself, and therefore it's safe to say that in a true war story nothing is ever absolutely true," wrote Tim O'Brien in "How to Tell a True War Story." In this national and personal confusion, every veteran was left to try, alone, to find a reason for what had happened to him. Many could not. "I want it to have been worth *something*," the poet W. D. Ehrhart, who was badly wounded in the war, burst out to a friend after coming home, "and I can't make myself believe that it was."

Along with incoherence, another odd trait of the popular literature and movies of the Vietnam war was how commonly war crimes were presented as the typical—and symbolic—experience of American soldiers. Sometimes a war crime was a central element of the story, as in the climactic scene of the movie *Platoon*. But atrocities also appeared in a kind of careless, routine way, as if they were simply taken for granted, an accepted feature of the historical landscape.

In the movie *In Country*, for example, there's a snatch of dialogue between Sam, a teenage girl seeking to learn about her father's death in Vietnam, and her mother. In their conversation, the mother mentions another veteran who came home tormented because he once killed a peasant family. "Did my daddy do things like that?" Sam asks. The mother shrugs. She doesn't know, she answers, but it could be. "That's what they were sent over there to do." The subject of killing civilians had, in fact, nothing to do with the story and is not mentioned again in the movie; it's probably a safe bet that the exchange hardly registered at all in the minds of most viewers. Those who did notice, though, might have wondered how *this* came to be the stereotype of American soldiers, appearing again and again in the popular literature of the war—that they were regularly involved in massacring civilians. Such crimes happened, of course, most spectacularly in the killing of several hundred villagers in the coastal hamlet of My Lai. But the actual incidence of GIs murdering or accidentally killing civilians was certainly a small fraction of the murder rate reflected in novels and movies and television shows.

Showing atrocities as routine, or carelessly assuming that murdering peasants was "what they were sent to do," was not only a terrible injustice to all those Americans who served in Vietnam and were not murderers. It also obscured the real issue of American responsibility for civilian deaths and suffering in Vietnam, caused, in the overwhelming majority of cases, not by the moral confusion or deadly impulses of scared young soldiers in the field, but by basic U.S. tactics, doctrines, and military technology.

The fact is that for every Vietnamese civilian killed by an American soldier with a rifle or grenade, thousands were killed by the profligate use of artillery and air power that characterized America's conduct of the war. The policy on using firepower was not indiscriminate, by any means. Commanders operated under rules of engagement meant to prevent needless civilian casualties. Plenty of GIs risked their own lives to avoid endangering innocent villagers. Still, in spite of all precautions, it remains true that U.S. firepower, employed in tonnages "unparalleled in military history," as one Army study put it, devastated large areas of rural Vietnam, with an unknown but certainly heavy toll of civilian lives.

American government statistics on civilian casualties were so sketchy, inconsistent, and confusing as to suggest that U.S. military and civilian officials were for the most part trying *not* to know the facts. Journalists and historians didn't show much interest in the subject, either. One Pentagon statistician did develop an estimate putting noncombatant deaths in South Vietnam at about twenty-five thousand a year, with a high percentage attributable to U.S. bombs and shellfire. Whether those deaths represented a crime or a tragic but unavoidable effect of modern war is, surely, the central moral question arising from America's conduct of the war in Vietnam—not the aberration represented by My Lai. Yet it is hard to recall a movie or novel showing villages shattered and peasants killed by shells or bombs as the result of standard U.S. tactics. Almost always, the images that reached American audiences were of young, low-ranking soldiers committing murder or accidentally killing villagers.

Why those images were so persistent is a matter of speculation. But they did help Americans duck some difficult questions—about our character as a nation, the moral standards of our leaders, the dehumanizing qualities of technology, and the way we chose to make war among people racially and culturally distant from ourselves. Just as the burden of national failure was largely displaced from the national leadership onto the soldiers, so was the burden of guilt; unfairly showing them (to themselves as well as to everyone else) as murderers seemed a way of escaping a responsibility that properly belonged to America's leaders and to American society as a whole. The movies and novels that made a cliché of atrocities drove another wedge between the country and its soldiers. They offered another way for Americans to tell themselves, as Bobby Muller pointed out from his wheelchair, "Hey, it wasn't my war! I didn't do it."

If you asked what was the single worst day for Vietnam veterans, a lot of them might pick January 20, 1981—the day fifty-two Americans returned home after being held captive for 444 days in the U.S. embassy in Iran.

The heroes' welcome for the hostages, the ubiquitous yellow ribbons, the extravagant national outpouring of sympathy and concern—all these represented a painful, even unbearable contrast with the treatment Vietnam soldiers had yearned for but had not received when they came home. "It still rankles me, the homecoming they got," Ron Zaczek, a former marine, wrote many years later in his memoir *Farewell Darkness.* "Not the hostages' fault, of course. There was no 'fault' to it at all, though I didn't think so at the time. Those poor bastards deserved their parade. Still, I've never forgotten how it was for us. Nothing seems to make up for that." Lily Jean Lee Adams, a former Army nurse, recalled: "I remember seeing them get into cars and seeing all the yellow ribbons and the wonderful reception they got, and I was really happy for them. Then, in the middle of all this, I said, 'Wait a minute. What the fuck did they do? They sat around for four hundred and some odd days reading magazines, and I worked my ass off three hundred and sixty-five days saving lives. . . . They are getting this homecoming, and I got beat up, psychologically beat up.'"

If it was a low point, though, the Iran hostages' homecoming may have also represented a turning. The day the hostages were welcomed with a ticker-tape parade in New York, Bobby Muller remembered, was also the day the phones finally began ringing in the Vietnam Veterans of America office:

> The first time ever, ever, ever that, unsolicited, we got calls. People were saying, "Not to take it away from the hostages, but I want you to know I'm thinking about you." My mother called from Houston, Texas, and she was outraged. She said, "One of the hostages came from Houston. They gave

him a Cadillac and free passes to the ball games. What did anybody ever give you? Nothing." And the contrast between America going gaga over the hostages and they never did anything for the Vietnam Vets was so great that they were compelled finally to try and balance the scales.

Less than two years later, the dedication of the Vietnam Veterans Memorial seemed, finally, to force the country to see and acknowledge those who had fought the war. The memorial, and the public response to it, released many veterans from their silence and offered them an expression of respect, however belated, for their sacrifice. It could not have been coincidental that Vietnam, for years virtually invisible on America's cultural landscape, suddenly began to appear in a steady stream of movies, novels, memoirs, and television shows—typically depicting the veterans in a favorable, even a heroic, light.

For most vets, this was a welcome change from the crazy or doped-up "psychotic killer" figure that had previously been the most familiar representation of the Vietnam vet in popular culture. But the veteran's new image, as a few shrewd critics commented, was not exactly in the tradition of earlier war heroes. "The stereotype has been shattered," Joseph Ferrandino of Columbia University pointed out. But instead of being transformed into a conventional patriotic hero, the "new" Vietnam veteran had become something quite different. "He is not a national hero in the traditional sense," Ferrandino wrote. "He is not a hero because he sacrificed himself for something 'larger.' He is a hero because he survived. He survived for no reasons other than he wanted to live, to raise a family, see the future, or just for the hell of it. . . . The Viet vet, as cultural hero, depends on no one but himself for survival. After having been fooled by his government and rejected by his peers, he holds everyone in equal distrust." The veteran, in other words, became an icon not of faith or selflessness or service to country or ideals, but of skepticism, alienation, and individual survival as the supreme value. He still symbolized courage, perhaps, but a courage divorced from any idealism, suited to a cynical, selfish era.

In no small measure, of course, this mirrored the soldiers' experience of the war itself, in which (especially for those who served after troop withdrawals began in 1969) it was hard to find any reason for fighting *other* than for survival—their own and their friends'. "I didn't care who won," recalled William Frassanito, who went to Vietnam in 1970. "I just wanted to make sure I got home. . . . I was taking one guy over, and bringing one guy back." In this there was also a message about the war itself. If bringing one guy back was the only real goal, then the war, by definition, lacked any purpose or meaning that could justify the loss of those who did not come back. And if fifty-eight thousand young Americans (and perhaps two million Asians) could be killed in such a war, then the world itself was similarly without meaning. It may not be too great an exaggeration to say that somewhere in the experience of nearly every Vietnam veteran, acknowledged or not, was the discovery that life is absurd. Sometimes that discovery emerged from the literal circumstances of the soldier's experience—though rarely, perhaps, with as much clarity as when one of the young marines in William Broyles Jr.'s platoon asked him one day, "Lieutenant, why are we here?"

It was, Broyles wrote, "the question none of us ever asked. We didn't want to know the answer. Harlan had broken the rules." The rest of the conversation, as Broyles recounted it in his memoir *Brothers in Arms*, went like this:

> "Well, Harlan, we're here to help South Vietnam stay independent," I said.
> "Sure, sure, Lieutenant. I know all that," Harlan replied impatiently. "But why are we here, right here?"
> "Oh. Well, our mission is to protect the Da Nang vital area."
> Harlan thought about that for a minute. "Okay, Lieutenant," he said, "but why is Da Nang a vital area?"
> "I guess it's because of all the American support troops back there."
> "Yeah, but why are they there?"
> "Well, to support us," I said, closing the circle.
> "That's what I thought. We're here to save the asses of those REMFs! Hell, they're supposed to be supporting us!" Harlan started to get mad. "They hog all the fucking socks! They hang the fucking nylon blankets from the ceilings of their hootches! They carry all the new fucking M-sixteens! They eat hot fucking chow! They eat cold fucking ice cream! They eat sweet pussy! They—"
> "Hey, Harlan," Hiers said, poking his head out of the tent. "Nobody said life was going to be perfect."

Among all the veterans of Vietnam, those who waited longest for recognition and respect were the women. Even long after the memorial and the emergence of the "new," sympathetic Vietnam vet, the women were still virtually invisible. "Vietnam was on TV, and there were all the

Vietnam movies," said Diane Carlson Evans, the former Army nurse who spent nearly ten years campaigning for a women's statue at the memorial, "but it was all about the men. . . . I didn't see anything to remind me that women were in Vietnam. . . . And the strangest thing. I started thinking, 'Maybe I *wasn't* really there. Maybe I am imagining it.'"

Women veterans were so invisible, indeed, that even twenty years later, no one seemed sure how many there were. The most exhaustive post-war study of the veterans' experience reported 7,166 women served "in or around Vietnam" during the war, though other estimates were several thousand higher. The great majority were nurses, most of them recently out of nursing school and only a few years older than the teenaged soldiers they treated. Eight women were killed in combat. However many women there were, it became clear—but only very gradually—that in many ways their memories of Vietnam may have been just as troubled as the men's. The combination of new medical techniques and quick helicopter evacuation from the battlefield meant that nurses regularly saw men so terribly wounded or burned that in any previous war, they would never have lived to reach a hospital. The fact that the Vietnam GIs were younger than soldiers in earlier wars carried a special pain, too.* "I thought of soldiers as grizzled John Wayne types," mourned Lynda Van Devanter many years after the war. "They weren't supposed to look like John-Boy. And they were supposed to get better."

Nurses went to war to heal, not to fight, and for many that was justification enough. "You knew what you were doing was right," said Jane Hodge, a nurse at the Ninety-fifth Evacuation Hospital in Da Nang in 1969–70. "The fact that we were in Vietnam might not have been right, but the guys who were being shot up weren't the ones that had that choice to make. That's why I think I was able to work and live under the conditions that we did for a year. It's because the kids—not all of them were kids, but a lot of them were—didn't have a choice about being there, and the least I could do was take care of them." Kathie Swazuk, who joined the Army at twenty-one right out of nursing school and was sent to Vietnam eight months later, told an interviewer: "Whether I believed in why we should be there or not had nothing to do with it. . . . What I did there helped save

---

*The average age of an American infantryman in World War II was twenty-six; in Vietnam, it was nineteen. "I was twenty-one years old at the time. I was one of the oldest people around," Ronald Ridenhour, the Americal Division veteran who brought the My Lai massacre to light, once told an interviewer.

lives and helped get some of these guys back in one piece. I feel like the medicine that I saw practiced over there was phenomenal for the conditions and for the flow of patients. I felt more needed, or more useful, there than I ever felt in my whole life. Really I did."

Like Swazuk, many nurses found their Vietnam service professionally rewarding. But the experience often carried a price. A high percentage showed symptoms of post–traumatic stress disorder (PTSD): anxiety, depression, insomnia, nightmares, flashbacks, numbness, thoughts of suicide. More than one-quarter of the former nurses surveyed in the National Vietnam Veterans Readjustment Study were reported to have had "full-blown PTSD at some time in their lives." But even those vet center counselors and other therapists who pioneered the diagnosis and treatment of PTSD for male vets were slow to recognize the same disorder in women. So, for that matter, were the women themselves. Technically, they weren't "in combat"—so how could they have the same problems that were usually identified with combat experience?

Besides, these women were nurses; their training and instincts were to help others in need, not to look for help themselves. And their culture—not just American culture but the religiously and politically conservative Middle American–Roman Catholic background that so many nurses shared—led them to stifle many of the emotions that sprang from their experience. Doubts about U.S. policy, for example. Or anger: "Girls don't get angry. When they do, they're called crazy, hysterical, and out of control." The sight of teenaged soldiers shredded by shrapnel or burned to blackened lumps left many nurses full of rage but with no place to let it out. Instead, typically, they buried that anger within themselves, in a place so deep and dark it could be seen only in the lurid light of their nightmares.

Even more than the men, women came home from Vietnam and found no way to speak about it, either about the things they were proud of or about the things that haunted them. "I guess some people did ask me about Vietnam, and I would say things like 'It was okay.' Or 'Actually it was the pits.' That's all I said for ten years," a former Army nurse named Anne Simon Auger told interviewer Keith Walker for his collection of women veterans' oral histories. (At the beginning of the interview, Walker noted, Auger "put one hand over her eyes, and it stayed there during the entire ninety minutes the tape recorder ran.") Kathie Swazuk remembered: "It was strange. There was no one to talk to. So basically I never talked to anyone about Vietnam for years and years and years. . . . It's something that you kind of locked up, at least that's what I did. I don't know if that's normal, but I didn't talk about it much. . . . I don't think I've ever not thought about Vietnam. I just know I never expressed it."

III

When the U.S. Naval Academy's Class of 1968 held its twenty-fifth reunion, one of the returning graduates was Bill Sullivan, who served during the war aboard the USS *Vancouver* and later became a psychiatrist. "I work in a veterans hospital," he told a reporter at the reunion. "We're still hearing about [Vietnam]. About half the people I see hated the war and are angry with the government. The other half hated the hippies."

A major opinion survey conducted for the Veterans Administration reported in 1979 that although the great majority were proud of their own service, "Vietnam era veterans are more alienated from and cynical about the nation's political institutions than is the public as a whole . . . much more alienated than a comparable cross section of the public of a similar age and level of education." A sizable minority said they would refuse to serve again, and nearly 60 percent of veterans agreed with the statement that the men who served in Vietnam "were made suckers, having to risk their own lives in the wrong war in the wrong place at the wrong time."

Anger gave a kind of strange unity to the veterans who disagreed most profoundly on everything else about the war. The poet W. D. Ehrhart and the novelist and former Navy Secretary James Webb, for example, both combat-wounded marine veterans, reached exactly the opposite conclusions about Vietnam. But their views sprang from virtually identical feelings of anger and betrayal. Not only that, Webb and Ehrhart were angry at exactly the same people, too—the national leaders who had led the country into its Vietnam disaster. To Ehrhart, the betrayal was in sending him to fight (and narrowly escape death) in a war he had come to see as unjustified and immoral. To Webb, it was in letting him and millions of others fight without giving them the support and leadership necessary to win.

Webb's anger was unmistakable in his first novel, *Fields of Fire*. "Fuck 'em. Just fuck 'em. Fuck everybody who doesn't come out here and do this," says one of his characters—a lieutenant commanding a rifle platoon, just as Webb did in real life. In his public life, Webb became a passionate spokesman for the soldiers whose service had been repaid with indifference or contempt by people like the Georgetown University law

professor who baited Webb with a taunting exam question about a hypo-
thetical marine sergeant named Webb who uses the bodies of dead comrades to smuggle some pieces of jade out of Vietnam. (After seething for
two days, Webb confronted the professor in his office. "I went over to Vietnam with sixty-seven lieutenants, twenty-two died, and it wasn't funny,"
Webb told him.) The same national leaders and institutions that had sent
American soldiers to Vietnam, Webb once declared, "have now decided we
should be ashamed of our scars. Well," he went on defiantly, "I'm not
ashamed of mine." Webb's mission was to demand respect for the marines
he'd served with and for the rest of the veterans. He was not interested in
reconciling with those who, he believed, had dishonored them.

Bill Ehrhart wasn't interested in reconciliation, either. He was fed
up, I once heard him say, with people telling him to stop talking about the
war and go on. "I keep getting my face rubbed in the Vietnam war every
time I turn on the TV or open the newspaper. . . . When we wise up I'll let
it go, and we all know how long that'll be. By healing, they mean stop
disturbing us by talking about this," he went on, his voice rising. "By reconciliation, do they mean I should embrace Henry Kissinger and Robert
McNamara? I don't want to reconcile with people like that. . . . I'm going
to keep talking about this till I think we learned something from it—and
that means I'm going to keep talking until they're shoveling dirt in my
mouth! Go on to what? Go on to Mogadishu? Go on to Baghdad? Not me!"

When the newspaper columnist Bob Greene asked veterans to
write in to his nationally syndicated column about their experiences, the
letters—later collected and published as a book—were shot through with
the same anger. Often it was impossible to tell whether the writer opposed
or supported the war, but the rage was unmistakable. "The American people can go to hell before I or my sons fight another war for them," said
Alvin L. Long of Wimberley, Texas, and Sam Maggio of Wheaton, Illinois,
wrote: "Almost every male in my family has been in the military, but it
ended with me. They'll have to kill me to get at my son." Ron Ferrizzi said
nearly the same thing when I visited him in Philadelphia, twenty-three
years after watching him throw away his decorations in front of the Capitol in Washington. He wouldn't fight "even if they invade Atlantic City," he
declared. "They can have it. They'll have to come across the Delaware River
and come down my street before I pick up a weapon."

Men like Ehrhart and Webb and Ferrizzi and many of Greene's
letter writers, divided in their opinions about the war but united in their
anger, were also united in being quite sure of their views. No doubt, plenty

of veterans were equally certain of one partisan viewpoint or the other. But just as certainly, there were many others occupying the middle ground (like the country itself) with complicated, contradictory feelings about the war. Randy Russin, for one, who says reflectively, "it was no fun being part of the first losing team" and thinks his government "fought that war not to lose" instead of fighting to win—but also wondered, twenty-six years after coming home, if the war was winnable, and if it wasn't, why the United States persisted in it so long.

Nearly three decades after shipping out to Vietnam as a nineteen-year-old marine in the spring of 1966, Russin—now Captain Randall B. Russin of the Baltimore County Police Department—remembered that when he went to Vietnam, he didn't doubt his government's purposes in the war, or that Americans would win. In 1966, of course, U.S. ground forces had been in combat for only a year. Most people still trusted the national leadership. And the national goal was still to win, not just to find a face-saving way out. Winning the war was his goal, too, Russin said, but in Vietnam, it was hard to tell if we were winning or not. His combat engineer unit was constantly shifted from one area of operations to another, supporting different infantry units. But wherever they went, the fighting "didn't seem to have any relation to the overall picture." Instead, every battle seemed an isolated engagement, without any connection to the fighting anywhere else, or to anything that happened before or after it.

In his thirteen months in Vietnam, Russin also said, after a brief pause to reflect on the question, there was never a single moment when he felt that he, personally, was involved in a successful effort. Even when the marines captured a hill or some other terrain feature, they didn't stay there. Instead, after a few hours or days they would leave, so that sometime in the future, they or some other marines would have to take the place all over again. "I had uncles in World War II, in the army in Europe and in the marines in the Pacific," Russin said, "and I remember from their stories that at times they didn't know whether they were winning or losing. . . . When you're that close to what's going on," he went on, now obviously speaking of his own war, too, "you might not know whether you're winning or losing as far as the big picture is concerned. You just went out and did your job and hoped it was part of a plan to win the war." When he left Vietnam, Russin still hoped someone, somewhere, had an idea how to win. But it was a matter of faith, not evidence—sort of like belief in God. Nothing in his own experience suggested that anything had changed during his tour, or that the marines (or the country) were any closer to victory.

As I listened, I found myself thinking that perhaps the country's division over Vietnam wasn't the only reason so many veterans shut up about their experience. Maybe they also stayed silent because they didn't have a language that could describe or explain this war. Americans understand war as narrative and use narrative language to describe it. Like millions of others in his generation, Randy Russin would have absorbed from history classes, from movies and books, no doubt from his uncles' recollections, too, that war is linear, something that progresses through successive battles and campaigns toward a conclusion. But Vietnam had no story line, just fragments of violence. It was random, chaotic, without narrative logic. That meant, among many other things, that the war American soldiers found in Vietnam turned out to be something almost entirely different from the idea of war most of them brought with them. Perhaps it was not surprising that few could find words to explain it—even to themselves.

The most surprising thing I learned from Randy Russin was that the silence began even before he left Vietnam. We were sitting in the Double T Diner on U.S. Route 40 just west of the Baltimore city line. Russin grew up near here; his high school, Woodlawn High, is only a mile or so away. The diner was a local institution even then; he and his friends often came here for a late-night snack or just to hang out. More than a quarter-century had passed since his homecoming from Vietnam, but when he spoke about it, he recalled the details with such clarity it might have been only a few weeks.

He had to turn in all his field gear when he left his battalion, Russin said, so he arrived at the Da Nang processing center with no rifle, no helmet, and no unit, which for a marine was something like losing his identity altogether. Da Nang felt like "no-man's-land . . . we weren't part of any organized company or battalion. It was kind of unnerving." And everyone was a stranger. When he boarded his flight for Okinawa a couple of days later, Russin said, "I didn't know anybody on the plane. Everybody was coming from different units." When the men boarded, he remembered, there was an eerie hush. "There was no sound on the plane except the shuffling of everybody getting on. . . . It was an unearthly silence, almost like everybody was holding their breath." Only after the plane—a civilian jet airliner, chartered by the military—actually left the runway did the men break into loud, boisterous cheers. On Okinawa, Russin waited another ten days or so for his flight back to the States—still surrounded by strangers. "It lent itself to isolation," he said. "There was almost a reluctance to talk. You didn't know where the other guy was coming from, he didn't know where you were coming from." The men bitched about the delay and swapped ribald fantasies about coming home, but as Russin remembered it, they hardly mentioned where they had just come from. "Everybody was reluctant to talk about their experiences."

Another thing Russin remembered about that homecoming was how quickly he came to feel reluctant to be identified with the war. In his memory, he said, it seemed he felt that way even before he got home and saw the "Welcome Home Randy" banner in front of his parents' house, while he was still standing in the Baltimore airport in his dress uniform with his lance-corporal's stripes on the sleeves, waiting for his wife and parents to come pick him up. "It was a hope that nobody would associate you with being a veteran. It was like you wanted to go home, take your uniform off, and hope nobody noticed how short your hair was."

Why? I asked. And where did the feeling come from?

It was because the country seemed to be blaming the veterans for the war, Russin answered after a pause. He felt he had done nothing shameful in going to Vietnam, and neither had the other veterans. They went "for what they thought were the right reasons," he said, "doing your duty to your country." But now he thought they were being criticized, unfairly, for an unsuccessful policy. American soldiers "went over there with honorable intentions—and came back almost as a scapegoat for the political decisions that were made to involve the country in the war to begin with." It was hard to identify when that feeling began, or what caused it, he added. But it was no doubt part of the reason he, like so many other veterans, tended to remain silent about the war. He said very little to his family: "I have the feeling if someone wasn't there, you're never going to make them understand."

Every so often, something brings Vietnam back to mind—a television show or movie, or perhaps a news event like the Persian Gulf War or the U.S. military disaster in Somalia. But Russin still doesn't find himself talking about his memories very often. "The consensus in the country was that nobody wanted to talk about it. . . . I don't know," he said, "I just suppressed it, kept it to myself, I guess."

Twenty-four years after he came home from Vietnam, Randy Russin buried his oldest son.

Chris Russin died of leukemia at nineteen, the same age his father had been when he went off to war. In high school, Russin said, Chris's two main interests had been playing the drums and associating with a group of students who were interested in pacifist ideas and the peace movement. For a couple of years he usually wore a necklace with the peace symbol (although, in the contradictory way of teenagers, he also thought on and off about joining the Marine Corps). Chris also wore his hair long, to cover a slight deformity in one ear. The hair and the peace sign both stirred uncomfortable memories for his father. When he looked back on the peace movement of the Vietnam era, Randy Russin could find no distinction between opposing the war and opposing the veterans. Critics of the war were blaming the soldiers "for something that wasn't our fault," he thought. And beyond that, beyond the specific issue of the war, there was something troubling at the antiwar movement's core—something in conflict with Russin's character and most basic beliefs. Randy Russin was and is a man who deeply believes in duty and responsibility, and it seemed to him the movement believed in neither.

"I viewed the peace movement almost like a kind of drop-out-of-society kind of movement," he said. "Like, I'm not going to accept any responsibility for supporting the country's effort"—meaning not just the war, but any effort for any national purposes. Yet even if the symbols made him uncomfortable, Russin also respected his son and his son's beliefs, and he believes his son respected him. And that is why, when Chris died and Russin's wife suggested putting the peace sign on his grave marker, he eventually swallowed hard and agreed. At first, he told her, "I don't know if I can go down and look at that every time I go to the cemetery." But after thinking about it for a few days he gave his assent. "We went ahead and did it, and to this day he's got the peace sign on his grave."

When I asked if it still bothered him, Russin shook his head. "No, because I knew my son." The peace symbol and the long hair "reminded me of something that was offensive to me from the sixties," he said. "But because of who he was and what I knew about him, they were never offensive." He paused and then added: "They kind of gave me a different perspective. Like maybe that's what the kids were like then, and it just didn't look that way to me."

After we parted that day I drove out and found Chris Russin's grave. The cemetery lies alongside a two-lane highway in Maryland's Carroll County, seventeen miles west of downtown Baltimore and just past the dividing line where suburban sprawl peters out and the landscape turns green and rural. It was a bright, warm September afternoon, with a caressing breeze that rippled the waters of Liberty Reservoir nearby. I found the marker, with a vase of fresh white and pink flowers on it and a pair of wooden drumsticks, one at each side of the vase. Chris's name and birth and death dates—April 15, 1972; May 20, 1991—were inscribed on a bronze tablet placed flat on the neatly clipped grass. Above the inscription to the right of the flowers was an image of a drum and drumsticks, and to the left, the peace sign.

I stood in front of the grave, grieving for Randy Russin and trying to imagine how any parent could bear such a loss. Somewhere, not in the foreground of my mind but floating at the edges, was a memory of the wall in Washington and all the dead sons whose names are inscribed there, and the parents who still grieve for them. Some birds chattered and there was a low hum of cars passing on the road outside the cemetery gates, but where I stood it was hushed, as if there were a bright little tent of silence over Chris's grave. Looking at the marker and the flowers and the peace sign, I remembered how Randy had linked this private tragedy to that other national tragedy he had been part of so many years ago. I had asked if he had felt anger about Vietnam. "Bitter," Randy replied, and when I asked if it had gone away, he said "No, just mellowed."

The country had more or less apologized for all those years of blaming the veterans for the war, he said, and he had finally more or less accepted the apology. But, he went on, "it's like losing a child. You're different because of it, you'll never be the way you were before. But you learn to live in spite of it."

3
THE GENERATION

*There's a wall ten miles high and fifty miles thick between those of us
who went and those who didn't, and that wall
is never going to come down.*
—Milt Copulos

*We all had our reasons for taking up our battle cries, and
I believe our battle cries very cleverly fooled us all.*
—Greg Schlieve

I

Not just the veterans but an entire generation of Americans found
it hard to turn the page on Vietnam. Many former war protesters looked
back with a chastening sense that the issues had been more ambiguous than
they had been willing to see at the time. Often their own motives for protesting seemed, in retrospect, to have involved as much pleasure-seeking and
self-preservation as moral principle. "What disturbs me about the war is,
even though we were right, we really didn't mean it," one man told Myra
MacPherson. Men who had avoided service often were troubled, like the
veterans, by their Vietnam history—particularly those who felt, as many
did, that they had benefited from a system that favored the upper-middle

class and the college-educated over those from less privileged backgrounds.

The text for this viewpoint was an article by the writer James Fallows, published in 1975 in *The Washington Monthly* under the barbed title "What Did You Do in the Class War, Daddy?" Fallows's mea culpa recalled how he escaped the draft during his final year at Harvard University by starving himself below the 120-pound weight requirement. It didn't take a Harvard degree to use that technique, to be sure. But boys from farms or from working-class or black or Hispanic neighborhoods weren't as practiced or diligent in searching out the draft law's many loopholes; nor did they as easily find the sympathetic doctors and psychiatrists who helped large numbers of college graduates to avoid the draft on medical grounds. On the day of his own draft physical at the Boston Navy Yard, Fallows recalled, while he and his friends pursued their various strategies to beat the system, another busload of young men arrived from the working-class neighborhood of Chelsea. "I tried to avoid noticing," Fallows wrote, "but the results were inescapable. While perhaps four out of five of my friends from Harvard were being deferred, just the opposite was happening to the Chelsea boys."

Fallows did not feel he and his friends had been wrong in opposing the war. But letting less privileged young men go in their place hardly seemed an honorable way of opposing it. Unlike their antiwar heroes Gandhi or Thoreau, Fallows noted dryly, "most of us managed without difficulty to stay out of jail. . . . The practical model for our wartime conduct was our enemy LBJ, who weaseled away from the front lines during World War II."*

Though it originally appeared in a magazine with a circulation of only about twenty-five thousand, Fallows's confession was widely quoted and reprinted in the following two decades—evidence of how painful a nerve he had struck. Twenty years after his article was published, a number of Fallows's Harvard classmates were evidently still anguished by the same

---

*Johnson, a thirty-three-year-old congressman from Texas when the United States entered World War II, held a Naval Reserve commission but spent only a few months on active service. His actual combat experience consisted of flying as an observer on a single bombing mission in the South Pacific. For that feat, he was awarded a highly suspect Silver Star—a fairly obvious attempt by the Navy to ingratiate itself with a member of Congress. (Johnson, whose only role was as a passenger, was the only man on the plane to get a medal for that mission. The pilot was not decorated, nor was a gunner who shot down an attacking Japanese fighter.) Soon afterward, having established his politically desirable status as a war veteran (and decorated hero), Johnson resigned his Navy commission and reassumed his seat in Congress.

issues of privilege, guilt, and regret. The draft issue had left "substantial confusion and inner conflict that persists to this day," one graduate commented in response to a questionnaire circulated before the class's twenty-fifth reunion. Another wrote: "I should have gone but didn't. It's beyond politics. I was too stupid at 18-21 to see that the deferment made it a 'class-based' military so LBJ could avoid college protest. I failed, he failed."

The class difference between those who protested and those who fought the war was not lost on "ordinary" Americans, either. "I'm bitter. You bet your goddamn dollar I'm bitter," a firefighter whose son was killed told the author Robert Coles. The grief and anger in his words still seemed to burn on the page, more than a quarter-century after the interview was recorded:

> It's people like us who give up our sons for the country. The business people, they run the country and make money from it. The college types, the professors, they go to Washington and tell the government what to do. . . . But their sons, they don't end up in the swamps over there, in Vietnam. No sir. They're deferred, because they're in school. Or they get sent to safe places. Or they get out with all those letters they have from their doctors. . . . The whole thing is a mess. The sooner we get the hell out of there, the better. But what bothers me about the peace crowd is that you can tell from their attitude, the way they look and what they say, that they don't really love this country. Some of them almost seem *glad* to have a chance to criticize us. . . . To hell with them! Let them get out, leave, if they don't like it here! My son didn't die so they can look filthy and talk filthy and insult everything we believe in and everyone in the country—me and my wife and people here on the street, and the next street, and all over.

His wife added:

> I told him I thought [the protesters] want the war to end, so no more Ralphs will die, but he says no, they never stop and think about Ralph and his kind of people, and I'm inclined to agree. They *say* they do, but I listen to them, I watch them; since Ralph died I listen and I watch as carefully as I can. Their hearts are with other people, not their own American people, the ordinary kind of person in this country. . . . Those people, a lot of them are rich women from the suburbs, the rich suburbs. Those kids, they are in college. . . . I'm against this war, too—the way a mother is, whose sons are in the army, who has lost a son fighting in it. The world

hears those demonstrators making their noise. The world doesn't hear me, and it doesn't hear a single person I know.

In giving voice to the vague guilt a lot of men his age felt about not having served (or about how they escaped serving), James Fallows opened a window on the split in his generation. But his article pointed at another split, too: between the men of the Vietnam generation and their fathers, and the meaning of the wars each had fought.

Military service in World War II was a unifying experience for the country (with the significant exception of African Americans consigned to segregated units—and some sense of sharing a common experience with their countrymen existed even in the segregated army). Seventy percent of draft-age men were in uniform. The burden of sacrifice seemed to be spread reasonably fairly: college graduates were overrepresented, not underrepresented, in the riskiest combat assignments. A dashing, twenty-four-year-old PT-boat commander named John F. Kennedy, Harvard '40, was something of an archetype of the nation's elite in uniform. So was Lt. George Bush, Yale '48, who enlisted out of Phillips Andover Academy to become the youngest flier in the Navy. At Kennedy's alma mater, only 11 men of the entire Harvard class of 1944 were present at commencement. All the others had already left for military service. Two years later, when the class of 1946 should have graduated, so many had interrupted their studies to serve in the war that only 28 men received their degrees on schedule.

Altogether, nearly 27,000 Harvard students, alumni, employees, and faculty members served in the armed forces; 691 of them lost their lives, including John Kennedy's older brother, Joseph P. Kennedy Jr., class of '38. The classes of '41, '42, and '46 each had 37 men killed in the war.* Two years after the war ended, 4,000 of Harvard's 5,300 undergraduates were veterans. Very few men from comparable social or educational backgrounds served in Vietnam. Only 19 Harvard alumni died there, fewer than were lost by many high schools in working-class neighborhoods. (Dundalk High School in Dundalk, Maryland, for example, attended mainly by children of steelworkers at the nearby Sparrows Point steel mill, counted 23 former students killed in Vietnam, from a male student body perhaps one-

---

*By comparison: West Point's class of '41 also lost 37 men killed in action; the highest toll of any West Point class was 57 killed from the class of '43. West Point's classes in that era were much smaller than Harvard's, so its casualties were proportionately far greater; still, the fact that the nation's military academy and its most prestigious civilian university lost roughly comparable numbers of graduates is a stunning contrast with the Vietnam era.

sixth the size of Harvard's.) In James Fallows's class, only a little more than 10 percent of those men who answered the reunion questionnaire had served in the military at all. An astonishing 27 percent had, like Fallows, failed the Selective Service physical exam, though twenty-five years later only 1 percent reported themselves in poor health. Only one-half of 1 percent—that is, two men!—had been drafted and served in Vietnam. No one in the class of 1970 died in the war; nor did anyone graduating in 1969, 1971, or 1972. "Those who were better off economically did not carry out their obligations," declared former Navy pilot and POW (later U.S. Senator) John S. McCain. Instead, America's elite left the fighting and dying to the less privileged. That, to McCain, "was the greatest crime and injustice of the Vietnam War."*

The national leadership was unquestionably an accomplice in that crime, if that's what it was. President Johnson and his defense secretary, Robert McNamara, might have been the most villainous of enemies, in the eyes of antiwar youth. But Johnson's and McNamara's policies were crucial in letting millions of middle-class, better-educated young men escape the Vietnam draft. Because of the huge boom in births right after World War II, America had many more young men than it needed to fight the war in Vietnam. Had they chosen to do so, McNamara and his colleagues could have raised intelligence and education standards and still have drafted more than enough men for the war. Instead, they chose to lower standards. From 1966 to 1971, a program called Project 100,000—hailed as, of all things, a kind of progressive social welfare program for the underprivileged!— *required* the armed services to draw one-fifth of all recruits from those in the lowest qualifying tier of general aptitude test scores. Another one-tenth would be drawn from men with scores so low they would have been rejected under pre-1966 rules. Once in the service, a disproportionate number of these "New Standards" troops (about 350,000 were recruited altogether) became infantrymen, since few could qualify for specialist training.

Not surprisingly, the Project 100,000 and New Standards troops were overwhelmingly from poor families. And while it might not be true

---

*Of the nineteen Harvard casualties, two were civilians (one a State Department official, one described somewhat mysteriously in his class's twenty-fifth anniversary report as having died "on a government mission against the Vietcong"). All but two of the others were commissioned officers, including four career officers with ranks of captain or above (including one major general) and eleven lieutenants. One of the two enlisted men was a corporal in the Marine Corps (almost entirely a volunteer force) and one was an Army Pfc., whose class records do not indicate if he volunteered or was drafted. If the former, that would mean that apparently *not a single Harvard man was killed as an enlisted draftee* in the entire war.

that every one of them took the place of a richer family's son who was not drafted, it is still clear that draft policies, not just the greater ability of middle-class youths to find loopholes, contributed to the skewed makeup of the Vietnam army. Whether those policies were purposely calculated to spare the elite and the middle class and thus keep the "silent majority" from turning against the war, as some have theorized, remains a matter of speculation. Robert McNamara, an enthusiast for Project 100,000 and the New Standards program when they were introduced, made no mention of either in the memoir he published nearly thirty years later as a kind of public expiation for his role in the war. The entire subject of the Vietnam-era draft, in fact, is nowhere mentioned in McNamara's 400-page apologia. Nor, in his lists of America's mistakes and the lessons that should be drawn from Vietnam, is there any hint that draft policies were unjust or that the country should try, in any future war, to spread the burden of sacrifice more fairly among its citizens.

It is symbolic that the best-known lieutenant of the Vietnam War, rather than an Ivy League–educated aristocrat like John Kennedy or George Bush, was a "below-average, dull, and inconspicuous" young man named William L. ("Rusty") Calley from Miami, Florida, who flunked out of Palm Beach Junior College with two Cs, a D, and four Fs in his first year and reportedly managed to get through officer candidate school without even learning to read a map or use a compass. In Vietnam, on the morning of March 16, 1968, between 7:30 and approximately 11 A.M., Calley's platoon massacred several hundred unarmed Vietnamese civilians in a place called My Lai, leaving a dark, permanent stain on the reputation of the U.S. Army and on that of all the soldiers who served in Vietnam and were not murderers. If Calley, who dismissed the massacre as "no big deal," should never have been an officer, as many observers felt, it followed that he was commanding an infantry platoon that morning only because too many of his more intelligent and capable contemporaries had found ways not to serve. In that sense, it could be said that the best and brightest shared some of the blame for My Lai. Author James Webb, who commanded a marine rifle company in Vietnam, declared long afterward: "I think the people who went to those schools—Harvard, MIT, whatever—are collectively responsible for William Calley."

The social differences between the World War II army and Vietnam's reverberated far from the battlefields, and long after the shooting ended. The aftermath of World War II gave rise to the greatest burst of upward social and economic mobility America, or any other society in the world, had ever experienced. The blurring of class lines in military service during the war certainly played a part in that phenomenon, raising the aspirations and broadening the horizons of millions of young men. The GI Bill, paying the way for more than two million ex-servicemen to go to college, extended that wartime experience on into the postwar years. For two decades after the war, too, the peacetime draft brought together American men from different regions, educational levels, and social backgrounds. For many draftees of that era, that broader experience of their own society was one of the relatively few compensations for the boredom and discomforts of peacetime army life. By contrast, the makeup of the Vietnam-era army contributed to widening class divisions among Americans—a widening that was already under way, to be sure, as the result of other postwar trends, including the bifurcation of cities and suburbs, the loss of upward mobility as well-paid factory jobs grew scarcer, and an educational system that increasingly seemed to serve the nation's haves far better than the have-nots.

The all-volunteer army, a direct legacy of the Vietnam War, perpetuated that growing social gap. Without the draft, few men (or women) from upper-middle-class backgrounds or with college educations chose to accept the regimentation and relatively modest compensation of a military career. Seven years after the draft ended, college graduates had virtually disappeared from recruiting rolls. In 1980, of 340,000 enlisted soldiers serving their first enlistment in the army, only 276 had graduated from college. In the combat arms (infantry, armor, artillery), out of 100,860 first-term enlisted men, the number of graduates was only 25! Fourteen years later, the services still drew their enlisted personnel overwhelmingly from those who had never gone beyond high school. Among enlisted recruits in all services in 1994, according to the Defense Department's annual report on "Population Representation in the Military Services," fewer than 5 percent had any college experience, compared with nearly 50 percent of civilians in the same age group.

At the same time, the armed forces also increasingly shut their doors to Americans from the poorest backgrounds, for whom military service had once been one of the most accessible routes to education, economic security, and higher social status. New battlefield technology demanded better-educated soldiers, while lower force levels enabled the services to recruit much more selectively. School dropouts or young men with minor criminal records rarely qualified for enlistment. The Defense

Department's statistics showed that fewer than 1 percent of recruits accepted in 1994 had aptitude test scores in the lowest passing category. Only 1.4 percent of new enlistees lacked a high school diploma, compared with nearly 20 percent of civilians in the same age group.

Thus, by the 1990s, with very few exceptions, neither the elite nor the very poor were to be found in uniform at all. The absence of that shared experience also meant, almost surely, a weakened sense of common citizenship or a shared destiny as Americans. Also weakened was the connection between the country's armed forces and the rest of society. The new, professional army of the post-Vietnam era "withdrew into itself," wrote the commentator William Pfaff, "with new ideas about its duty to a civilian government which it believed had betrayed it in Vietnam. . . . Military communities," he continued, "more than ever came to resemble a dream of America's past, fenced off and self-sufficient, protected by military police posts from the turbulence of the surrounding American society."

If the Vietnam draft both created and reflected growing class and cultural differences in American society, so did the other formative experiences of Americans who came of age during that war. Their parents' generation, by and large, had been brought together, rather than divided, by the Great Depression and World War II. By contrast, the baby-boom children who grew up into the Vietnam era—already more segregated by social class than their parents as a result of the great postwar shift to suburban housing—lived in a landscape of issues that split the country.

The civil rights struggle, the women's movement, environmentalism, new codes of speech and manners and sexual conduct—all of these, like Vietnam, pried open deep, jagged fault lines across the terrain of American society. They did so, moreover, at the exact moment when the profoundly revolutionary force of television began to show Americans to themselves in a very different way. Television unified in some ways but also magnified the images and voices of division and, by its sheer power to transmit directly to the emotions of the viewer, often seemed to destroy patience, thought, and the capacity for compromise that had been essential in American political life. The generation that grew up with Vietnam was also the first to grow up with this new medium; together, its experiences and the way it saw them contributed to a "heritage of division," as the political writer David Broder called it, that overtook post-Vietnam America.

As members of the Vietnam generation began to climb the rungs of America's political ladder, there were insistent echoes of the divide between those who had served in Vietnam and those who had not.

When it was discovered during the 1988 campaign that George Bush's running mate, Sen. Dan Quayle of Indiana, had done his wartime service in the Indiana National Guard instead of the regular armed forces, many critics instantly concluded that Quayle had intended to dodge Vietnam and had succeeded in doing so only because he came from a wealthy and influential family. Quayle insisted he had not been trying to avoid the war, but most men of his age remembered that joining the National Guard was a virtual guarantee against being sent to the war zone—and, largely for that reason, it was also an option rarely available to young men facing the wartime draft unless they had fortuitous friendships or connections. High-level influence helped in some cases, as with the professional athletes who benefited, quite openly, from preferential arrangements with local guard or reserve commanders. "We have an arrangement with the Colts," the head of Maryland's National Guard told a national magazine. "When they have a player with a military problem, they send him to us." The Detroit Lions management got two star players into an army reserve unit in return for letting the unit provide the honor guard for the pregame salutes to the flag. This open favoritism was in sharp contrast with World War II, when hundreds of professional athletes—including many of the most prominent stars—were drafted. (There was another contrast, not lost on African Americans: while virtually all prominent white athletes escaped the Vietnam-era draft without penalty, boxer Muhammad Ali was denied conscientious-objector status, stripped of his world heavyweight title, and sentenced to prison for refusing induction in 1967. Four years later, Ali's conviction was set aside by the U.S. Supreme Court, which found unanimously that the Justice Department erred in refusing his original application for CO status.)

Other draft-eligible men managed to get into a National Guard or reserve unit simply by having friends already serving who could tip them off in advance when a vacancy was about to open up. At the time, there was little pretense about why most men joined the guard, or that it was an almost certain safe haven from the war. Of slightly more than one million men who served in the National Guard or reserves during the Vietnam era, only thirty-seven thousand were mobilized—and only fifteen thousand of those went to Vietnam.

The Quayle controversy was a curtain-raiser for the similar but larger furor that erupted four years later when Bill Clinton's draft record burst into the 1992 presidential primary contest. As the story finally emerged, after a good many misleading and in some cases flatly false explanations by Clinton,* the future president had received a draft notice in April 1969, while he was in the first year of his Rhodes Scholarship program at Oxford University in England. That summer, after unsuccessfully looking for a National Guard or Army Reserve vacancy (shades of Dan Quayle!), Clinton avoided induction by promising to join the Reserve Officer Training Corps program at the University of Arkansas after completing his second year at Oxford. A few months later, however, in a letter from Oxford, he reneged on that commitment, and shortly thereafter escaped the draft altogether by receiving a high number, 311, in the new draft lottery, held on December 1.

It was technically true, as Clinton later claimed, that in backing out of his ROTC commitment he gave up his deferment and voluntarily reentered the draft pool. It was also true, however, that he did so only after arranging to miss a definite induction date, and at a time when lower draft calls, more flexible rules for graduate students, and the impending change to a lottery system all substantially improved his chances of avoiding the army after all.

Twenty-two years later, early in Clinton's presidential campaign, his Vietnam past reappeared in the form of a long letter he had written two days after the lottery to Col. Eugene J. Holmes, director of the University of Arkansas ROTC unit and the man who had agreed to take Clinton into the program, qualifying him for a deferment. The letter (which Clinton thought he had arranged to be removed from the files and destroyed during his 1974 campaign for Congress) was Clinton's mea culpa for having misled Holmes on his true feelings about the war. Taken as a whole, the letter was a serious expression—in places, an eloquent one—of the anguish Vietnam represented for Clinton and many other young men of his generation. But in the style of the 1990s, when both political discourse and journalism relentlessly sought to compress every issue or thought or event into

---

*The fullest and probably most authoritative account is the one pieced together by David Maraniss in his 1995 Clinton biography *First in His Class*. Maraniss convincingly demonstrates that Clinton's own various accounts of his draft history fell somewhat short of the full truth—and that in some instances, his claims to have been honestly mistaken about certain key details were, to put it mildly, highly implausible. For example, for many years Clinton never volunteered the fact that he had actually received a draft notice. It had just slipped his mind, he claimed later, an assertion that is almost impossible to believe.

a single, simple, unambiguous, and provocative phrase, two short fragments of Clinton's letter were spotlighted so intensely that the rest of it
faded rather quickly from public view. One was Clinton's admission that
he had chosen not to resist the draft openly, in spite of his beliefs, "for one
reason: to maintain my political viability within the system." The other was
his comment in the letter's closing lines that he hoped Colonel Holmes
would come to understand how the war had left "many fine people . . . still
loving their country but loathing the military." The first left a lasting impression that Clinton was an opportunist; the second branded him as a
left-wing, unpatriotic, antimilitary radical.

Both those perceptions, in varying ways, would hover over the rest
of the campaign and over Clinton's presidency. But his Vietnam record did
not derail his quest for the Democratic nomination, despite the predictions
of his primary opponents, one of whom was Sen. Bob Kerrey of Nebraska,
a Medal of Honor winner in Vietnam. Nor did charges of draft dodging
seem to have a major effect on Clinton's contest with President Bush, a decorated hero in World War II. As with Quayle, the issue left traces on voters'
minds but, apparently, did not have a direct, appreciable impact on their
decisions. Nor, for that matter, did Kerrey's heroic war record, or Bush's.

Running for reelection four years later, Clinton faced another World
War II veteran, Sen. Bob Dole of Kansas, whose right arm and shoulder
were permanently impaired from wounds he suffered while serving with
the Tenth Mountain Division in Italy. Dole and his campaign staff did not
bring up the draft issue as explicitly as the Bush campaign had in 1992. But
Dole, who had previously been quite reserved about his wartime experiences, spoke about them frequently during his run for the White House.
His advisers, clearly, hoped that the public would draw its own conclusions
from the contrast between the president's record and Dole's, and vote
accordingly. But the great majority of voters found other issues more important. Though Clinton's draft record no doubt cost him some votes and
contributed to a residue of doubts about his honesty and character, most
Americans seemed not so quick, after all, to judge decisions made years
earlier by young men in a troubled time.

Because he had opposed the war, Clinton was at least spared the
charge of hypocrisy that was leveled at Quayle and a long list of other conservatives who justified the war even though they had, by one means or
another, avoided serving themselves. The list included such conservative
luminaries as Newt Gingrich, William Bennett, and Sen. Phil Gramm of
Texas. Strikingly, few in this group shared, or at least acknowledged, any of

the guilt that pained James Fallows and some of his antiwar colleagues. The most brazen was Gramm, a vociferous member of the Republican Party's right wing and a competitor for the 1996 Republican presidential nomination. Gramm had a habit of attacking opponents for their lack of military service but explained his own string of deferments during Vietnam by saying—without apparent embarrassment—that although he supported the U.S. effort in the war, "I thought what I was doing at Texas A&M was important." Gramm also offered the explanation that his brother and many of his students served in Vietnam, implying that his own obligation was thereby somehow lessened, and declared that "the difference between Bill Clinton and me is I wasn't out protesting against the war," as if it were somehow more honorable to duck a war one believed in than to avoid a war one thought was wrong!

Quayle, Clinton, Gingrich, and Gramm might all feel themselves on the defensive about avoiding Vietnam, along with other politicians with similar histories and with millions of their less-celebrated countrymen. But theirs was the common experience of their generation. Of the nearly twenty-seven million American men who reached draft age between 1964 and 1973, only 40 percent served in the military. Of those, only about 25 percent went to Vietnam, representing just one-tenth of the draft-age male population. Among the college-educated, which included both Clinton and most of his visible critics, the percentage was far lower.

The number of young Americans who actively protested the war was, relatively, quite small too, despite the popular cliché of a generation split between veterans and protesters. Fewer than half of American campuses experienced any form of organized antiwar activity. Those who adopted the rhetoric of anti-imperialist revolution and marched under Viet Cong flags were never more than a small fraction of their age group, even if theirs became the image popularly associated with the antiwar movement. Active draft resisters were a small minority, too. Approximately 210,000 men were reported to federal authorities for violating one or another provision of the draft laws, though nearly 90 percent of the cases were never prosecuted. Only 3,250 went to prison.* A substantial majority of the generation neither served nor resisted nor demonstrated, but stayed out

---

*Some accused draft evaders avoided prosecution by reporting for induction. But many cases were dropped because of procedural errors by draft boards or for other reasons. In addition to the 210,000 cases referred to federal prosecutors, the authors of one postwar survey estimated that an additional 360,000 men violated draft laws but were never reported, either because draft boards simply didn't bother or because their offenses were never discovered.

of the army if they could, went about their own lives, and voted for Richard Nixon for president in both 1968 and 1972.

The Vietnam draft was in fact quite small, by historical standards. The highest yearly draft during Vietnam (340,000 men in 1966) was lower than many monthly draft calls during World War II. Nearly twice as many had been drafted in 1951—from a much smaller pool of draft-age men—for Korea. Remarkably, the percentage of twenty-six-year-old men who had done military service was actually lower in 1973 (40 percent) after seven straight years of wartime conscription than in 1962 (58 percent) after nearly a decade of peace.

Among a good many Vietnam veterans, there was a lingering bitterness at those—including Clinton—who hadn't gone. "There's a wall ten miles high and fifty miles thick between those of us who went and those who didn't," a badly wounded combat veteran named Milt Copulos told the writer (and fellow veteran) Robert Timberg, "and that wall is never going to come down." The fact remained, though, that nine out of ten American men in that generation were on Bill Clinton's side of the wall. And Dan Quayle's. And Newt Gingrich's and Phil Gramm's. On both sides, there were some who found moral clarity in the wartime choices they had made, or that circumstances had imposed on them. But for most, as the generation moved on through middle age, the issues of an anguished time continued to defy easy or comfortable judgments, remaining as painful and morally confusing—or more so—as during the war itself.

In the end, soldiers and protesters alike often found it hard to face the inner truth of their experiences. Students hid from the truth that they were protesting because they were afraid of dying in the war and to earn the approval and acceptance of their peers, a veteran named Greg Schlieve told Clinton's biographer David Maraniss, "and vets had their own smokescreens. We couldn't see the truth about ourselves, either. We would say we were patriotic, responsible young men. That's bullshit. Maybe ten percent of the true story. For a lot of us who went, we were going after the same thing—approval. We were trying to get it from our peers, from our father who had been in World War II. . . . It doesn't matter if you were a soldier fighting the war or a student fighting against it. We all had our reasons for taking up our battle cries, and I believe our battle cries very cleverly fooled us all."

III

America's long, bitter wrangle over Vietnam kept reappearing so insistently because, at its heart, the dispute was not about the specific rights or wrongs of a war that had ended twenty years earlier or about what certain Americans had or hadn't done in that war. The national argument on Vietnam was really about America's vision of itself: about conflicting ideas on who we are, as a people, and what we value and believe. That underlying issue explains why the country's deep divisions over Vietnam lingered on in a cultural clash that still reverberated, a full generation after the war ended, in America's political life, its arts, and its popular culture.

In 1980, 1984, and 1988, voters chose conservative presidents at least partly because of "values" issues arising directly from the turmoil of the war years. The same issues continued to hover over Bill Clinton. Fairly or not, millions of Americans continued to associate liberalism, and to some extent the entire Democratic Party, with lack of patriotism, too much permissiveness about sex and drugs and crime, contempt for traditional beliefs and tastes, and disrespect for authority and its symbols. Linking the upheavals of the 1960s with contentious matters in the eighties and nineties, the "values issue" extended old clashes into the present—connecting, for example, Clinton's draft record and youthful antiwar protest to his policies more than two decades later on issues such as welfare benefits for single mothers or the controversy over homosexuals in the military.

If the Vietnam era saddled liberals with a lasting image of cultural radicalism, it also burdened conservatives, miring them in nostalgic myths that disregarded the great changes taking place in American life and had "little basis," as the commentator Kevin Phillips once acknowledged, "in the political and economic facts of the world we live in today." Nor, at least as far as Vietnam was concerned, did those myths have much basis in the facts of yesterday, either. The politics of nostalgia demanded, among other things, a revised, highly selective memory of Vietnam as a righteous effort, staunchly supported by the vast majority of patriotic Americans and opposed only by the "counter-culture McGoverniks" (to use a phrase from a later era) who, like their liberal descendants a quarter-century later, were an out-of-step fringe group in no way representing "real" American beliefs. The revisionist view of the war, as expressed by politicians and also in popular movies such as *Rambo*, reflected, as one scholar put it, "a need to show we have the will and the character we had before Vietnam . . . a need to rethink ourselves to the basic American good guy."

The power of nostalgia in post-Vietnam America was embodied most of all by Ronald Reagan. Personal and political instinct, ideology, and a notable capacity to ignore inconvenient or unwelcome facts made Reagan the ideal spinner of the new Vietnam fable. The classic expression of the revisionist myth came during an appearance before the Veterans of Foreign Wars early in his 1980 run for the presidency when, against the advice of his campaign strategists, Reagan declared—to thunderous applause—that America's effort in Vietnam "was, in truth, a noble cause."

The applause was understandable. If Reagan was right, there was no need for any more self-doubt or self-reproach or moral confusion about the war in Vietnam. We had failed to win not because our policies were misconceived, but only because we had not stuck to them resolutely enough. And if the failure was partly due to timid leadership in Washington or to misguided military strategy, most of the blame could still be shoveled off onto the McGoverniks—the same liberals who were also to blame for pornography, poor test scores and discipline problems in schools, street crime, desecrating the flag, high divorce rates, and failed welfare programs. In this vision, Vietnam could be inscribed, after all, on that scroll of righteous, patriotic wars going all the way back to the Revolution. And America could still be the unblemished, innocent country of Reagan's imagination, a country that trusted its leaders, honored its symbols, exulted in its power, and harbored no doubts of the special moral standing it had long claimed among the nations of the world.

The real war in Vietnam was, however, more complicated and more ambiguous than Ronald Reagan ever seemed to understand. And so was the task of vanquishing Vietnam's legacy.

If nothing else, Reagan did a service to the soldiers who had been in Vietnam, and who could now take from his "noble cause" speech a belated acknowledgement of their honor. Reagan was "a one-man welcome-home parade," said Robert Timberg, whose sympathetic and sincere respect reassured veterans who had been "stunned into silence" by the indifference that greeted them when they came home. Reagan's words told them that there was no shame in their service; that they weren't criminals or losers; that it was all right to take pride in their service and sacrifice. Reagan's Democratic opponents and many reporters ridiculed his VFW speech. But to veterans it was a welcome message, telling them, as Timberg observed, that "even if the national goal was later tarnished beyond redemption, that in a distant land under the most brutal of circumstances their friends and comrades, in some cases they themselves, had often acted with a raw courage that by any measure qualified as noble."

But comforting the country about its *policy* in Vietnam, which Reagan's storybook version of history also tried to do, was another matter. If Reagan's distortions pleased those who did not want to remember painful truths, there was a kind of eerie justice in the fact that the war, and distorted memories of the war, also played a crucial role in his presidency's greatest scandal. Vietnam was the common link in the backgrounds of Lt. Col. Oliver North, his boss Robert McFarlane, former Air Force Maj. Gen. Richard Secord, and others involved in the secret arms sales to Iran and the murky "Enterprise" network that illegally supplied arms to Nicaraguan rebels fighting against the left-wing Sandinista government in Managua.

The war wasn't just a line in North's and his associates' résumés. It shaped, in crucial ways, their political values and view of the world and many of the particular acts that came together to make up the Iran-Contra affair. "I became convinced that Vietnam and its aftermath lay at the heart of the matter, that absent Vietnam there would have been no Iran-Contra," wrote Timberg, who covered the scandal as a journalist but also brought to the story earlier experiences identical to North's and McFarlane's: the Naval Academy, the Marine Corps, combat service, and a Purple Heart in Vietnam. As the story unfolded, Timberg wrote in his book *The Nightingale's Song*, "I kept picking up echoes of Vietnam. . . . I remember thinking that perhaps Iran-Contra was at least in part the bill for Vietnam finally coming due." If North and McFarlane and their fellow Annapolis graduate Rear Adm. John Poindexter rather easily fell into a pattern of misleading Congress about what the Reagan White House was up to in Iran and Nicaragua, it was in no small part because Vietnam had taught them and millions of other veterans to distrust civilian politicians. If they skirted or broke the law to keep the anti-Sandinista Contra rebels in the fight, it was at least in part because of a bitter determination not to reenact America's broken promise to South Vietnam.

The link between Vietnam and Iran-Contra was most evident in the case of North, the most celebrated and flamboyant figure in the affair. Risking his neck in Vietnam and then seeing his country and its leaders abandon the cause had left North "quite cynical about government," his fellow marine and National Security Council boss McFarlane told congressional investigators. Honor, to North and others seared by Vietnam, did not lie in observing the letter of laws written by timid politicians. It was in making sure the United States did not betray others as, North believed, it had betrayed its Vietnamese allies. His defiant opening statement to the congressional hearings resonated with that belief. Congress's "fickle, vacillating, unpredictable" policies on financing the Contra rebels was the real crime in the affair, North suggested; in alternately authorizing and shutting off funds, lawmakers had unconscionably toyed with the lives of real, flesh-and-blood men and women facing death or wounds on the battlefield.

"Armies need food and consistent help," North lectured the committee members in his memorable appearance before the Iran-Contra investigating committee. Speaking about the Contras but surely remembering the South Vietnamese as well, he went on: "They need a flow of money, of arms, clothing, and medical supplies. The Congress of the United States allowed the Executive to encourage them to do battle and then abandoned them. The Congress of the United States left soldiers in the field unsupported and vulnerable to their Communist enemies. . . . It does not make sense to me."

North's zealous commitment to the Contras and the deceptions he committed on their behalf may have been rooted in honorable motives—so it seemed, at least, to millions of Americans who made him an instant symbol of patriotism and national honor. But the Vietnam echoes that sounded so insistently as the record of the Iran-Contra affair became known recalled another truth that could also have been learned from the nation's painful experience in Vietnam: that good intentions, even if accompanied by energy and courage, are not enough to make mistaken policies wise or failed ones successful.

IV

If those on one side of the national divide sentimentalized the war and the values of a more innocent time, there were plenty of sentimental myths on the other side, too. Celebrating the 1960s as a mythical era of peace, love, pleasure, and political idealism became a staple of American popular culture. "The Way We Were: How It Looks from Middle Age," declared the headline printed across a photo of frolicking hippies on a 1994 *Newsweek* cover commemorating the twenty-fifth anniversary of the Woodstock rock festival—as if the image in the photo stood for everyone's experience, not just that of a privileged minority. The coverage inside the magazine, like most other commentary on the anniversary, barely acknowledged that anyone in the generation did not share the values and outlook of the "Woodstock nation." In part, no doubt, this was because the people who grew up to write for national magazines tended to come from precisely the class of Americans whose sons and daughters congregated on elite college campuses and saw their era's experience from that perspective. *Newsweek's* essayist, after commenting that "some of us were damaged" by drugs and other excesses of the era, went on to say that "others of us now write the movies and TV shows, run the record companies and radio stations and ad agencies." Those who grew up to become police officers or drive buses or run gas stations rated no mention in the article, as if they somehow didn't really count as members of the generation—or exist at all.

The myths of the sixties were sustained both by those who romanticized the era and those who demonized it. Former protesters sentimentalizing the drama of their youth and right-wingers bent on blaming liberal ideology for every flaw in American life joined together in odd alliance to support the belief that the antiwar movement was decisive in ending U.S. involvement in Vietnam, and that the liberal social policies and programs of the era represented the agenda and influence of hippies and McGoverniks. Conservatives assailing "big government" three decades later regularly invoked long-out-of-date images of counterculture radicals, as when the right-wing commentator and presidential candidate Pat Buchanan, promising to abolish the federal Department of Education, declared: "We don't need some character in sandals and beads telling us how America's children should be educated." Sandals and beads may have been useful symbols for conservative rhetoric. But, as even Pat Buchanan should have realized, they were hardly the dress code in the Department of Education or other federal agencies in 1995.

In fact, the counterculture's real impact on American politics (as opposed to its cultural effects, which were profound) was far less than either the New Right or nostalgic former flower children customarily claimed. The War on Poverty and the related cluster of federal social welfare programs identified with the sixties and sweepingly denounced by conservatives in the nineties—Head Start, Model Cities, Legal Services, Medicare and Medicaid, and so on—were conceived, promoted, and put into effect not by sixties radicals but by their most vilified enemy, Lyndon Johnson.

Nor did the peace movement have much to do with the other great struggle of the era: the campaign for civil rights in the segregated South.

Even though the words "Vietnam-and-civil-rights" would later be carelessly run together as a kind of shorthand caption for protest politics in the sixties, the two struggles remained quite separate. They weren't even simultaneous: the 1960s civil rights movement, touched off by sit-ins at segregated lunch counters at the very beginning of the decade, reached its zenith before any large-scale Vietnam protests had begun. The peace movement—then still focusing mainly on nuclear disarmament, not Vietnam—was present but barely visible on the national political scene during 1963 and 1964 and 1965, the years that saw America's racial landscape transformed by the climactic demonstrations in the Deep South and the answering fire hoses and police dogs, the March on Washington, the civil rights "freedom summer," and the great debates leading to congressional enactment of the Civil Rights and Voting Rights Acts.

Early in 1967, the Rev. Martin Luther King Jr. lent his voice and moral authority to those opposing the war, calling it "a blasphemy against all that America stands for." Other black leaders, with some hesitation, eventually took a similar stand. But the civil rights and antiwar movements did not merge or develop common purposes. African Americans were by and large more opposed to the war than whites, according to opinion polls. Still, blacks remained all but invisible in peace demonstrations and the counterculture. Though the peace movement continually proclaimed racial justice as one of its goals and its adherents were virtually without exception sympathetic to the civil rights struggle, the mass of war protesters were almost entirely white and middle class, as were the crowds at Woodstock and the hippies who congregated in the Haight-Ashbury section of San Francisco or in communes in Vermont.

It is not even clear that the peace movement was actually decisive in turning national policy around on its own issue: the war in Vietnam. The idea that an idealistic new generation of Americans rose up in moral outrage at an unjust war and forced a corrupt, oppressive Establishment to change course is appealing, but is also to a large extent a sentimental fable. (So is the same story seen through different political lenses, which show a valid, patriotic, and honorable effort doomed because a bunch of long-haired radicals, assisted by timid politicians and a misguided or even disloyal press, fatally undermined public support for a worthy cause.) It wasn't even true that young people were more opposed to the war than their elders. Throughout the war, opinion polls showed exactly the opposite: consistently, support for the war was highest among those under thirty, and lowest among those fifty or older. It was also true, despite the conventional stereotypes of antiwar intellectuals and prowar, flag-waving "hard hats" from the working class, that highly educated Americans, as a group, were *more* likely to support the war and those with only a grade-school education were the group most opposed to it (while intensely disliking antiwar demonstrators, too).

Nor did young people turn against the war any more quickly than older Americans. A Gallup survey in August 1965, shortly after U.S. ground forces entered the war, found the policy was supported by 76 percent of young respondents, 64 percent of those aged thirty to forty-nine, and 51 percent of those over forty-nine. Three years later, after the shock of the Tet Offensive and President Johnson's withdrawal from the 1968 election, 45 percent of young Americans still approved of the war, compared with 39 percent of the middle-aged and 27 percent of the older respondents. Even in the late stages of the U.S. effort, the pattern was the same. In May 1971, Gallup reported, approval rates were 34 percent among the young, 30 and 23 percent among the middle-aged and older groups.

There is no way to separate out the disparate causes for the steady downward trend in support for the Vietnam effort. Certainly the peace demonstrations had some part in the decline. On some level, the protests compelled the country to face uncomfortable questions about what it was fighting for in Vietnam and how its military and civilian leaders had chosen to conduct the war. If nothing else, the tumult must have forced many members of the American elite to ask themselves why their children had turned so strongly against national policy and the symbols and traditions and values of their society. But it also seems likely that a great many Americans changed their minds for reasons almost entirely unrelated to the moral and ideological issues raised by the organized peace movement—which was, in fact, even more unpopular than the war.

The most important reason for the shift in attitudes may have been a very simple one, having nothing to do with politics or ideology at all: that the war wasn't succeeding.

I began to realize this on a bright fall afternoon in 1969 on Cliff Avenue in Winthrop, Massachusetts, where I had gone to report on the nationwide day of protest known as the Vietnam Moratorium. For a couple of hours that day, I accompanied a pleasant, middle-aged woman from a local peace committee who was going from door to door with a petition calling on President Nixon to set a date for complete U.S. withdrawal from Vietnam. In one house after another, to my growing amazement, those who came to the door nodded and signed—including one woman who began by saying suspiciously: "This whole thing [the Moratorium, or maybe the peace movement in general] is Communist-inspired" but hastily added, "Of course, I'm not for the war or any of that business." A man named William Pallin read the petition on the cement walk in front of his home and, without a word, took out a pen and signed his name. "I was in two wars," he said as he handed it back. "I was in World War II, I was in the whaddyacallit, Korean War. We don't need it over here." A few doors away, Elizabeth Fucillo, wife of a local firefighter, signed after only a quick glance, saying firmly: "I can't believe there's anyone who wants this war to go on any more."

It was a weekday, and more women were home than men, which no doubt affected the results. Still, the unanimity was startling. Eventually we came to the door of a sixtyish woman named Alice Baldinell, who was obviously vague about the details of Vietnam and whose first reaction, I guessed, could probably be traced back to the image of satanic Communism that all Boston Catholics of her generation would have absorbed in countless sermons and parochial school lessons of the 1940s and 1950s. America couldn't just get up and leave Vietnam and leave millions of innocent people to have their throats slit, Mrs. Baldinell said in the flat, sharp-edged accents of working-class Boston. Kind of like Hitler, she went on, and if we'd got into that war earlier, maybe we could've saved all those people who got killed in that one. Well, *here's* someone who's not going to sign, I thought. But at her own mention of World War II, an expression of doubt began to form on Mrs. Baldinell's face. "I dunno," she said after a moment. "I remember that war, we had to get in, so we got in and we fought and we won it, and then it was over." Her accent clipped off the final *r*s, making the words come out "remembah" and "ovah." This one, she went on, this one heah, seems like it's gonna go on forevah. She paused again for a moment, then reached for the clipboard. Maybe you're right, she told the woman from the peace committee, and put down her name.

In that short, confused conversation with herself, lasting no more than a minute or two, Mrs. Alice Baldinell of Winthrop, Massachusetts, raised on a vision of Communists as diabolic, bloodthirsty fiends, had made a complete, 180-degree turn on the war. Her quick reversal left me dumbfounded. But I also remember thinking that here on the doorsteps of Cliff Avenue, rather than in noisy campus rallies or marijuana-laced protest marches in Washington, I had found the true cause of the great change in public opinion on Vietnam. The turmoil on the campuses notwithstanding, Americans had actually been remarkably patient about the war. By October 1969, they had given their national leaders four and a half years—already a year longer than the entire period of American engagement in World War II—to achieve success in Vietnam. They had given more than thirty thousand young men's lives, many more thousands wounded, and scores of billions of dollars. But the national leadership was still not able to show that the war was getting anywhere, and now millions of people like Mrs. Baldinell on thousands of streets like Cliff Avenue no longer believed it ever would.

They didn't learn this from the peace marchers, whom they liked even less than they liked the war. They didn't think their country was evil or imperialist. But they had come to see the war as futile. It seems likely, though not provable, that if any convincing policy for winning the war had been offered to them, a great many might have supported it, even this late in the game. But there was no plausible plan for victory; just month after month after month of inconclusive battles and weekly casualty reports and young men coming home in coffins and the same rancid, angry arguments. Not in the streets or on campuses but quietly at home, reading their morning newspapers or talking with husbands or wives or friends or thinking about their own and their neighbors' sons reaching draft age, Americans reached a kind of silent but potent consensus: going on with the war was pointless. The country could not keep throwing good lives after bad. It was time to cut losses and bring the rest of their sons home.

V

For all its radical rhetoric, the true revolution of the sixties was in personal life, beliefs, behavior, and relationships, not in the political or economic system. The war was the emotional engine of the peace movement, and when the engine ran out of steam, as troop levels and casualties and draft calls dropped, the movement subsided too, without having put down any real political roots or become a true radical alternative to conventional two-party American politics. Long before the war was over, the mass fervor on the country's campuses evaporated. Only a small core of activists remained, trying to keep the flame alight. With them, radical ideas about political and economic change also fell back into the outer margins of America's political landscape, where they had traditionally languished. What remained in the foreground were new, free-wheeling styles, different values and standards of personal conduct, and a deep cynicism about authority that was, by the 1990s, often associated with conservative, not revolutionary, ideology. Rather than liberating the oppressed, the peace marchers chiefly liberated themselves, from a vast array of taboos and conventions that had set boundaries for earlier generations. It was their symbols—their clothes, their shaggy hair, their dope, their music and language—that turned out to be the substance of their revolution, while their political ideas (other than on the war) proved to have been mostly fantasies, unconnected to American political realities.

In the spheres of private behavior and attitudes, the movement had a reach and influence its political ideas never achieved. Millions of young Americans who were never politically involved at all were swept up into the great cultural changes that grew out of the sixties, and those changes were still having a profound impact long after the era's radical politics were a faint, slightly embarrassing memory, like teenage pimples. To some extent, this was no more than the triumph of hedonism. The "Woodstock agenda" had won after all, *Newsweek*'s anniversary essay declared: "The Dionysiac triad of sex, drugs and rock and roll now dominates private life and popular culture." More than just pleasure-seeking was involved, however. The legacy of the sixties was a more tolerant society, less bound by tradition and arbitrary social rules. Women in the post-Vietnam decades escaped from the kitchen and the handful of occupations traditionally open to them; a growing number of homosexuals aspired to the right to live free of discrimination, secrecy, and shame. Following the path blazed by the civil rights movement, other groups—the physically disabled, for example—realized they no longer had to silently accept exclusion or social or economic handicaps. Embracing diversity became a goal in workplaces and universities and in American popular entertainment, too. And while the change was accompanied by considerable rancor and backlash and abrasive collisions between one group and another, it was still the case that workplaces, universities, and political institutions in the 1990s all represented a much more varied cross-section of America than they had thirty years earlier.

If some doors opened, though, others were swinging shut. The same class and economic differences that largely determined who went to Vietnam and who went to Woodstock in the 1960s still split American society, even more deeply, as the Vietnam generation reached middle age. By most measures, economic inequality grew sharply during the two decades following Vietnam, with those in the top income brackets enjoying ever more affluence while those on the middle and lower rungs slipped back, or at best struggled harder and harder just to stay even. Barriers to upward mobility grew steadily higher, as rapid economic and technological change made it increasingly more difficult for those left behind to catch up. Moving into the new American elite were millions from precisely the population that had partied at Woodstock and marched against the war: upper-middle-class, college-educated men and women, born between the mid-1940s and early 1950s. Yet the social conscience that was supposed to have been their generation's hallmark, together with sex, drugs, and rock 'n' roll, was hardly visible in the political life of the 1980s and 1990s. Looking back on the protest era from a radical viewpoint, a good many might agree with the sour remark of a character in Richard Barre's novel *Bearing Secrets*: "As for the sixties, all they did was make the ruling class stronger, like the antibodies after a vaccination."

Middle-aged baby boomers, even if they had spent their college years marching against the war, imperialism, and injustice, now seemed unapologetically satisfied with their affluence and privileged status. Or perhaps they took their privileges so much for granted they didn't even recognize them for what they were. Writing about the twenty-fifth reunion of his Harvard class ('71, a year after James Fallows's), *New York Times* columnist Frank Rich compared his overwhelmingly white, male class with the more diverse Harvard student body of the 1990s and proclaimed victory for his generation, whose fight, Rich noted, had been not only against the war in Vietnam but also against "a white male hammerlock on privilege." Some might consider that breaking a white male hammerlock and replacing it with an equally strong (or stronger) hammerlock by a somewhat more diverse ruling class wasn't actually much of a revolution. If any such thought occurred to Rich in the nostalgic warmth of reunion with his classmates (median net worth in 1996, $831,000; average salary, $124,000 a year), he did not mention it in his column.

Counterculture celebrities embodied the change in values: Jane Fonda selling fitness videos and marrying a television tycoon; Jerry Rubin, formerly of the Chicago Eight conspiracy trial and the Yippies (Youth International Party), selling stocks. The ironies even reached Woodstock itself: at the twenty-fifth anniversary concert there in August 1994, a reporter found an enterprising young man named Bob, "standing tall with a fistful of fives, surveying a line of kids waiting to pay him for the use of the satellite phone in his backpack." The profits, Bob explained, would go to "the betterment of my enjoyment."

As the "love-and-peace" generation hit middle age, issues of growing inequality and the needs of those who were losing out in the new economic order—the urban poor, factory workers thrown out of steel mills and auto plants into poorly paid service jobs, young men and women without the education or skills now required even for relatively undemanding occupations—commanded comparatively little attention or energy from the nation's political, cultural, and opinion leaders. What was now called the liberal agenda was largely devoted to middle-class causes such as environmental protection, abortion, and gay rights. A supposedly liberal media gave almost no coverage to issues of economic justice that had once been at the heart of liberalism. In the celebrity-driven journalism of the 1990s, a subject like sweatshop labor, for example, became news only when linked to a prominent personality such as TV's Kathie Lee Gifford, whose embarrassment, rather than the plight of the exploited workers, was usually the main point of the story. Blue-collar discontents generally got reporters' notice only when someone raised them as a campaign issue, as conservative Pat Buchanan did in his run for the Republican presidential nomination in 1996. When Buchanan's candidacy faltered and he dropped out of the news, so did the workers he had claimed to champion.

A quarter-century after the protest era, the popular stereotype was of a generation seduced by materialism and greed into betraying its youthful ideals. Like most stereotypes, this one had an element of truth. But it could also be argued that the generation's political evolution was not really so contradictory, after all. Despite its red flags and socialist slogans, the protest politics of the sixties was, at its core, much more individualist than collectivist, more about self-realization (self-indulgence, too) than about social or economic justice. "Just Do It," a well-known advertising slogan in the 1990s, could have also been a perfectly apt catchword in the 1960s. In that sense, the path so many in the Vietnam generation traversed, from flower child to yuppie, was straighter than it seemed.

In other respects, too, the political atmosphere in the 1990s was a legitimate descendant of America's experience in the 1960s, despite the apparent vast change in the political climate. Both eras were characterized by distrust of government and a sense that national leaders were taking the country down the wrong road. The Vietnam-era radicals' vision of the "Establishment"—conceived as a secret, behind-the-scenes elite, wielding its influence against the real interests of the American public and the nation—was mirrored almost exactly in the conservative politics of the 1990s. In both its right-wing and left-wing versions, this vision of America permeated the popular culture. Thus, a cynical post-Vietnam consciousness circled back on itself to remold the popular image of the war itself and recent American history—a process epitomized in the 1992 movie *JFK*, whose director, Oliver Stone, had served in Vietnam and also made the most realistic of all Hollywood's movies about the war. In *JFK*, Stone asserted that senior members of America's military, intelligence, and foreign-policy leadership successfully carried out a gigantic conspiracy to murder President Kennedy *to keep him from ending the war in Vietnam*. Millions of Americans apparently found nothing preposterous in that premise or in the movie's utterly cynical view of American leaders and institutions—just as millions were ready to believe that a large number of senior military and civilian officials had engaged in a twenty-year cover-up of evidence that U.S. prisoners were still held in Vietnam.

What was most striking in *JFK*, though, was not its cynicism alone, but the fact that its underlying political vision was identical to that of novels and movies that seemed to express exactly the opposite views. Stone showed a secret, sinister Establishment conspiring to kill a president to keep the war going; other movies such as *Rambo* showed their audiences essentially the same sort of conspiracy—carried out by the same sort of conspirators and for similarly indistinct reasons—to keep the war from being won. Despite the disagreement on the war, the underlying messages were identical: government is corrupt, untruthful, and immoral; democracy and the power of a sovereign people have been subverted by unseen enemies; bad things happen not because of honest mistakes but because of evil conspirators who, in most cases, have so much power they can only be fought outside the law.

On the extreme fringes, as many observers noted, the far-right militia groups that sprang up in many states in the 1990s to oppose gun control and a threatened takeover by "world government" were driven by violent fantasies and paranoid suspicions strikingly similar to those that had inspired would-be revolutionaries of the 1960s. Change a few words, and the inflammatory pronouncements of right-wing radio talkers such as G. Gordon Liddy would not sound too different from the rhetoric of such groups as the Weathermen or the Black Panthers. Indeed, right-wingers who saw government conspiracies behind the deaths of Branch Davidians in Waco, Texas, or the wife and teenaged son of survivalist Randy Weaver at Ruby Ridge, Idaho, sounded exactly like their opposite numbers a generation earlier talking about the police shooting of Chicago Panther leader

Fred Hampton in 1969 or the FBI's 1975 shootout with Native American activists at Wounded Knee, South Dakota.

In the turmoil of the 1960s, that part of the peace movement that emerged from the religious community was only intermittently visible on the national stage. Those who came to the movement out of religious conviction were never more than a small fraction of the hundreds of thousands demonstrating against the war. Yet, a quarter-century later, it was mainly that small group—almost alone among former peace marchers—who kept alive the movement's visions of nonviolence and a revolutionary transformation of American society. In part, this may have been because the religious left, unlike many student protesters, had always seen the issues as much wider than just the war in Vietnam. "The Vietnam war could end tomorrow and leave undisturbed the quality of our society, and its world role," declared the Catonsville Nine, a group of activists led by the radical priests Philip and Daniel Berrigan who carried out a celebrated raid on a local draft board office in Catonsville, Maryland, in May 1968. To the Berrigans and others in their loose network of activists, the true struggle was to abolish militarism and nuclear arms—a cause that did not disappear with the end of the fighting in Vietnam.

That alone, though, did not seem enough to explain why those in the religious left were still in the trenches long after so many other former radicals had settled comfortably into America's consumer society. Perhaps religious conviction was a stronger motivating force to begin with. And religion may have provided better armor against discouragement at the lack of concrete results. "As Buddhists say, one does the good because it is good, not because it goes somewhere," Dan Berrigan told a 1993 Baltimore reunion commemorating the twenty-fifth anniversary of the Catonsville raid. Printed in the program for that meeting—attended by six of the Nine, including both Berrigans*—was a verse from the Book of Revelation: "You have persevered and have endured hardships for my name, and have not grown weary." The Berrigans and their associates had persevered, certainly.

---

*The six were Daniel and Philip Berrigan, Tom Lewis, George Mische, Thomas Melville, and John Hogan.

Daniel Berrigan, a Jesuit, was living in New York in 1996, where he worked at an AIDS hospice. Philip Berrigan, a Josephite, left the priesthood, married Elizabeth McAlister, and founded Jonah House, a Baltimore community dedicated to "a simple lifestyle and Gospel nonviolence."

But some of them did sound a little weary. "Where are all the professors who led teach-ins in the sixties?" George Mische asked rhetorically, tartly answering his own question: "The campuses are full of professors worrying about their retirement pay." John Hogan, another of the Nine now working as a carpenter in New Haven, Connecticut, said, a little sourly, that the 1990s made it "difficult to pick and choose what to protest—the world's sickness is enormous."

For all its dedication, the post-Vietnam religious peace movement was a tiny group, rating occasional local headlines for acts of civil disobedience at missile sites or submarine bases but having no visible impact on national opinion or policy. Particularly discouraging for its activists was the experience of the Persian Gulf War, when it became painfully clear that almost no one not already committed to the movement was listening to their message. For some, doing right for the sake of doing right was motivation enough, even if there was no apparent result. "What I'm doing is really a prayer, and you never know how God will answer prayers," one demonstrator said about a civil-disobedience protest at the White House just before the Gulf War began. But others felt isolated and useless. "I've been in the peace movement for twenty-seven years," one woman from a suburban Maryland peace group said a few months after the Gulf War ended, "and I'm looking for the strength to go on."

Most disheartening, possibly, was the indifference of the authorities themselves. The same government that hounded the religious left with FBI agents and informers (and once attempted to prosecute Phil Berrigan and six others on a bizarre charge of plotting to kidnap President Nixon's national security adviser) now treated the peace movement like a band of harmless cranks, something like the people who see UFOs and visitors from outer space. On Independence Day 1996, when Phil Berrigan led a group of protesters onto the grounds of the National Security Agency, instead of being arrested they were greeted by a public affairs officer who told the group cheerily: "Thank you very much, we appreciate all your efforts. We'll do our best," he added, while security guards watched from the other side of a fence, "to bring your concerns to the attention of the proper authorities."

No TV crews had shown up for the event, but a *Baltimore Sun* reporter was present to record the denouement: "Berrigan stood outside . . . and calculated the prospects of a 72-year-old man successfully scaling 10 feet of chain-link fence and barbed wire to force his own arrest. He considered the placid, clean-shaven faces of the young military policemen on the other side. Then he looked into the pure blue of heaven on a perfect day. 'To hell with it,' he said, and walked away." *

At the Catonsville Nine reunion, Brendan Walsh, a long-time activist in poor neighborhoods in Baltimore, said he was worried that the peace movement had become self-righteous, intolerant, and elitist. He was not even sure any longer that nuclear weapons were the biggest danger. "Maybe it's not nuclear weapons," he said. "Maybe it's what we do to each other [in] everyday life." Change needs to begin at the bottom, Walsh concluded: "That's where the suffering is." And he ended with a quote from William James that sounded almost like an elegy for a lost dream of revolution: "I am done with great things and big things."

There's another passage from James that brings to mind the Vietnam generation and its troubled journey through the last one-third of what was once called the American Century. "I have often thought," James wrote in 1878, "that the best way to define a man's character would be to seek out the particular mental or moral attitude in which, when it came upon him, he felt himself most deeply and intensely active and alive. At such moments there is a voice inside which speaks and says: 'This is the real me!'"

The country's long Vietnam agony brought some—but only some—to that moral attitude in which, as James said, they could discover their real selves. The Berrigans did, no doubt, as did other men and women who risked their freedom to resist the war and found, in doing so, their true convictions and capacity for sacrifice. And (even if many in both groups would reject the comparison) so did many of the young men who fought the war, honoring their obligations, as they understood them, to the country and to the men they served with.

For most, though, the legacy of the Vietnam era was moral confusion, not clarity. If anyone typified the generation's experience, it would be neither a soldier nor a true resister but someone like Bill Clinton, who, as the cultural historian Paul Lyons noted, "neither served nor took many risks as an activist, always, as his now famous letter states, maintaining his

---

*The authorities were less indulgent when, on Ash Wednesday 1997, Berrigan and five companions broke into the Bath Iron Works shipyard in Maine, boarded a guided-missile destroyer, and pounded with hammers and poured symbolic blood on missile hatches and navigational equipment. After a three-day trial, the six were convicted for conspiracy and damaging government property. Sentenced to two years, Berrigan served just over twenty months (including his time in prison before trial). As in previous demonstrations, the Bath protest, the trial, and Berrigan's conviction and imprisonment received almost no national news coverage.

options." The feverish attempts by his right-wing critics to tar him with the excesses of the counterculture, or to paint him as extreme or even disloyal in opposing the war, missed the point. Clinton's moral caution was the exact opposite of extremism. Understandably, if not heroically, he attempted—in the end, successfully—to make the minimum sacrifice for his convictions. Millions of others did the same.

In avoiding Vietnam, though, for good reasons or bad (or both), Clinton and many like him also avoided other questions: What *is* worth fighting for? When is sacrifice necessary or justified? And if a country finds nothing worthy of sacrifice, what does that say about its culture, its values, and its people? Those issues, too, were churned up in the political and cultural confusion of the Vietnam War and its era. And long after the war and the draft and the protests, those were the questions that still haunted Bill Clinton and his generation, and the uneasy, skeptical, divided nation that they inherited.

THE SYNDROME

We are not looking at another Vietnam. . . . This is not another Vietnam. . . .
It is not going to be another Vietnam.
—George Bush, December 18, 1990

The Vietnamese may be in terrible shape, but they have certainly got their
revenge. Merely mention the possible use of our military now any place on
Earth and you will hear the pessimistic refrain: It will mean 500,000
ground troops, the military will fail, the wily enemy will prevail,
the terrain is inhospitable, we will be hated etc. It is
believed all this will be an inevitable outcome.
—Meg Greenfield

I

Three days after the shooting stopped in the Persian Gulf War—a war that had quite clearly been fought not just against Iraq and its leader Saddam Hussein but also against America's troubling memories of Vietnam—George Bush declared victory against that opponent, too. "The specter of Vietnam," Bush proclaimed in a radio speech broadcast to U.S. troops in the Gulf, "has been buried forever in the desert sands of the Arabian Peninsula." Interred with Vietnam's ghost, presumably, was its legacy of public hesitancy about any commitment of U.S. forces in distant and confusing conflicts.

But the ghost did not stay buried. The same public that celebrated U.S. success in the Gulf War remained, after the victory parades, skeptical about military intervention and unwilling, by all appearances, to accept any but the most nominal U.S. casualties in any military operation. The boundaries of public attitudes were clearly reflected in the summer of 1994 in a comment by an American Special Forces captain named Dave Duffy, commander of a nine-man Green Beret detachment sent to assess the refugee crisis that had erupted in the central African nation of Rwanda. "We are here to help," Duffy told reporters as his group headed for the teeming refugee camps in neighboring Zaire, and then added, "but not at any cost to the American soldiers."

In a small way, Captain Duffy's mission (like his statement) embodied the contradictory impulses that had beset his country's foreign policy decisions through five administrations: a sense that the United States, as the world's leading superpower, must be willing to use its military power when necessary for national goals, and a conflicting sense that after Vietnam, Americans simply would not tolerate any intervention that seemed, however remotely, to foreshadow a repetition of that disaster. The Rwanda crisis in mid-1994 led to such powerful (though fleeting) televised images of need that U.S. policymakers felt compelled to make some response; at the same time, they were equally compelled to reassure the nation that, as Captain Duffy put it, there would not be "any cost" to the Americans involved.

There was, of course, an inherent illogic in the notion that the United States could use military power to serve national policy without any risk that American soldiers might actually be killed or wounded. But illogical as it was, for years that idea dominated every discussion of possible U.S. military action anywhere in the world. America seemed unable to forget Vietnam, one commentator wrote in 1982, "but it doesn't know what exactly to remember. It sees Vietnam everywhere, a ghost in every conflict. Vietnam in Angola. Vietnam in Nicaragua. Vietnam in El Salvador, in Guatemala, in Beirut. The ghost whispers contradictory messages. To some it says, 'Stay out.' To others it says, 'Fight this one to win.' . . . From time to time, politicians have proclaimed that we have finally put the war behind us. But we have always proven them wrong." The place names changed in subsequent years, but the arguments, in many important respects, did not.

Not surprisingly, Americans tended to interpret Vietnam's lessons, and apply them to later foreign policy choices, in the light of their own ide-ologies. During the 1980s, with the Cold War still dominating the inter-national landscape, those Americans most strongly in favor of an activist national policy backed by the use, or at least the threat, of military force were also those who tended to believe that Vietnam had been lost by timid-ity in Washington, rather than by flawed policy. To them, America's post-Vietnam reluctance to use force represented a crippling continuation of the same mistaken timidity, and the "Vietnam syndrome," which severely con-strained U.S. leaders from using their own power, was a self-inflicted weak-ness that had to be overcome if America was to regain its rightful role and influence in the world.

Vietnam, complained the neoconservative writer Norman Pod-horetz, had "canceled out" the historical lesson that aggressive totalitarian power must be resisted, not appeased. Having become "perhaps the most negatively charged political symbol in American life," Podhoretz contin-ued, Vietnam turned into "what Munich had been to an earlier generation: the self-evident symbol of a policy that must never be followed again." (Historian Morton Keller, writing in 1978, also harked back to Munich. "It is not too much to say that Vietnam was the last effort of a generation of policymakers determined not to repeat the mistake of Munich," Keller observed. "Nor is it too much to say that for years to come, foreign policy will be shaped by a generation of policymakers determined not to repeat the mistake of Vietnam." One wonders if Podhoretz or Keller—or those U.S. leaders who consciously sought to avoid "another Munich" in Viet-nam—were aware that the Vietnamese Communists were haunted by a Munich analogy of their own, arising from a history few Americans knew anything about. "Never Munich again, in whatever form," North Vietnam's Prime Minister Pham Van Dong vowed in 1966, referring to the Vietnam-ese revolutionaries' conviction that they had been betrayed after making diplomatic concessions in 1945 and 1954.)

A classic version of the "Vietnam syndrome" thesis was stated by Richard Nixon, who once said the biggest mistake of his own presidency was failing to order full-scale war against North Vietnam as soon as he took office. "The willingness to use power to defend national interests is the foundation of any effective foreign policy," Nixon wrote in a 1985 book entitled *No More Vietnams*, "but our ineptness in Vietnam led many Amer-icans to question the wisdom of using our power at all. . . . Many of our leaders have shrunk from any use of power because they feared it would bring another disaster like the one in Vietnam."

On the opposing side of the debate were those who had come to see the war as the tragic result of overreaching by leaders who had an exaggerated estimate of America's power and its ability to control events elsewhere in the world. "The disease of victory," the writer Neil Sheehan called it: an illusion of supremacy nurtured by America's towering success in World War II and the unprecedented prosperity and world dominance Americans enjoyed in the following decades. For Sheehan and others with similar views, the overriding lesson of Vietnam was that future U.S. leaders must avoid the mistakes of arrogance and ignorance that had led us into that war: a misplaced confidence in military force; a distorted strategic vision that saw only externally instigated "Communist aggression" and not the local roots of Third World revolution; a wilful failure to see that smaller countries can also have will and inflexible purpose of their own and that, as the historian Barbara Tuchman wrote, "problems and conflicts exist among other peoples that are not soluble by the application of American force or American techniques or even American goodwill."

Vietnam's ghosts also whispered to the American military itself, which had come out of that war so "confounded, dismayed, and discouraged," as one general put it, that even more than twenty years afterward, the scars still seemed fresh. Vietnam had been a painfully harsh test of nearly every aspect of U.S. military practice and doctrine. As early as 1969, while the war was still at its height, a Pentagon consultant's study ruefully observed that "the enemy, on purpose or not, has managed in the course of the Vietnam war to pulverize almost all of our military and strategic concepts." In what amounted to a Vietnam syndrome of their own, senior U.S. military leaders in the post-Vietnam era were extraordinarily unwilling to engage in any war that might prove long or inconclusive or ambiguous in result, or that might not have the unqualified support of the American public, or that would be waged under unwarranted constraints ordered by Washington.

This last reflected the fact that America's professional officers, despite a two-hundred-year tradition of civilian control of the military, had come away from Vietnam with bone-deep doubts about the country's political leadership. "Those conscience-stricken pissants who ran our government," Vice Admiral James Bond Stockdale, who won a very hard-earned Medal of Honor for his bravery during seven and a half years as the highest-ranking Navy prisoner of war in North Vietnam, wrote about the national leaders who, he felt, had sent him to war and then left him "stranded high and dry." Other officers might not have stated it quite as pungently, at least not in public, but a great many of them came to exactly the same conclusion: that their civilian superiors had disregarded military realities and thrown away an attainable victory by imposing unnecessary and ultimately crippling restraints on their soldiers. The "Vietnam nightmare" that haunted the post-Vietnam military leadership, wrote Bob Woodward in his 1991 book *The Commanders*, was embodied in the figure of "President Lyndon Johnson leaning over maps in the White House, circling specific targets" for air attacks in Southeast Asia.

Professional officers tended to see this interference as the result of a lack of military knowledge and experience on the part of those governing the nation. Speaking about Presidents Kennedy, Johnson, and Nixon, and notwithstanding that all three were World War II veterans, an infantry colonel who had served in Vietnam scornfully asked: "What the hell did we have? . . . A PT-boat commander with a talent for self-advertisement and a couple of Navy logrollers who never saw action. How do you expect them to make intelligent military decisions, even if their advisers are smart and forceful, when they have no background that helps them understand the situation? No way, Mac." There was little doubt that most of his military colleagues would have expressed much the same view, reflecting a gap between the military and civilian worlds that would grow even wider after Vietnam and especially during Bill Clinton's presidency.

Such attitudes were by no means unknown in earlier times, of course. Gen. Joseph W. Stilwell, the memorably plain-spoken World War II commander whose troubled tenure in Chiang Kai-shek's China was an eerie forerunner of Vietnam, regarded Franklin D. Roosevelt as a "rank amateur in all military matters," prone to "whims, fancy and sudden childish notions" about waging war. But if the military "has traditionally regarded their politicians and political appointees with some apprehension," as the authors of one mid-1980s think-tank paper noted, Vietnam dramatically deepened that mistrust.

Following the war, there was virtually no impulse to look back at the armed forces' own performance in Vietnam, or to consider that the military leadership might have made any mistakes except in failing to resist civilian meddling. Instead, the professional officer corps and its strategists and planners quickly returned, almost with a sigh of relief, to the familiar conceptual terrain of the "big war" against the Soviet army in Europe: the war that never happened but was at the center of U.S. military thinking before and after and, to a considerable extent, even during Vietnam. Only a few voices in the wilderness suggested trying to find out what had gone wrong in Southeast Asia. The more popular view was that, although pain-

ful, Vietnam had been an aberration without lasting relevance, like an ill-
ness that had run its course and now needed only to be forgotten as quickly
as possible. Shortly after the U.S. troop withdrawal in 1973, an instructor
at one of the service schools was said to have greeted a new class by saying:
"Now that Vietnam is behind us, we can get back to the real world." The
story may have been apocryphal, but it accurately reflected the military's
attitude in Vietnam's aftermath and its apparent determination to sweep
the whole mess under a rug of official forgetfulness.

In subsequent years, the military—like the rest of American society, if for somewhat different reasons—largely kept silent about Vietnam.
The service academies and other service schools made little effort to teach
about the war or to encourage officers to reflect on the issues it had raised.
Nor were many officers inclined to do so. To some extent, the military's
postwar amnesia about Vietnam reflected a powerful need among a whole
generation of officers to feel that they had done their job as military pro-
fessionals, and that the ultimate defeat of national policy, caused by factors
beyond their control, was not their responsibility or concern. Some were
disconcertingly offhand about the subject. "I licked everybody I was supposed to lick," one retired officer (who had risen to become a very senior
army general) told me, in effect shrugging off the larger failure and the ultimate futility of his own efforts.

I was startled at the general's detached tone, but when I mentioned it to a friend who had gone to West Point, he didn't share my surprise. When he sent me a copy of his thirtieth-anniversary yearbook, where
every member of the class of 1960 was given space for a three-hundred-
word essay on his life since graduation, I saw why. Two-thirds of the men
in the class had served in Vietnam, many for several tours. Twelve of them
died there. Yet entry after entry in the 1990 yearbook mentioned the war
only as another duty assignment, recalled with no more emphasis or feeling than tours in Georgia or Germany.

There were a few exceptions. One graduate wrote that Vietnam was
a "burden on my heart that just won't go away. . . . I am not bitter. I am not
frustrated. I have not been mistreated because I am a Vietnam Vet. I am not
second-guessing the policy makers. I just get very, very, sad when I allow
myself to think about Vietnam and the human tragedy it caused." Another
wrote: "I suppose that my several years with the Big Red One in Vietnam
taught me the most about myself and my fellow man. Nothing since then
has seemed very important to me!" Others must have had similar feelings,
but almost none expressed them. More surprising was how few comments

were directed against the political leadership or those who had opposed the war at home. Some may have felt that their opinions were so widely shared by their fellow graduates that there was no need to state them. Some, no doubt, thought of their yearbook entries as a simple summary of their careers, not a place for opinion or introspection. One could only guess what feelings lay behind the bland entries submitted by all but a tiny handful of graduates. But it did not seem plausible that the great majority of the West Point class of 1960 were truly so matter-of-fact about the war that had touched so many of them and had so deeply troubled their profession, their generation, and their country.

If some soldiers masked their feelings—perhaps from themselves—there was no doubt that the post-Vietnam military harbored a considerable store of resentments about its experience in the war. "There existed considerable bitterness toward the political leadership that had committed the Army to the conflict and then, seemingly, abandoned it," an Army major, Andrew F. Krepinevich Jr., wrote in a 1986 book called *The Army and Vietnam*. "There was also bitterness toward the American public for its lack of support or appreciation for the sacrifices made by the nation's men and women in uniform."

In expressing that bitterness, few soldiers seemed to remember that in fact, the American public had been quite patient in giving its military and political leaders the chance to gain the success they kept promising but never achieved. Americans gave fifty-eight thousand young lives for the cause, ambiguous though it was. They footed more than $150 billion in war costs and gave their military forces the greatest conventional destructive power and the most advanced and expensive technology ever used in the history of war. And, by any fair judgment, they gave their generals plenty of time to justify those sacrifices with a victory. Major U.S. forces had been in battle for nearly three years before public doubts reached a significant level, and after that Americans accepted, if reluctantly, five more years of fighting in an effort to salvage some kind of honorable outcome.

Yet the professional officers of the Vietnam era, seared by having fought for their country without receiving the public respect and gratitude they felt they deserved, persisted in their reluctance to blame military mistakes or flawed policy for the lack of success in Vietnam. The failure, they continued to believe, wasn't theirs; instead, the war was lost because a misled public and a timid leadership hadn't allowed its soldiers to win. That view, which was passed on virtually intact to the post-Vietnam generation of officers, underlay the new military theology that any future war must be short, with an absolute minimum of American losses, with dependable, overwhelming public support, and with a virtual blank-check authority for commanders to "fight to win" without restrictions imposed by civilian authorities. Believing their hands had been tied in Vietnam, U.S. officers harked back to the philosophy articulated nearly a century earlier by the British admiral Sir John Fisher, who declared in 1905: "The essence of war is violence. Moderation in war is imbecility. Hit first. Hit hard. And hit anywhere."

To Fisher's list of injunctions, American planners added one more: Hit fast. The new U.S. doctrine called for maximum force to be wielded as soon as hostilities began. The policy of gradual escalation—attempting "to use force sparingly, to hold back, to gradually put pressure on the enemy," as Gen. Frederick Weyand, the last U.S. commander in Vietnam and later the Army's chief of staff, described it—was now seen as one of the fatal mistakes of the Vietnam War, one that must at all costs be avoided in any future conflict. Also essential, the post-Vietnam military concluded, were clear-cut objectives, an "exit strategy" (that is, a clear understanding of how and under what circumstances military action would be ended) and restrictions on news coverage tight enough to assure, insofar as humanly possible, that any conflict would be reported in a manner casting the military and U.S. policies in a favorable light.

It was unclear, of course, exactly how long a war or how many casualties would be acceptable to the public and thus approved under the military's post-Vietnam standards. Nor was it clear how public support could be guaranteed in advance or how, in a complicated and dangerous world, any war could really be fought without political constraints. And the commandment to avoid "gradualism" often led the military to propose such impossibly apocalyptic plans for any possible intervention (the "bomb Moscow option," former Secretary of State George P. Shultz called this practice) that no president would ever actually approve them. To some interventionists, it began to seem that the military's new doctrine set requirements that could never be met in the real world, and that America's senior military leaders had become so gun-shy that they would never actually support using force to back national policy. "I cannot concur," former Defense Secretary James Schlesinger declared, "with the emerging belief that the United States must only fight popular, winnable wars. The role of the United States in the world is such that it must be prepared for, be prepared to threaten, and even be prepared to fight those intermediate conflicts that are likely to fare poorly on television."

The man who emerged as the leading apostle of the new creed of caution was, somewhat surprisingly, President Reagan's secretary of defense, Caspar W. Weinberger. In a National Press Club speech in November 1984 (the most important speech of his tenure, Weinberger was said to believe), the secretary set out his criteria for the use of military power: U.S. armed forces should be committed to combat only when the purpose was "deemed vital to our national interest" and there was a "clear intention of winning"; a war must have "clearly defined political and military objectives"; the policy of using force "must be continually reassessed and adjusted if necessary"; the commitment should be approved by the American people "and their elected representatives in Congress"; and going to war must be "a last resort" after all other possible policies had been tried and failed.

The country's senior military leaders may have had some reservations about stating the new doctrines publicly, as Weinberger had done. But there was little doubt that at heart they largely shared the defense secretary's attitudes and took similarly cautious positions during the administration's internal debates. Wary of being called on to fight when the public, too, mistrusted its leaders' ability to use force, the service chiefs and other officers were also deeply worried that, in Central America and elsewhere, U.S. forces would be sent to deal with crises whose roots were social and economic and political, not military, and which could not be solved by military power.

The disastrous "peacekeeping" mission to Lebanon, where a suicide-bomber succeeded in blowing up a barracks and killing 241 marines in October 1983, heightened military caution and deepened the services' misgivings about deploying military forces for unclear goals in muddled, complicated foreign conflicts. "In almost every instance in which the President and his advisers wanted to exert military force," wrote one knowledgeable observer, "the military officers advised against it or, at least, urged extreme caution." This was in the same Reagan administration that poured hundreds of billions of dollars into a huge military buildup and proclaimed a muscular, activist foreign policy intended to roll back Communism worldwide, strike back at international terrorism, and vigorously challenge other enemies. The continuous clashes between Weinberger's cautious views and those of the administration's more intervention-minded ideologues produced a kind of schizophrenia in foreign policy that persisted for the entire Reagan presidency. Brutal bureaucratic struggle raged inside the government (and at times in public) whenever the use or threat of military force was at issue: over opposing left-wing insurgencies in Central America; over the ill-fated peacekeeping effort in Lebanon; over covert operations in Nicaragua, Angola, and Soviet-occupied Afghanistan; over attempts to strike back at terrorism and hostage-takers and particularly at those states (most prominently Iran) which sponsored or shielded the terrorists. Each time, Weinberger's list of rules seemed to his activist opponents to be an excuse for inaction. It was "the Vietnam syndrome in spades, carried to an absurd level, and a complete abdication of the duties of leadership," George P. Shultz, Reagan's secretary of state and Weinberger's most prominent opponent inside the administration, complained in his memoir. Nor was it just in Weinberger's Defense Department that an overcautious view prevailed, Shultz added: "On Capitol Hill and in the Pentagon, among Democrats and Republicans, on the left and on the right, all too many people of influence and authority seemed to have an endless litany of reasons to refrain from the use of power as an instrument of American foreign policy."

Through all the years of debate on these issues, no consensus was ever reached, inside the Reagan administration or in the country. And that meant, as the *New York Times* defense correspondent Richard Halloran pointed out in a book published shortly after the halfway mark of the Reagan presidency, not just that there were continuing disputes and wrangling over particular foreign policy problems. It meant that the leaders and the public of the United States could not agree on the fundamental premises of national security policy. Five years after Reagan came into office, Halloran observed,

> there was no agreement within the administration, or between the administration and Congress, or among political leaders and senior military officers on basic principles governing the use of military force. There was, therefore, no agreement on national strategy to defend the fundamental interests of the United States, and no agreement, beyond a vague fear of the Soviet Union, on the threat to the United States. There was little consensus on the proper size of the armed forces, on the contingencies for which they must be prepared, or on the priorities with which those forces were to be acquired, trained, and deployed.

What was most remarkable about that passage was how true it still sounded a full decade later. Through four years of Bill Clinton's presidency, and long

after the Soviet Union's collapse and the end of the Cold War had completely transformed the international strategic landscape, none of the issues
on Halloran's list seemed any closer to being settled. Except that there was
no longer even a "vague fear of the Soviet Union" to provide some common vision of the possible threat to American security, Halloran's observations could have been republished, without changing a syllable, as a perfectly accurate description of the muddled state of American strategic
thinking in the profoundly changed world of the mid-1990s.

II

If Vietnam memories had provided the subtext of military policy
debates during the Reagan administration, it was left to Reagan's successor,
George Bush, to confront the ghosts directly.

The 1989 invasion of Panama, mounted during the first year of
Bush's presidency to capture the unsavory Panamanian leader Manuel
Antonio Noriega and bring him back to the United States for trial on drug
trafficking charges, was, like the Reagan administration's invasion of the
Caribbean island of Grenada six years earlier, a quick and successful operation carried out with overwhelming force for a purpose the American
public generally applauded. It thus met the standards of the military's post-
Vietnam doctrine—but, as was also true in Grenada, the issue was not truly
serious enough, and the enemy forces involved were so laughably infe-
rior, that neither the public nor the military itself could really feel that the
self-doubt and nagging confusions of Vietnam had been overcome. Seven
months later, though, when the Iraqi dictator Saddam Hussein suddenly
sent more than one hundred thousand troops to seize and occupy Kuwait,
the United States faced a military challenge of a completely different order.

The crisis in the Persian Gulf in August 1990 coincided exactly
with a moment of stunning change and enormous uncertainty about every
aspect of world politics and international strategy. "Year Zero of the post–
Cold War world," one analyst called it. The timing made the confrontation
with Iraq particularly crucial, in Washington's eyes: now, if ever, seemed
a time when the United States, suddenly the world's only superpower,
could set a new pattern and begin to define a new international order
shaped under U.S. ground rules and hospitable to U.S. interests. To do so,
though, it would be necessary to escape the post-Vietnam strategic paralysis about using military power. "Administration officials worried," one
commentator wrote,

that failure to use American military power in a just cause, blessed by the United Nations, at a time when the Soviet Union was immobilized by its domestic turmoil would confirm the pessimistic judgments of the "declinists"—those at home and abroad who spoke of the United States as if it were a fading empire. . . . It quickly became the Administration's credo that the nation must exhibit that willingness to resort to war which is the ultimate foundation of diplomacy, law, and the political order itself.

Thus, as President Bush and his administration set out to mobilize national opinion in support of a possible new war, a key part of that effort, from the very beginning, was a conscious, explicit campaign to free the country, and its leaders, from the legacy of that earlier conflict in Vietnam. Indeed, it was hard to escape the impression that laying the Vietnam syndrome to rest was itself a major administration goal, perhaps even equal in importance to the goal of defeating Iraq. By one account, in the very earliest White House deliberations immediately following Iraq's seizure of Kuwait, Bush's national security adviser, Brent Scowcroft, saw "another, larger principle" at stake in the coming decisions: overcoming the "paralysis" he felt was epitomized in Caspar Weinberger's doctrines and the military's own reluctance to fight except under conditions Scowcroft and others believed would almost never be met.

Bush and his senior aides incessantly promised that war against Iraq would not be "another Vietnam." In repeating the promise so often, in fact, they came close to sounding frantic—as in one press conference in December, when the president managed to say it no fewer than three times in the space of seven sentences: "We are not looking at another Vietnam. . . . This is not another Vietnam. . . . It is not going to be another Vietnam." The same words rang in the minds of the country's military leaders, who almost seemed more preoccupied with avoiding a repeat of Vietnam than with achieving the country's objectives in this new conflict. Under the influence of Gen. Colin Powell, the politically adroit chairman of the Joint Chiefs of Staff, the military was determined that U.S. forces should, above all, avoid any prolonged entanglement that might erode public support. The consensus, by one postwar account, was that "Americans would enter the enemy's territory in force and leave as soon as possible, with no entangling occupation duties or alliances with Iraqi insurgents who might take up arms against the Iraqi dictator. The stain of Vietnam would be removed by a rapid victory, and American forces would exit swiftly. Anything else was a potential snare."

As the buildup in the Gulf continued, the words "not another Vietnam" took on a meaning beyond the simple promise that the administration would not let the war against Iraq, if it happened, turn into another drawn-out, inconclusive quagmire. They also meant that this time, there would be a different relationship between the country and its soldiers. The political authorities would allow its military leaders to fight without unwarranted interference. And, quite explicitly, the impending conflict was presented as a chance for Americans to atone for their failure to honor and respect the Vietnam veterans.

To the extent that the country remembered its treatment of the Vietnam vets as shameful, the chance to expiate that shame in this new war was welcomed. And, as was no doubt intended by the Bush administration and its publicists, to the extent that opposing the *policy* in Vietnam had been interpreted (particularly after the fact) as dishonoring the soldiers who fought there, this time support for the soldiers would have to be expressed as support for the policy as well. Groups supporting the administration distributed millions of red-white-and-blue bumper stickers proclaiming "Support Our Troops." Forests of U.S. flags flew in front of homes and public buildings; miles of yellow ribbon—previously an emblem of love and loyalty for hostages or prisoners, not soldiers—festooned mailboxes and storefronts.

These and other expressions of solidarity with the soldiers, in repudiating the antiwar demonstrators of the Vietnam era, also implicitly discredited anyone who might protest the planned war in the Gulf. "I came down to protest the protesters," one woman said fervently at a support-the-troops rally in Worcester, Massachusetts, organized by a group called Operation Eagle. "That's the only reason I came. . . . I want the boys over there to know that there *are* people over here who are behind them and they're not going to have to come home ashamed of their uniform; they're not gonna be having to take their uniform off at the airport so they can sneak into their own country and not be called murderers and everything."

Backing America's sons and daughters in the Gulf—and thus making up for the country's shabby treatment of its Vietnam veterans two decades earlier—became a powerful issue for the Bush administration as it moved closer to hostilities. None of the government's other stated reasons for going to war (defending Saudi Arabia, protecting oil supplies, freeing Kuwait, destroying an aggressive Iraqi military machine) could mobilize the kind of emotions that would overcome public skepticism about sending U.S. forces into battle in a distant, dangerous, and confusing region.

Support for the troops could—although, as sociologist Jerry Lee Lembcke pointed out, this was a "purely emotional and symbolic" issue that blotted out any distinction between the instruments of war and the reasons for fighting it. "The means of war, the soldiers themselves, became, in the popular mind, the ends of the war," Lembcke observed. It almost seemed that American troops in the desert had been transformed into hostages, who could be rescued and brought home only by defeating the enemy—as if Saddam Hussein had kidnapped four hundred thousand Americans and the United States had to go to war to get them back. (Something like this logic underlay the Nixon administration's effort to make recovering U.S. POWs the central aim of the Vietnam War.) The unspoken and illogical but powerful association of U.S. soldiers with hostages may have been reinforced by the geographic coincidence that this new conflict was taking place in a region and landscape Americans associated with past hostage crises. It was also curious that the symbol of supporting the troops was the yellow ribbon, the same emblem used to display support for the hostages seized by Iran.

This process of blending the means and ends of the Gulf buildup was illustrated in remarkable fashion in newspaper and television advertisements paid for during the climactic stage of the national debate on the Gulf by a group called the Coalition for America at Risk. The newspaper version was a full-page ad placed during December 1990 in such papers as the *New York Times* and the *Wall Street Journal*. As Lembcke recounted, the ad

> featured a large photo of barren ground with a curvy line running across it. Beneath the photo, in mid-sized type justified to the left margin, was the caption: It's not just a "line in the sand" . . . it's . . . Then, in large block type beneath the caption and centered on the page, was the single word: PEOPLE. The bottom half of the page addressed itself to "all the men and women participating in Operation Desert Shield," with the words "we are behind you and support you 100%!" Reading down, the ad passed along a "special hello from home" to sixty-three nicknamed soldiers in a unit identified as HMLA-367: Slick, Max, Rooster, Elvis, Bilbo, Badfinger, Fuzzy, The Dakota Kid, etc.

A decision about going to war that was based on "people," not just on drawing a line in the desert, was essentially an emotional, not a rational, decision, Lembcke went on. "But which people should this war be about? Who are the people in this ad? Not Kuwaitis. Not Saudis. This war is about Fuzzy and Bilbo, the boys from down the block. The war is about the soldiers who have been sent to fight the war." It was also, clearly, about those soldiers who had been sent to that other war and who had been let down so badly by a country now remorseful enough never to let such a shameful injustice happen again.

When the first U.S. cruise missiles streaked out of a black sky to explode on Baghdad shortly after midnight on January 17, 1991, announcing the start of the shooting war after months of preparation and suspense, the national impulse to demonstrate sympathy and support for the more than half-million U.S. servicemen and women in the Gulf quickly overwhelmed the policy debate that had gone on almost to the eve of the assault. And along with the sympathy for the troops, there was a palpable national thirst to make the war a successful and satisfying event—the exact reverse of its experience in Vietnam, so that the shadow that war had cast over the country's image of itself and its military could be pushed back into history and forgotten. "It's Vietnam revisited as it should have been," commented historian Robert Dallek, "Vietnam: The Movie, Part II, and this time it comes out right."

News coverage of the war was more celebratory than skeptical, only partly because of the tight controls the U.S. command put on reporters in the field. During the buildup, journalists in the field and major news organizations at home protested the restrictions. Once the war began, though, reporters and their producers and editors at home gave an impression of being cowed by a sense that their audience was in no mood for bad news, and that critical reporting, with its echoes of Vietnam, would further alienate a public that was already quite mistrustful of the media. Television newscasts, particularly, seemed in all kinds of ways to be intentionally giving viewers the triumphant story they clearly wanted. This was true not just in the reports themselves. The glitzy, eye-catching montages used to open and close news shows, for example, displayed the most romantic possible images: soldiers and weapons silhouetted against desert sunsets, sleek jets thundering off carriers into crystal-blue skies, ranks of rippling American flags. Television's images of the home front had the same character: flags, yellow ribbons, parades; faces of soldiers' families and others aglow with firmness and patriotic fervor, like Norman Rockwell's sentimental but immensely popular portraits of home-front America during World War II. The techniques were identical to those used in broadcasting major entertainment or sports events: a World Series, say, or a Superbowl. The purpose

seemed identical, too: to attract and excite viewers and to frame a particular mood concerning the event itself. The use of dramatic montages to open
and close news shows was standard TV practice, so it may be that the engineers and producers who assembled the Gulf War titles were not conscious
of deliberately trying to inspire positive, patriotic reactions to their reporting. Still, the images they chose were completely consistent with the positive story the administration and the military wanted to have told about
the war. (There was no outcry, or at any rate none that drew significant public attention, about the overwhelmingly positive images television chose to
accompany its reporting on the war. One can imagine the storm of denun-
ciation that would have fallen on the industry if it had regularly opened
and closed its newscasts with, say, images of wounded soldiers in agony, or
of screaming, terrified children under U.S. bombs in Iraq.)

The vision of the war reaching the home front was pretty clearly
just what the public wanted. What it did *not* want, unmistakably, was the
kind of painful, morally confusing information it remembered receiving
about Vietnam. In the minds of all Americans who remembered that war,
as the historian Marilyn B. Young observed, "there remained a thick residue
of feeling, too deep for easy articulation," that could be traced back in part
to the memory of specific images that were "iconic in their power": Saigon's police chief shooting a captured guerrilla in the head; a naked little
girl running in terror and agony from a napalm strike; South Vietnamese
soldiers clinging to helicopter skids to escape from their disastrous offensive into Laos; returned American soldiers with faces full of bitter disillusion hurling their medals toward the distant dome of the U.S. Capitol.
"One index of the power of such images," Young wrote, was the clear wish
of Americans during the Gulf War not to see anything like them again. In
this new war, Americans did not want to know things resembling those
they "had been forced to know about Vietnam."

For the military, the Gulf War was (as Grenada and Panama were
not) a satisfying reversal of Vietnam. The terrain was a metaphor. In Vietnam, American soldiers fought in tangled, dense, concealing jungles, or
hunted an invisible enemy in suffocating, black tunnels under the earth.
Literally and metaphorically, Americans experienced Vietnam as a darkness; in Iraq, the landscape was open, bright, an expanse of sand and sky
where everything was visible and clear. American officers gratefully and
enthusiastically echoed Britain's Field Marshal William Slim, who had

written in his memoirs about the desert campaigns in World War II: "You can see your man."

The clear, unobstructed light of the desert also seemed to show Americans at home a more gratifying vision of their country at war: crisp, uncomplicated, morally unambiguous. The war on Iraq was everything Vietnam had not been: a triumphant display of American resolve, skill, and technology, responding to a clear-cut act of aggression and waged against a dictator who could plausibly be pictured as a sinister thug. The Gulf conflict was consistent with America's national tradition of regarding its wars as moral crusades. And, as the Iraqi forces swiftly disintegrated under the American assault, the war also satisfied a palpable wish for an unequivocal national success. "This has reasserted our preeminence of a sort," one man told a reporter. Maybe all the television sets and video recorders in American homes came from Asia, he went on, and German and Japanese cars might have captured much of the auto market, "but what's going on in the Middle East is undeniably made in the U.S.A." The Gulf crisis let Americans see themselves "as the leaders of the world again," columnist Anna Quindlen wrote in the *New York Times*, "assured of their inherent greatness and the essential evil of the enemy." For many Americans, she went on, "the war in the Persian Gulf has made the world a simpler place. Black and white. Good and bad. Win and lose." (With more prescience than many of her fellow pundits, Quindlen added: "But not for long.") Advertisers and merchandisers jumped to capitalize on the nationalistic mood. Bloomingdale's, the fashionable New York department store, opened a "Stars and Stripes" department on the second floor where shoppers could express their patriotism, if they chose, by buying ties, T-shirts, denim and leather jackets, even towels and pillows, all decorated with the U.S. flag.

U.S. military leaders were lionized. General Powell and the theater commander in the Gulf, Gen. Norman Schwarzkopf, became instant popular heroes, a status that made both of them rich men after the war. (Schwarzkopf, following his retirement from the Army, signed a book contract said to have been worth several million dollars; Powell reportedly got an even fatter $6 million advance for his memoir. Both men reaped huge speaking fees, reported to range as high as $60,000.) Public affairs officers in the Pentagon and Saudi Arabia also became national stars as military news briefings dominated the TV ratings.

Watching the war in their living rooms, Americans exulted in extraordinary televised images of computer-guided missiles streaking unerringly toward their targets. In those images there was hardly anything to suggest that those missiles and bombs were falling on actual human beings. As many commentators pointed out, the war Americans saw on their television screens bore an eerie resemblance to a video game. Television did report from Baghdad, showing destruction and casualties. But those reports made only the slightest dents in the sanitized, antiseptic image fostered by U.S. officials. When American bombs killed more than two hundred Iraqi civilians in a Baghdad bunker that U.S. intelligence had identified as a key military command post, there was hardly any discernible impact on American public opinion. Eight out of ten Americans blamed the Iraqis, according to a poll taken soon after the raid's gruesome results were broadcast on CNN. Only 13 percent thought the U.S. command needed to take more precautions to avoid civilian casualties—or "collateral damage," as military briefers preferred to say.

American commanders declined, as a matter of policy, to estimate enemy casualties; that would just bring back unwelcome memories of Vietnam's notorious "body counts," they believed. That policy was largely successful in keeping dead Iraqi soldiers out of the news, or at least in avoiding any discomforting focus on the amount of killing wrought by American firepower. The result was a war "relatively innocent of dead bodies," at least as Americans at home experienced it on television. With death and agony largely kept off camera, it became possible, as Marilyn Young observed, "to believe that the enemy were not people at all, but machines; that the tanks, buses, cars, which jammed the highway out of Kuwait City had fled on their own, that their charred hulks contained no human remains."

While reveling in their soldiers' success in the desert, Americans exulted, too, in their own mood of unity, pride, and patriotism—a mood reflected back to them in the cascade of words and images poured out by television, newspapers, and magazines. "The sour, deeply divided nation of a few months ago, worried about economic decay and political paralysis, has received a remarkable lift" from the war, a *New York Times* reporter wrote in that paper's "News of the Week In Review" section as the war neared its climax. "It is as if all the confusion and pain of recent decades have melted, leaving the nation with its reassuring images from World War II intact." In contrast to "the ambiguity and humiliation of Vietnam," he added, "the gulf war seems a model of clarity and success, a war portrayed as being fought with the most efficient weapons and greatest resolve against the vilest of villains. . . . Many believe that if the war ends in a low-cost triumph, it could affect the American mood for years."

The war did come to a quick, triumphant conclusion, at relatively light cost. Total U.S. casualties, killed and wounded combined, were fewer than a thousand, out of a force of more than half a million. But far from affecting the national mood for years, the surge of patriotic spirit proved remarkably short-lived. This perhaps reflected the fact that the war had been fought for goals distant from anything Americans were truly concerned about, or that made a discernible difference in their lives. To the extent that the war for the vast majority of Americans was "about the soldiers who have been sent to fight," as Jerry Lembcke pointed out, its purpose ceased to exist as soon as the victory was celebrated. For the public, the war was, in a sense, only about itself. None of the realities that had troubled Americans before the war—economic dislocation and insecurity, a sense of sterile and mean-spirited national politics, widening class and racial and cultural divisions, weakening families, and a loss of moral and ethical anchors—were any different afterward.

This was in sharp contrast with the national experience during World War II, the mythical model Americans consciously or unconsciously tried to recreate on the home front in the Gulf War. Often obscured in the sentimental haze that has come to surround that experience is the fact that along with all its loss and sacrifice, World War II also ended the years-long misery of the Great Depression, bringing full employment and unprecedented prosperity to many millions of Americans. In addition, victory in that war yielded immensely satisfying gains for the United States, which emerged, as one commentator pointed out, as "the only undamaged power, the world's banker, the sole possessor of the atomic bomb, and the producer of half of the world's goods." The effects of World War II went a long way, for most Americans, toward vindicating its cost. The home-front spirit of unity and patriotism we now remember so nostalgically might have been quite different if that had not been true.

The burst of patriotism during the Gulf War was not tested by any significant hardship or sacrifice. The few hundred families mourning lost loved ones were an infinitesimal fraction of the population; for the overwhelming majority of Americans, the war was almost completely painless. There was no disruption of civilian life: no rationing, no shortages, not even (because the land battles were over so quickly) the kind of agonizing suspense soldiers' families lived through for months or years in World War II or Vietnam. As a result, while the outpouring of national pride and support and respect for the troops was unmistakably spontaneous and genuine, the country's experience of the Gulf War seemed to have little depth. In the parades and flags and other displays of patriotism, there was a feeling of something contrived and artificial and self-conscious. Even as they celebrated the victory, Americans seemed connected to it through televised imagery rather than by any more authentic experience of their own. The war collapsed into its own televised narrative, and took on an unsettling resemblance to other TV spectaculars. It was entertainment at the same time that it was history: the war and the war movie blended into one.

The country's mood turned out to be insubstantial and fleeting too. Like the glitzy images on its television screens, the national euphoria faded with surprising swiftness, barely outlasting the victory celebrations. In opinion polls, the percentages on a host of questions relating to patriotism, trust in the national leadership, and satisfaction with the state of American society fell back almost as fast as they had risen. Seventy percent of poll respondents said they felt "strongly patriotic" in February 1991; only 55 percent still felt that way in June. Immediately following the victory in the desert, nearly half of those polled agreed that the government "does what is right most of the time"; by mid-1992 that had fallen to only 23 percent, about where it had been before the Gulf crisis began. Similarly, the percentage who felt too much money was spent on the military, only 28 percent at the time of Iraq's surrender, climbed back to 43 percent two years later, almost exactly the same as before the war. "Like a rock falling into a pond," one analyst wrote on the war's third anniversary, "the gulf war tossed public opinion about, but the waters soon settled down and the pond no longer shows signs of the rock's splash."

Meanwhile, the impression of a clear, unequivocally righteous victory in the Gulf—the outcome that was supposed to banish the Vietnam legacy—also began to evaporate. Despite his army's quick collapse, the Iraqi dictator Saddam Hussein, whom President Bush and other national leaders had likened to Hitler, remained in power. Beyond restoring a somewhat unsavory (and pretty clearly undemocratic) monarchy in Kuwait, it grew less and less clear what the United States had actually fought for, or what it had really achieved.

It became a cliché after the Gulf War that the military's success was achieved because commanders were given a clear goal, which they lacked, according to the conventional military wisdom, in Vietnam. This is a particularly mystifying piece of mythmaking because even the most cursory analysis suggests that in fact, almost exactly the opposite is true. The mission in Vietnam was to destroy the enemy forces, or wear them down to the point that they could no longer seriously threaten the government and army of the Republic of Vietnam. This goal seemed (despite innumerable after-the-fact statements to the contrary) perfectly clear at the time. In many conversations with U.S. officers in Vietnam, I do not recall discovering any who were in doubt about what they were supposed to do there. The trouble was in figuring out how to do it.

By contrast, in the Gulf, American objectives were never completely clarified. The only unambiguous goal was to free Kuwait. It was left quite unclear whether the war was supposed to change the regime in Iraq, what responsibility the U.S. would assume for anti-Hussein movements among the Shiites in southern Iraq or the Kurds in the north, or even how far the military campaign was supposed to go in destroying Iraqi military capability. U.S. commanders seem to have been mainly interested not in clarifying the objectives but in making sure that the war would be concluded in the shortest possible time and that U.S. forces would avoid any entanglement in subsequent events. There was considerable controversy after the war, in fact, over whether the White House and General Powell, essentially for public relations reasons, called off military action "one goddamn day too soon," as one Army officer put it. In a bizarre way, the military's approach was proof that the Vietnam syndrome was still alive and well, even in the midst of the triumph that was to put it to rest.

Just two months after the war ended, polls indicated that few Americans cared about its outcome—or about any other international issue, for that matter. Only an almost invisible 2 percent of the public identified the Middle East as America's "most important problem." The Bush administration responded weakly and equivocally when, within weeks of the surrender, Saddam Hussein sent his remaining forces to put down uprisings by Shiites in southern Iraq and Kurds in the north. This was followed by an embarrassing series of disclosures confirming that the administration had given extensive support to the Iraqi dictator until almost the eve of his occupation of Kuwait. In fact, American actions both before and after the war reflected the reality that, notwithstanding all its efforts to demonize Saddam Hussein, the U.S. government actually preferred to leave him in power rather than risk Iraq's disintegration and a greater regional role for the Islamic revolutionary regime in Iran. These events clouded the image of unambiguous national righteousness President Bush had tried so hard to promote in order to vanquish the moral confusion left by Vietnam, which, he and others felt, had tied the hands of America's leaders for much too long. In the end, instead of rewarding Bush for his success in the Gulf, Americans punished him for neglecting the far more important issues they faced at home. His popularity, as measured by opinion polls, suffered the steepest decline ever recorded: from an astronomical 89 percent approval rating at the height of the conflict all the way down to 29 percent in mid-1992. A sardonic bumper sticker summed up the change in mood: "Saddam Hussein still has his job. What about mine?" Bill Clinton's victory in the presidential election that year (despite his Vietnam baggage) reflected, in no small part, the perception of millions of voters that Bush was too involved with foreign affairs and too unconcerned about the problems of ordinary Americans.

The election came less than two years after the war, but the victory in the Gulf already seemed irrelevant and almost forgotten. So did the great surge of pride and patriotism that had accompanied it. It was the memory of the Gulf War, not of Vietnam, that had been left under the drifting desert sands. "The war that was intended to wipe out the memory of Vietnam," Marilyn Young noted, " . . . has instead itself disappeared."

III

After an election campaign shadowed by the Vietnam ghosts in his own past, Bill Clinton took office only to find Vietnam still hovering, as it had for twenty years, over the defense and foreign policy issues of his presidency. In case anyone still thought the Vietnam syndrome had been vanquished, the events surrounding the bungled U.S. intervention in Somalia brought it back, with a vengeance, less than a year into the Clinton presidency.

The Clinton administration did not originate the Somali debacle. Clinton inherited the crisis from President Bush, who, six weeks before leaving office, ordered U.S. troops to Somalia, in response to television and news reports of the horrifying anarchy and starvation that were ravaging the country. It was under Clinton, though, that what had begun as a humanitarian effort to rescue terrorized and starving people turned into a clumsy and ill-conceived campaign against one of the rival faction leaders, adding the phrase "mission creep" to America's vocabulary. In the end, events in Somalia came to represent the very nightmare Americans and their military leaders had dreaded for twenty years: U.S. soldiers dying in an unwinnable conflict in a confusing and violent Third World country, for no explainable reason—in other words, as Senator Fritz Hollings of South Carolina declared, "Vietnam all over again." Exactly like Vietnam, Somalia became a symbol of everything that could go wrong in a foreign military operation; it seemed, indeed, to revalidate the Vietnam syndrome for a new generation.

The benevolent image of American soldiers bringing food and hope to a stricken land—"God's work," President Bush called it—lasted only a few months. The military codename for the intervention, Operation Restore Hope, indicated the message meant for the rest of the world: America and its armed forces would be a powerful force for good in the "new world order" that had replaced the Cold War. But just as in Vietnam, the United States found that in intervening for what it saw as an uncomplicated good cause, it had assumed responsibility for a situation that offered no good solution, or perhaps no solution at all. The notion that Americans could carry out what one official described as "a limited operation, strictly humanitarian," without getting entangled in Somalia's murderous politics, proved false. Starvation, terror, and anarchy existed *because* of the violent struggle between rival clan leaders, whose power rested on the support of the same armed gangs who were preying on the population. To truly restore hope to Somalia, there needed to be a settlement among the factions and their gangsters had to be disarmed. Otherwise, God's work would turn out to be no more than supervising aid shipments for a few months and then delivering Somalis back into the same chaos that had created their misery in the first place.

Some Clinton administration officials had even loftier aims in mind. The Somalia effort, declared Madeleine K. Albright, U.S. ambassador to the United Nations, was "an unprecedented enterprise aimed at nothing less than the restoration of an entire country as a proud, functioning and viable member of the community of nations." That and similar statements represented, in a way, a new version of the old Cold War attitudes and rhetoric, exaggerating foreign policy goals by presenting them as a moral crusade. But America's actions were a lot less bold than its promises. U.S. forces would not even undertake to disarm the Somali gunmen before handing over the peacemaking mission to the United Nations. Rather than risk involving Americans in combat, the Clinton administration chose to declare victory and let the United Nations take over. "The mission is accomplished," Clinton declared in a White House welcome for returning U.S. servicemen.

In fact, at least in the sense that there was no repair of the political breakdown that caused Somalia's crisis to begin with, the mission hadn't even begun. The contradictory impulses driving U.S. policy had left it with the worst of both. A desire to assert world leadership led U.S. leaders to commit troops to a dangerous and difficult task, but an equally strong desire to avoid even minimal casualties made it virtually impossible for American goals to be achieved. And, despite their intense preoccupation with avoiding a repeat of Vietnam, U.S. military and civilian leaders—products of their culture—did repeat many of the same mistakes, especially in underestimating the threat from what seemed a poor, backward opponent. "The American command," wrote one observer, "believed the Somalis to be intellectually primitive, culturally shallow, and militarily craven. All three beliefs proved expensively incorrect."

Control of the Somalia operation was formally transferred to the United Nations in early May, but the United States, which had initiated the international rescue effort, could not escape continuing responsibility for its outcome. Some five thousand U.S. troops remained deployed under U.N. command and an American officer, retired Navy admiral Jonathan Howe, was appointed U.N. "special representative" in Mogadishu, the Somali capital, overseeing efforts to arrange a political settlement and disarm the gunmen. But promoting a settlement also meant, unavoidably, that some Somali leaders would see their interests advanced and others would feel threatened. Somali politics having become what it was, it should have surprised no one that those who felt threatened would respond with violence. On June 5, forces controlled by Mohammed Farah Aidid, one of the competing clan leaders, ambushed Pakistani peacekeepers, killing twenty-three of them.

The Clinton administration, seeing its own image at risk if the U.N. mission failed, pushed through a U.N. Security Council resolution calling for the arrest, detention, and prosecution of those responsible for the ambush. In Mogadishu, Admiral Howe, widely regarded as a competent and intelligent officer but clearly disastrously out of his depth in Somalia, announced a $25,000 reward for Aidid's capture. At Howe's urging, four hundred Army rangers and a detachment of Delta Force* commandos were sent with the express mission of arresting Aidid. Their operations in Somalia, unlike those of the U.S. units assigned to the peacekeeping force, remained under American, not U.N. command.

To the increasing embarrassment and frustration of U.S. commanders, Aidid escaped repeated American forays to capture him, but hundreds of Somali civilians, including women and children, died in the raids.

*The Army's secret counterterrorist unit.

Americans died, too. By the end of September, eleven U.S. soldiers had been killed and a number of others had been wounded. Just as in Vietnam a generation earlier, U.S. casualties, even in small numbers, raised the stakes for the leadership in Washington. Like Lyndon Johnson before him, Clinton needed a success to vindicate the losses already suffered. And also like Johnson, he needed to explain those casualties to a public that, reasonably enough, wondered why their soldiers should be getting shot at in Somalia at all.

The answer was exactly the same that had been given to a skeptical public (and perhaps to quiet self-doubt in the national leadership, too) about Vietnam. America's strength and will were being challenged, and the challenge needed to be met; abandoning the manhunt for Aidid or pulling out of Somalia altogether would be an unacceptable loss of face. Even General Powell, the embodiment of the military's obsession with avoiding another Vietnam, ended up articulating the quintessential Vietnam argument on behalf of the Somalia policy: "You don't cut and run" just because things had gotten difficult, Powell told the National Press Club.

As with Vietnam, too, this rationale for U.S. policy was completely self-referential. Whether the original decision to send troops was wise or not had become irrelevant. Somalia was important because Washington declared it important, not from any attributes of its own; the United States had to persist in its effort there not because there was any intrinsic U.S. interest worth the cost of pursuing, but only because it had to finish what it had started, for the sake of its international reputation and to prove that the soldiers who had already been killed had not died for a mistake.

Unhappily for the Clinton administration, the public's response to its Somalia policy also echoed the experience of Vietnam. Increasingly, Americans rejected the abstract goal of saving face and concluded it was folly for their leaders to risk more American lives in a distant, murky conflict of no real interest to the United States. Sending soldiers to Somalia to feed starving people might make sense to Americans at home; sending them there to take sides in clan warfare did not. Military ineptitude in Mogadishu did not help. On a couple of occasions, U.S. troops pursuing Aidid stormed into the wrong buildings, one of them a compound that turned out to be occupied by U.N. aid workers. Every time Aidid escaped capture, his prestige increased among his Somali followers.

Mounting unease at home was already weighing on Clinton and his advisers when, on the afternoon of October 3, elements of the ranger force and the Delta commandos attempted to seize Aidid and his top lieutenants in a helicopter assault on Mogadishu's Olympic Hotel. Once again, Aidid escaped, while his armed supporters succeeded in shooting down three helicopters and trapping the raiding party. Other gunmen ambushed relief forces attempting to drive in from the city's outskirts. In fighting that lasted until the following morning, eighteen Americans were killed, seventy-eight were wounded, and one, Chief Warrant Officer Michael Durant, was taken prisoner. Somali casualties were in the hundreds.

Also fatally wounded in the botched battle was Washington's Somalia policy. Television, which had seemed a magnifying mirror for Americans' feelings of patriotism and pride during the Gulf War, now reflected back and magnified their growing doubts about Somalia. The most shocking image showed exultant Somalis dragging the corpse of a dead American soldier through the streets; another showed Durant in captivity, with fear-filled eyes staring from a bruised, bloody face. For many Americans, there was a direct, instant, intuitive connection between those images of dead and captured Americans in Somalia and the memory of Vietnam. Durant's capture, particularly, evoked the Vietnam POWs and their long, painful captivity, as well as more recent memories of Americans kept captive in the U.S. embassy in Teheran or kidnapped by terrorists and held hostage in Beirut.

Like those earlier captives, too, Durant became a metaphor for a whole country imprisoned in a bungled policy. The relentless spotlight of modern media coverage meant there was no escape from the symbol, either. CNN broadcast its clip of Durant more than thirty times in twenty-four hours; his battered face, in a grainy close-up taken from the TV tape, stared out from magazine covers, among them that of *Newsweek*, which opened its cover story by recalling the famous 1968 photo of a South Vietnamese general executing a bound Viet Cong prisoner on a Saigon street. Like that scene, the magazine's writers went on, the images from Somalia served to "define the horrors of an unpopular war." The issue's package of Somalia stories ended with an essay by *Newsweek*'s military commentator, retired Col. David Hackworth, who also saw the Vietnam nightmare coming back to life in Somalia. "It took almost 400,000 dead and wounded in Vietnam before we admitted our error there," Hackworth's piece concluded. "In Somalia, let's reclaim hostages and go home. Mogadishu is still a long way from the Mekong Delta, but let's not take even one more step in that direction."

Durant was quickly released, sparing the Clinton administration a drawn-out hostage drama. As a face-saving show of force, Clinton ordered reinforcements to Somalia. With no other rationale at hand, he too fell back on the credibility argument. In a televised speech, he repeated what General Powell had said five days before the Mogadishu disaster: "'Because things get difficult, you don't cut and run.' Our own credibility with friends and allies would be severely damaged." At the same time, though, yielding to congressional and widespread public outrage, he announced that all U.S. troops would be pulled out in six months.

The Somalia debacle cost more than face. It also weakened U.S. ability to intervene in other crises. A kind of reverse domino theory was at work: one failed peacekeeping mission spawned so much doubt and distrust that it would become much more difficult for a U.S. president to undertake another—at least, without a virtual guarantee that there would be no American casualties. Inside the Pentagon and the military services, the disastrous Somali experience reinforced chronic suspicions of the civilian leadership and a powerful aversion to any military operation except with the use of maximum force. The very concepts of relief or peacekeeping missions, especially if they were under multinational command, became something close to anathema. So strong was the military reaction that one analyst later argued that the battle in Mogadishu, lasting only a matter of hours and involving no more than a few hundred combatants on all sides, "has in many respects had a bigger impact on military thinking than the entire 1991 Persian gulf war"—a startling thought, but not entirely implausible, either.

Eighteen months after the botched firefight in Mogadishu, a force of eighteen hundred marines returned briefly to the Somali capital to cover the withdrawal of the remaining U.N. forces. During the evacuation the marines swapped a few shots with Somali gunmen, but suffered no casualties: the only result, it seemed, that Americans would now accept.

Even more than in Somalia, Vietnam's ghosts hovered over the agonizing war in Bosnia.

In that war, brutal Serb policies of "ethnic cleansing" in Bosnian villages, documented cases of mass rape of Muslim women, and regular and deliberate Serb artillery and sniper fire on unarmed civilians in the city of Sarajevo and other surrounded towns represented a test of the promise the world's leaders had repeated literally thousands of times since the Nazi slaughter of Europe's Jews during World War II: "Never again."

Serb atrocities in Bosnia were not, in fact, the worst the world had seen after the Nazi era. Cambodia's fanatical Khmer Rouge regime in the late 1970s carried out far more murderous policies; so did the leaders who deliberately unleashed waves of tribal butchery in Rwanda, to name just two examples. Nor was the siege of Sarajevo the worst such event of the 1990s. At exactly the same time the world's eyes were riveted on Serb shellings of the Bosnian capital, far worse destruction and civilian casualties were occurring, with only the scantiest news coverage, in Kabul, the capital of Afghanistan. But the horrors of Cambodia and Rwanda and Afghanistan took place among people racially, geographically, and culturally distant from the West. The war in Bosnia, taking place among Europeans on European soil and with significant historical roots in World War II, awakened sharper memories of Nazi crimes—not sharp enough, though, to sting anyone into actually intervening against the Serbs. For more than three years, U.S. leaders joined the worldwide wringing of hands over Serb outrages in Bosnia, but recoiled from any policy that might put American lives at risk to stop them. Even while criticizing President Bush during the 1992 election campaign for failing to respond strongly enough to the Bosnian tragedy, Bill Clinton was compelled to declare that sending U.S. ground forces to Bosnia was out of the question. Once in office, Clinton's policies for most of his first term were as cautious—and ineffective—as Bush's had been.

From its beginning, America's debate on the Bosnian tragedy resonated with eerily exact echoes of Vietnam, although the political lineup was oddly reversed. It was as if an old tape were being played but at the wrong speed, so that the words were familiar but the voices sounded distorted and strange. Those pushing for a stronger, if riskier, U.S. role in Bosnia came largely from the liberal side of the American political spectrum (though not all liberals took that view, by any means), which almost unanimously looked back on Vietnam as a terrible mistake. Conservatives, with few exceptions, opposed deeper involvement in the Balkans. Both sides offered, often virtually word for word, the same arguments they had vigorously opposed a generation earlier. Liberals who had scoffed at the old domino theory (stop Communism in Vietnam or it will roll over the rest of Southeast Asia) now espoused a new version of the same dubious logic (stop ethnic violence in Bosnia or it will spread to the rest of Eastern Europe). Conservatives who had called it fainthearted not to stay the course in Vietnam now declared the United States must at all costs avoid the risks of any commitment in Bosnia. Liberals who had insisted the Vietnam conflict was a local civil war that should not have been of concern to outsiders now found compelling reasons why Americans and their allies should interfere in Bosnia; in the more far-fetched formulations of this argument, the stakes were presented as nothing less than ethnic peace, stable boundaries, and the rule of law throughout post-Communist Europe and as far away as the former Soviet republics of central Asia. In a parallel backflip, conservatives who had declared that larger international interests and moral principles justified intervening to protect the Vietnamese from Communist tyranny now argued that it was not America's responsibility to police the whole world or protect the Bosnian Muslims from Serb barbarism.

In yet another ironic reversal, liberal interventionists regularly proclaimed that American credibility was at stake in the Balkans, and that the United States could not appear irresolute or ineffective there without weakening its influence everywhere else in the world—precisely the logic they had opposed so bitterly when it was presented as the reason the United States had to continue pursuing success in Vietnam. Putting a different twist on the credibility issue, Georgetown University's Charles A. Kupchan, who served on the National Security Council staff early in the Clinton administration, acknowledged that "just because the West has not stopped Serb aggression in Bosnia does not mean ethnic groups all over Eastern Europe will rise up and commit genocide against their neighbors." But, Kupchan contended, that was beside the point. The credibility that had been lost in Vietnam and needed to be restored was at home, not abroad: the U.S. government's credibility with its own people. After Vietnam, "Americans lost faith in their government and in their country's mission," he wrote, and they would not regain it if U.S. leaders continued to avoid their moral responsibility to step in against the slaughter in Bosnia. Even in turning the credibility issue around, however, Kupchan still arrived at an absurd overstatement of the goal in Bosnia: "It is not just the fate of Muslims or stability in the Balkans that is at stake. . . . It is the future of the West."

Liberals favoring a stronger Bosnia policy even adopted the Vietnam era's wishful myth that an unfavorable military situation could be changed tidily and cleanly by bombing, without the mess and bloodshed of fighting on the ground. Conservatives, meanwhile—in some cases exactly the same people who had spent the last twenty years insisting that the Vietnam War could have been won easily and quickly by the proper use of air power—warned gloomily that Bosnia would become a quagmire, bogging down tens or hundreds of thousands of U.S. troops indefinitely if Washington made the mistake of intervening in the conflict.

The recycled arguments also recycled old fallacies, on both sides. The new version of the domino theory, for example, was as overstated and plainly wrong-headed as the old one, disregarding the local roots of conflict and mistakenly assuming that all states and peoples in a region are subject to the same forces and will consequently act alike. The concept "required a combination of maps and rhetoric and ignorance," one critic had written about the domino theory as it was applied to Vietnam. Exactly the same could be said of the frequent fatuous assertions that democracy and ethnic peace in Eastern Europe would be decisively affected by what the West did or didn't do in Bosnia, or that America's worldwide credibility was on the line there. If a U.S. demonstration of force in one place could deter violence someplace else, asked Fareed Zakaria, editor of the journal *Foreign Affairs*, why hadn't the enormous U.S. military effort in the Persian Gulf deterred the Serbs, or aggressors in other conflicts from Azerbaijan to Sudan? Recalling that U.S. and allied aircraft had dropped more than a quarter of a million bombs on Iraq, Zakaria added: "Does anyone really believe that if that did not deter the Serbs, dropping a few hundred bombs in southern European mountains would stop the next war in its tracks?"

It was also a fallacy, though, to pretend that Bosnia had no claim on America's conscience at all. Comparisons with the Holocaust may have been overdrawn, but if there were any standards of international conduct worth enforcing, as the United States and its allies had been insisting since World War II, Bosnia made a persuasive case for intervention.

As with nearly every other U.S. policy issue in the 1990s, the Bosnia debate, like that on Somalia, seemed mainly driven by television coverage. Whenever events in Bosnia put images of civilian suffering on the screen, American political leaders issued statements declaring that something must be done—or pretending that something was. When the cameras were turned elsewhere, the issue subsided. Bosnia was on camera, as it happened, in April 1993 as European and Jewish leaders assembled to dedicate the Holocaust Memorial Museum in Washington. Television newscasts that week were full of horrifying scenes from the Muslim town of Srebrenica, under siege by Serb forces. At the Holocaust Museum ceremony, the Nobel Prize–winning author and Auschwitz survivor Elie Wiesel took the occasion to put the issue publicly, passionately, and starkly to President Clinton. "Mr. President, I cannot *not* tell you something," Wiesel told the president in front of the television cameras. "I have been in the former Yugoslavia. I cannot sleep since for what I have seen. As a Jew I am saying that we must do something to stop the bloodshed in that country." Clinton's reply was ambivalent, as was the country. (One poll that same week reported that on the question "Do you agree or disagree that the fighting in Bosnia is not America's problem?" Americans were split with metaphorical exactness: 47 percent agreed, 47 percent disagreed.) Even among those who could not escape some sense of responsibility, though, there seemed almost no support for military intervention. "It should be stopped," one woman in Kansas City, Missouri, told a *New York Times* reporter, "but we shouldn't try to stop it on our own. . . . Maybe we can help out a bit through the United Nations. But no more than that." And a tobacco company executive, succinctly summing up the conflicting memories that made Bosnia so disturbing, said: "I know about the Holocaust and I certainly don't denigrate it as a concern. But I also know about Vietnam and what a hopeless quagmire it turned out to be for us."

From time to time, especially when the Bosnia story was playing prominently on television, Clinton and his advisers attempted to take stronger action in the Bosnian tragedy, or at least to look as if they were acting strongly. But for most of Clinton's first term, domestic political reality always prevailed over any impulse to use significant force, even after it became clear that neither diplomacy nor economic pressure on Serbia was overcoming Serb defiance. Years of pious pronouncements from Washington could not conceal the truth that a half-century after the Nazis, the post–Cold War world's only military superpower was unwilling to use force to stop terrible crimes against humanity in Bosnia, largely because its experience in Vietnam a generation earlier had been so painful. It did not seem too fanciful to say that within the American conscience, the ghosts of Europe's murdered Jews struggled with the ghosts of Americans uselessly killed in Vietnam—and for years, Vietnam's ghosts won the struggle. It was also true, of course, that some unknowable number of other young Americans did not die to become ghosts of a war in Bosnia, which might or might not have achieved results justifying their sacrifice.

"The Vietnamese may be in terrible shape," the *Washington Post's* Meg Greenfield wrote in early 1994, "but they have certainly got their revenge. Merely mention the possible use of our military now any place on Earth and you will hear the pessimistic refrain: It will mean 500,000 ground troops, the military will fail, the wily enemy will prevail, the terrain is inhospitable, we will be hated etc. It is believed all this will be an inevitable outcome."

The debate over a possible U.S. intervention in Haiti to reinstate the deposed President Jean Bertrand Aristide bore out Greenfield's tart observation. Sen. John S. McCain of Arizona declared on the Senate floor that he could "almost" buy the argument that backing down from an invasion after repeated threats would damage America's credibility. But, McCain went on, "what happens to our credibility if we find ourselves in a quagmire?" McCain, a former Navy pilot who was shot down over North Vietnam and endured brutal torture during his five and a half years in prisoner-of-war camps, hardly needed to make explicit mention of the Vietnam experience: his well-known war record and the permanently stiff arm he bore from his captivity made the connection clearly enough. Nor did McCain make a habit of calling attention to his wartime ordeal. But, perhaps the more sharply because of having undergone so much in a war his country came to feel wasn't worth fighting, McCain chose to invoke Vietnam directly as a cautionary lesson for Haiti. "Everybody has their different view of the lessons of the Vietnam war," he told the Senate, but "there is one lesson that the American people are in agreement about . . . and that is you do not embark on a military exercise without the support of the American people." (McCain did not mention it, nor did the many others who in-toned the same mantra about the need for public support, but the truth is that Vietnam passed that test. When the United States began its interven-tion in Vietnam, the policy was overwhelmingly backed by politicians, the news media, and the public. It was only later, when the war seemed bogged down, that serious dissent developed.)

Like McCain, other critics summoned the memory of Vietnam—now yoked with Somalia, another symbol of a failed policy—in opposing the Haiti intervention. In the House of Representatives, shortly before the landing, Rep. Joel Hefley of Colorado took a dig at Clinton's own Vietnam history: "Well, I say it's never too late for Bill Clinton to get a little combat experience. If he's so sure we need to risk the blood of even one American soldier, let him lead the invasion." Hefley's colleagues, for the most part, were a bit more polite to the president but just as spooked by the memory of past failures. "Most foreign policy experts say a quagmire similar to Soma-lia awaits the United States in Haiti," warned Barbara F. Vucanovich of Nevada; Tim Hutchinson of Arkansas declared ominously that although the ramshackle Haitian army "cannot keep us out, they can inflict bloody casu-alties." It wasn't only critics of the Haiti mission who harked back to the Viet-nam debate. Administration officials defending the policy dusted off the all-purpose credibility argument. Clinton's ambassador to the United Nations, Madeleine Albright, even resurrected the old "the-president-knows-best" claim, with its echoes of Lyndon Johnson and Richard Nixon. Admonish-ing journalists not to be such skeptics about Haiti, Albright told a group of reporters and editors that "the president has more facts than you all have."

In defiance of the Vietnam syndrome, Clinton ordered the first of fifteen thousand U.S. troops into Haiti on the night of September 18. Paratroopers were already in the air headed for Haiti when, in a last-minute deal—negotiated, somewhat to the Clinton administration's embarrassment, by former President Jimmy Carter—the Haitian military junta was persuaded not to oppose the U.S. landing force. Even after the troops landed with no fighting and no losses, Clinton continued to reap surprisingly harsh commentary. The president had shown himself, said a particularly vicious essay in *Time* magazine, ready to "reach for anyone, and any deal, capable of saving him from the image of body bags returning from Haiti"—it having not occurred to the essayist, evidently, that the deal had spared the country not just from the image but from bringing home *real* bodies in real body bags.

Almost exactly a year after sending troops to Haiti, President Clinton finally decided to challenge the Vietnam syndrome in Bosnia. Between August 30 and September 14, 1995, in a bombing campaign intended to put serious military pressure, for the first time, on the Bosnian Serbs, U.S. and other NATO planes carried out nearly a thousand strikes against Serb positions. The immediate objective was to force the Serbs to move their heavy weapons away from the outskirts of Sarajevo. Beyond that, Clinton and his advisers hoped the bombing would open the way for a negotiated settlement between the Serbs and their adversaries and end the conflict at last.

The announced reason for the air campaign was a Serb shelling attack on August 28 that killed thirty-eight civilians in Sarajevo's main marketplace. Earlier, in July, the Serbs had committed what were thought to be the worst mass killings of the entire war, rounding up and slaughtering thousands of Bosnian Muslims fleeing the town of Srebrenica after its capture by Serbian forces. The new-found boldness of the United States and its allies, however, was inspired less by Serbian atrocities than by indications of Serb weakness on the battlefield. In early August, Serbian troops had been easily pushed out of the Serb-occupied region of Krajina, in eastern Croatia; they had also given up hundreds of square miles of territory in northwestern Bosnia and elsewhere. Suddenly, the Serbian forces—previously seen as tough, determined fighters in the mold of the Yugoslav partisans who had fought hundreds of thousands of German troops to a standstill in World War II—no longer appeared so formidable or tenacious. Only weeks earlier, the U.S. military leadership was still viewing a possible intervention in Bosnia with typical post-Vietnam wariness. "In the professional judgment of our military leaders," the Clinton administration informed Congress in June 1995, a U.S. decision to fight the Serbs "would entail the commitment of several hundred thousand troops, a long war, and thousands of casualties." In August, with the Serbs' reputation for toughness severely dented, the prospects for using force successfully and at low cost looked considerably brighter.

Whether because of the NATO air strikes, Serb setbacks on the battlefields, or both, the Bosnian impasse was finally broken, after years of disappointments, broken agreements, bungled opportunities, and international timidity. Days after the NATO strikes ended, the foreign ministers of Bosnia, Croatia, and Yugoslavia agreed to preserve Bosnia as a nominally unified state divided into two "entities," one under a Croat-Muslim alliance and the other under the Bosnian Serbs. Although the unity provided by this agreement was clearly more fictitious than real, it met the minimum U.S. condition that Serb aggression must not be rewarded by the formal dismemberment of Bosnia. Following that breakthrough, the warring sides agreed to a sixty-day ceasefire and then opened negotiations under U.S. auspices in Dayton, Ohio. On November 21, a peace plan was announced at Dayton, including an arrangement for an "implementation force" of approximately 60,000 NATO troops—about one-third of them Americans—to replace the ineffective United Nations peacekeepers already deployed in Bosnia.

Americans were still wary about sending U.S. troops to enforce a Bosnian peace agreement. "I've yet to hear from the first constituent who supports it," one congressman told senior Clinton administration officials at a House hearing. The administration, in turn, in its strenuous effort to allay fears of another Vietnam or Somalia, spent a great deal of time explaining what the peacekeepers would not do in Bosnia. The NATO force, known as IFOR, would not become involved in aiding refugees, or in monitoring elections or human rights violations, or in returning the victims of "ethnic cleansing" to their homes, or in rebuilding the Bosnian economy or political institutions, U.S. officials promised. Nor would IFOR troops risk combat and possible casualties to pursue wanted war criminals. Officially, U.S. policy favored prosecution of those charged with atrocities in Bosnia, among whom were the Bosnian Serb president, Radovan Karadzic, and his military commander, Gen. Ratko Mladic. But U.S. military leaders, no doubt remembering the ill-conceived effort to capture General Aidid in Somalia and its disastrous outcome, were extremely reluctant to take any responsibility for investigating war crimes or apprehending the criminals.

U.S. leaders were also firm in their insistence that American soldiers would not stay in Bosnia indefinitely. If the Bosnians resumed the war, Secretary of Defense William J. Perry said flatly, "we would withdraw." Even if the ceasefire held, the administration pledged that U.S. participation in the implementation force would not be open-ended. Appearing together before House and Senate committees, Perry and Gen. John M. Shalikashvili, chairman of the Joint Chiefs of Staff, declared unequivocally in their joint statement that IFOR "will complete its mission in a period not to exceed twelve months"—a time limit that from the beginning was seen by most experts as hopelessly unrealistic but that President Clinton and his advisers apparently regarded as a necessary promise to win congressional and public support.

While pledging caution, the administration also made a convincing argument that not only the Bosnian ceasefire but also U.S. stature as a world leader would be endangered if the United States failed to join the peacekeeping force. Secretary of State Warren Christopher and other officials insisted that the United States could not ask its allies to send their troops while refusing to send its own. To do that would be to abdicate U.S. leadership of NATO and, administration officials declared, gravely undermine broader U.S. interests in Europe. The argument that the United States had no choice but to act in Bosnia to preserve American world leadership may have been paradoxical ("Are we leading or being led?" one senator asked skeptically) but was nonetheless persuasive enough to win crucial support among Republicans—most importantly from Bob Dole, the Senate majority leader who was expected to be Clinton's opponent in the 1996 presidential election.

Though Dole's backing gave Clinton some protection against partisan attacks over sending U.S. troops to Bosnia, the political risks were still considerable. Opinion polls showed that only a bit more than one-third of the public supported the deployment, and there was no doubt that even that support would evaporate overnight if American soldiers were wounded or killed, or if the mission in Bosnia began to bear any resemblance to the disaster that had overtaken U.S. efforts in Somalia or Vietnam. As in Haiti, though, Clinton was lucky in Bosnia—luckier than he deserved, perhaps, after temporizing for so long while the dying went on. There were some embarrassing headlines in the first few days, when units of the U.S. First Armored Division coming from Germany were stalled on Bosnia's northern border because Army engineers were unable to bridge the Sava River on schedule. After that, though, IFOR's operations proceeded so uneventfully as to drop out of the news altogether for weeks at a time. The widely forecast outbreaks of violence and resulting U.S. casualties ("from snipers, from grenades rolled into bars, from firing from a crowd of civilians, from car bombs and those kinds of things," as former national security adviser Gen. Brent Scowcroft predicted) never materialized. No news from Bosnia was, of course, good news for the White House, as President Clinton and his advisers headed into the 1996 reelection campaign.

One reason things stayed so quiet in Bosnia was IFOR's determination to keep its mission within the narrowest possible limits. True to their vow to avoid "mission creep," once the warring Bosnian sides had complied with the cease-fire provisions and pulled their forces back from the boundary between the two zones, U.S. and other NATO commanders were less than forceful, to put it mildly, in promoting other objectives of the Dayton accord. IFOR took no responsibility for protecting Bosnians who had been displaced by the war and wanted to return to their homes. Instead, NATO commanders insisted that protection of returning refugees was up to local police—who were, in many cases, the very people who had driven the refugees away in the first place. Not surprisingly, only a handful of the million or so displaced Bosnians dared go back to their old homes. IFOR was similarly cautious about hunting down war criminals. Not only did it decline to send troops to arrest those under international indictment; on occasion, IFOR even refused to provide security for investigators digging up the killing fields in search of evidence.

Even had its policies been more vigorous, the NATO force by itself obviously could not bring about reconciliation among the Bosnians or restore true unity to their shattered country. But it also seemed true that NATO's extreme caution encouraged the ruling hardliners in all three ethnic groups to believe that, short of resuming the war, they could continue to act pretty much as they pleased, in spite of their pledges at Dayton. The "defining moment of the post-Dayton process," declared a former U.S. diplomat, "was the flat refusal of NATO to do anything other than defend itself and enforce the military separation line." The reason for IFOR's inaction, he added, "is Vietnam. The commanders were afraid of casualties." NATO's presence did little to loosen the grip of ethnic politics or foster a spirit of reconciliation. In elections in September 1996, Muslim, Croat, and Serb voters all gave large majorities to the same nationalist leaders who had inflamed the country's divisions during the war. A year after IFOR arrived, almost all accused war criminals not only remained free but hardly bothered to stay out of sight.

If the international effort in Bosnia had its shortcomings, at least the bloodshed had ended. The West's belated intervention might not have been enough to redeem the years of inaction by American and European leaders, but President Clinton could at least tell himself and his country that the United States had taken some risks to stop the killing. And if the ultra-cautious policies of U.S. and other NATO commanders had weakened the peace effort, as many critics charged, they had also avoided blunders that might have led to a hasty U.S. exit and the possible collapse of the entire process. Setbacks to an enduring Bosnian settlement were deplored by Balkan experts and commentators but drew little attention from the American public, which was more interested in the safety of U.S. troops than in Bosnian politics. With the Bosnia mission largely out of the headlines during his reelection campaign, Clinton was able to skirt the increasingly obvious fact that the administration's "exit strategy" had been unrealistic and the twelve-month limit it had placed on the U.S. presence in Bosnia would have to be extended. With the election safely behind him, Clinton announced on November 15 that about 8,500 U.S. troops would remain for up to 18 additional months to participate in a reduced NATO force that was needed, the president said, to preserve "the stability and the confidence that only an outside security force can provide."

Following the announcement, there was some grumbling from Republicans who had taken the political risk of supporting the original deployment. But there was no big public outcry, even though the majority of Americans were probably no more enthusiastic about taking responsibility for a Bosnian settlement than they had been a year earlier. Nor did Clinton receive much public criticism for failing to honor his original deadline, although many felt he had dissembled on the issue during the campaign. His opponents feared that if they insisted on bringing U.S. troops home and the war broke out again, they would be held responsible—and they knew that if things went wrong and some unforeseen military disaster occurred in Bosnia along the lines of those in Somalia and Vietnam, Clinton would get the blame.

Like Haiti, Bosnia could be counted a success, at least in the sense that it did not turn into a fiasco that undoubtedly would have further strengthened the most isolationist forces in American political life. If the Dayton agreement's promises of unification, democracy, justice, and national reconciliation in Bosnia remained largely unfulfilled, President Clinton could still point to the end of the fighting as a vindication of his policy and a demonstration that the United States could still act as a world power with global interests and influence. It could hardly be said, though, that America had vanquished its memories of Vietnam and Somalia and the cautious, contradictory attitudes that were, for good or ill, the legacy of those earlier conflicts. If anything, the interventions in Haiti and Bosnia appeared to reinforce the zero-casualties standard that now seemed to be set as the condition for public support of any military mission abroad. When American troops crossed over the icy Sava River into Bosnia in the last days of 1995, the end of the U.S. military effort in Vietnam lay nearly twenty-two years in the past. During that time, the international political and strategic landscape had changed almost beyond recognition. But Vietnam's ghosts still hovered as Clinton began his second term in office, which would take him and his country across the threshold of a new century. Amid the multiple confusions of the post–Cold War world, U.S. foreign and military policies continued, in many important respects, to be haunted by the past.

5

THE MYTH

The longing for recovery, retrieval, and reconciliation is so pervasive that it cannot be due merely to claims of some people, especially family members, that Vietnam is still holding MIAs in prison. It can only signify some deeper sense of loss associated with the war. We hated losing, and still hate the Vietnamese for it. Nobody knows how much.
—Leo Cawley

Some people just don't want this issue to go away, ever.
—Chuck Searcy

I

On Memorial Day 1993, the cover of *Parade* magazine—a national supplement distributed with more than thirty-six million Sunday newspapers across the United States—showed twenty-seven small black-and-white photographs, laid out as if for a page in a yearbook. Instead of new graduates, though, these photographs showed servicemen lost twenty or more years earlier in the Vietnam War. "Lest We Forget," proclaimed the headline. Above it, in smaller type, appeared this declaration: "On this Memorial Day, as we pay tribute to our veterans, it is fitting that we give special thought to the POWs and the MIAs of the Vietnam war. Their fate remains in doubt, and their families continue their vigil." Inside were three pages of text, written by author and Vietnam veteran Al Santoli and accompanied by still more yearbook-style photographs of the missing. Santoli's opening sentence declared, "Perhaps the most haunting legacy of the Vietnam war is the unresolved fate of American prisoners last known alive in Vietnam, Laos and Cambodia. After two decades of controversy, the Pentagon maintains as its official position: 'We cannot rule out the possibility of live Americans, although there is no evidence.'" However, Santoli went on, a "top secret" Vietnamese military report, found in Soviet archives, "declares that Hanoi withheld hundreds of captives 'for future negotiations with the United States.' And numerous intelligence documents and satellite images—as recent as mid-1992—indicate possible survivors."

The appearance of such an article in a mass-circulation magazine more than twenty years after the U.S. withdrawal from Vietnam was evidence, if any were needed, of the remarkable durability of the missing-in-action issue. Of all the war's legacies, the MIA story seemed to have the greatest staying power. In a sense, it became the central legend of Vietnam, represented in MIA-POW flags flying over state capitols, in countless novels and movies, and apparently in the minds of a substantial majority of Americans—two-thirds of whom, according to opinion polls, believed that the Vietnamese were still holding American prisoners two decades after the last U.S. troops came home.

The persistence of that belief was all the more remarkable because during those twenty years, although POW "sightings" and other sensational reports appeared regularly, none ever led to an actual prisoner, or to any convincing proof that there were (or ever had been) any prisoners to be found. The nearly six hundred American POWs who returned knew of no one still alive who was left behind; except for one defector,* not a single possible prisoner was ever positively identified, by the MIA activists or anyone else. Time after time, the "evidence" produced in support of the more lurid claims turned out to be fake. This happened so consistently one might think the press, at least, would have become less credulous. But on this issue, American journalism seemed to have lost its customary skepticism. Like the public, journalists appeared to have no memory of how unreliable past reports had proven. Each new sensation was presented as credible, if not proven, even when the evidence was flimsy on its face.

---

*In 1979, a former Marine private named Robert Garwood returned from Vietnam—the only U.S. prisoner to turn up alive after the war. Though Garwood claimed to have been held against his will, fellow prisoners testified he had defected to the Viet Cong long before the war ended. In 1980, a court-martial found him guilty of collaborating with the enemy.

For example, in the summer of 1991, newspapers across the country front-paged a photograph of three mustached men holding a handwritten sign with the date "25-5-1990." According to the accompanying article from the Reuters news agency, the three men in the photograph were identified by relatives as U.S. airmen who had been shot down during the war: Air Force Col. John Leighton Robertson, Air Force Maj. Albro Lynn Lundy, and Navy Lt. Larry James Stevens. Following the conventions of news-agency reporting, the Reuters report cited a source for each major point in the story and repeated, though far down in the text, the standard Vietnamese denial that they were holding any U.S. prisoners. Nothing in the report, however, conveyed any grounds for doubting the story. Its language and tone carried no suggestion of skepticism. The opening paragraph, for example, referred to the photograph as "a snapshot, apparently taken last year, of three U.S. servicemen who have been missing since the end of the war in Indochina and may have been held against their will."

Yet there were ample grounds for doubt. To begin with, no matter how firmly the three men's families may have believed they were the ones shown in the photo, one had to wonder how certain anyone could be in identifying, from a single and somewhat grainy photograph, men who would now be more than twenty years older than when they disappeared. In fact, it turned out that two other families claimed that the photo showed *their* missing relatives. Other doubts were raised by the photo itself. The handwritten numerals on the sign, particularly the 1s and 9s, were written in a distinctively Eastern European style that very few Americans would use, and the three men looked remarkably robust for men who had supposedly spent more than two decades in Asian prisons. The person who gave the photo to Reuters—a former POW and retired Navy captain named Eugene "Red" McDaniel—offered no information about where it was taken or by whom or how it reached the West.

Nor was it mentioned in the Reuters article (though the information was easily available) that none of the three men supposedly identified in the photograph had ever been reported as captured. In fact, Defense Department records showed that two of the three almost certainly died when they were first shot down. Colonel Robertson's weapons operator, who ejected, was captured, and was then freed in the 1973 prisoner exchange, told his Air Force debriefers after his return that Robertson never got out of their F-4 Phantom after it was hit over North Vietnam in September 1966. In Major Lundy's case, four other pilots saw his parachute falling with an empty harness after he radioed that he was bailing out of his damaged plane over Laos on Christmas Eve 1970—conclusive enough evidence for the Air Force to list him two days later as killed in action, rather than missing. The third officer, Lieutenant Stevens, was in an A-4 that exploded in midair, also over Laos, in February 1969, according to Navy records, with no evidence that he might have survived.

People familiar with the MIA issue were skeptical about the "Robertson-Lundy-Stevens" photo from the beginning. Government investigators knew, for one thing, that it originated with a group known to have circulated false evidence in the past—"a ring of Cambodian opportunists," according to the Pentagon, "led by a well-known and admitted fabricator of POW-MIA information." Eventually, the new photo was shown, beyond any possible doubt, to be a fake. Defense Intelligence Agency investigators even identified the actual photograph that had been doctored: the original was in an old copy of a Soviet magazine that the forgers apparently found in a library in Cambodia. Not even that disclosure, however, could quell the furor the photograph had raised. While MIA activists used it to generate a new round of publicity for their crusade, politicians of both parties clamored for yet another probe of the issue. The possibility of surviving prisoners "absolutely commands our attention," declared then-Senator Albert Gore, who added that the public did not trust the government's assurances that all apparent MIA information was being tracked down. "It has been clear for a long time," Gore said, "that the American people are not confident in those assurances, or in the conclusion that there are no MIAs alive." Within days, not visibly troubled by the fact that it was inspired by demonstrably false evidence, the Senate established the Select Committee on POW/MIA Affairs, which undertook to settle the issue "once and for all" but proved, in the end, as powerless as its predecessors to overcome the myth and its promoters.

After the debunking of the "Robertson-Lundy-Stevens" photograph, one might have expected journalists, if not politicians or the general public, to respond more cautiously the next time. But when the next sensational MIA story surfaced, the treatment was every bit as credulous, and in the nation's most prestigious newspaper, at that. In April 1993, the *New York Times* front-paged a report on a Russian translation of a Vietnamese document appearing to show that Vietnam actually held 1,205 prisoners in September 1972—more than three times the number they acknowledged holding at the time, and more than twice the 591 men who were eventually repatriated (including those captured after the supposed date of the document) when the prisoner exchange took place in early 1973. "Files Said to Show Hanoi Lied in '72 on Prisoner Totals," declared the *Times's* headline over the story, which appeared, coincidentally or not, just as the Clinton administration was reported to be edging toward further steps in its gradual rapprochement with Vietnam.

The document, purported to be a "top secret" translation of a high-ranking Vietnamese commander's report to a Politburo meeting in Hanoi, was discovered in a Moscow archive by a researcher named Stephen Morris.* Morris's find was full of errors and discrepancies that would have been immediately obvious to anyone familiar with the issue. But the initial *Times* article mentioned none of them, and neither did most of the feverish reactions and commentaries that tumbled off the presses and over the airwaves following Morris's disclosure. Former National Security adviser Zbigniew Brzezinski declared—without, as far as anyone could tell, any evidence whatsoever (his conclusion appeared to be based entirely on the Russians' massacre of Polish officers in the Katyn Forest in 1940)—that "the great likelihood is that the Vietnamese took hundreds of American officers out and shot them in cold blood." Two days after the *Times* article appeared, a *Washington Post* columnist wrote that the Russian document "has the air of authenticity," though he had no apparent basis for this opinion beyond the allegations in the *Times* article itself. In another column, the conservative commentators Rowland Evans and Robert Novak cited Brzezinski, Henry Kissinger, and "Soviet scholars"—but no Vietnam experts—as finding "the ring of authenticity" in the Russian document. MIA activists leaped to proclaim the "smoking gun" had at last been found, establishing that what they had claimed for so many years was now proved to be true.

Whatever the Morris document rang of, however, it wasn't authenticity. Detail after detail raised questions, beginning with the supposed author of the original Vietnamese document, identified as Lt. Gen. Tran Van Quang, deputy chief of staff of the North Vietnamese army. But Quang did not hold either that rank or that post in 1972 (he was promoted to the job two years later, in 1974). In September 1972, the date of the supposed report to the Politburo, Quang was a major general commanding the "B4 Front" in central Vietnam, a job that had no connection with POWs. He was not stationed in Hanoi and did not even visit the capital that month. In any case, Vietnamese records show no Politburo meeting was held on the date mentioned. Moreover, as was customary for key Communist commanders, Quang never used his real name on any documents or reports during that period.

Other discrepancies included repeated references to the "23rd Cen-

---

*This is the document alluded to by Al Santoli in his *Parade* magazine article, quoted above.

tral Committee Plenum" of the Communist Party, a meeting that actually took place more than two years later. Elsewhere, the document confused two prominent South Vietnamese who had similar given names: Ngo Dzu, a corps commander (one of only four) in the Saigon army, and Truong Dinh Dzu, a Saigon lawyer and opposition figure who ran against South Vietnam's President Thieu in 1967 and was later jailed for "conduct detrimental to the anti-Communist spirit of the people and the armed forces." Whoever actually wrote the Morris document apparently thought the general and the dissident were the same man—a mistake unlikely to have been made by a ranking Communist general or for that matter by any politically aware Vietnamese on either side in 1972.

There were additional misstatements: that American prisoners were segregated by rank and that they were dispersed after an unsuccessful 1971 U.S. commando raid on a disused North Vietnamese prison camp. In both cases, the truth was exactly the opposite. And experts familiar with Vietnamese Communist documents pointed out that the language Quang purportedly used—at least as it was represented in the Russian translation unearthed by Morris—bore no resemblance to the customary style. Reports by senior commanders to the Politburo were never written in the first person; nor did they contain the kind of bombastic propaganda phrases that are sprinkled through the Morris document. Although the translation repeatedly used the term "American prisoners of war," the Vietnamese Communists carefully avoided those words, which might imply that the Americans were legitimate combatants. Consistent with their view that U.S. forces were illegal aggressors in Vietnam, the Communists customarily referred to the POWs as "captured American military personnel."

Morris was a well-known critic of the Vietnamese Communist regime and a fervent opponent of normalizing relations with Hanoi. Dismissing attacks on the document as politically motivated and reflecting a soft-on-Hanoi agenda, Morris declared in an article for the *Washington Post* that his critics were "political activists identified with the cause of accelerated normalization." But Morris's defense of his discovery was itself a tad short of convincing, as when he argued, in print, that American prisoners "sometimes . . . gave false names" to their captors. That, of course, was the last thing any captured U.S. serviceman was likely to do: giving his name was not only authorized but was the only way his family might learn that he was still alive.

The most significant problem with the Morris document, however, was not in the details, clearly incorrect as most of them were, but in its basic premise. If its central allegation was true—that the Vietnamese had deliberately and in secret held back more than six hundred American prisoners after the prisoner exchange—then several other things would also have to be true: The Vietnamese would have had to set up a secret, parallel prison system virtually from the beginning of the American intervention; that is, more than seven years before Quang's alleged report to the Politburo and long before the POWs became a significant negotiating issue. They would have had to hide that system from U.S. intelligence during the entire war. They would have had to succeed in keeping the two groups of prisoners completely insulated from each other, beginning from the moment a man was captured—so that in all that time, not a single prisoner in one group would have had any contact with the other, not even so much as a glimpse. Even more remarkably, the Vietnamese would have had to segregate in the secret camps exactly those men whom U.S. intelligence didn't know had been taken prisoner, while sending all the POWs known to have been captured to the camps the Americans did know about.

Those suppositions defy common sense, and so did the numbers in the Morris document. If some eight hundred additional prisoners were being held in September 1972, beyond the approximately four hundred the Vietnamese acknowledged at the time, a very large majority of the missing-in-action would have had to survive not only the original incident in which they disappeared, but long enough thereafter to be still alive in the "secret" camps in 1972. If the Morris document's figures were accurate, that would mean that nearly all the men whose aircraft were shot down or crashed had managed to come out alive—and there would then have had to be a miraculously high survival rate among men with serious wounds or burns, despite poor medical care, primitive sanitary conditions, torture, hunger, and enormous physical and emotional hardships in the camps. No one not already wedded to the MIA mythology could believe such survival rates were plausible, and no one in the U.S. government had ever suggested that eight hundred men, or anything close to that number, might have survived and been taken prisoner in addition to those who were eventually freed in 1973. Over the years, different figures were given for MIAs who might possibly have been alive after being shot down, but the highest estimates were only a little more than one hundred.* The number of true discrepancies—in

---

*American military negotiators who dealt with the Vietnamese during the first two years after the prisoner exchange sought information about 107 men who, according to U.S. intel-

which there was some actual information that men may have been captured—was much lower. The historian H. Bruce Franklin, in his intensively researched book *M.I.A., or Mythmaking In America*, showed that U.S. records documented a dozen or so missing men as "definitely alive in enemy hands" after being shot down, and another eight "possibly" captured. Of the known prisoners, most were believed, on fairly strong evidence, to have died in captivity.

The doctored "Robertson-Lundy-Stevens" photograph and the Stephen Morris document were only two in a long list of sensational exposés supposedly revealing that American prisoners still languished in Indochina long after the war—and that U.S. officials had participated in an unconscionable conspiracy to conceal their existence and prevent their rescue. (This art form reached a peak of sorts in a 1990 book by Monika Jensen-Stevenson and William Stevenson called *Kiss the Boys Goodbye*, which propounds a conspiracy so convoluted that even the authors seemed to have considerable trouble keeping track of their own theory. To say that the Stevensons were loose with the facts is a considerable understatement. On one page, for example, they write that U.S. authorities listed "317 men missing in Laos." One page later, they ask: "So where were the 371 [*sic*] and possibly more men known by the U.S. government to have been captured by the Pathet Lao?"—thus, in a few paragraphs, converting missing men into known prisoners and fabricating another 54 men out of thin air, to boot.) Despite the fact that none of these exposés ever proved true, many of them received wide and uncritical coverage from the news media, which seemed to find the combination of lost American heroes, treacherous Communists, and a vast official cover-up absolutely irresistible.

No tale was too outlandish to get some journalistic attention. A California paper informed its readers that the U.S. Air Force had secretly recovered nearly one hundred prisoners from Vietnam years after the war and ordered them to assume new identities to avoid embarrassing the U.S. government and its leaders. (*Kiss the Boys Goodbye* has another version of this story, telling of emaciated Americans brought from Hanoi and Haiphong and confined in a "classified" ward of a U.S. military hospital in the Philippines.) When two retired Special Forces soldiers, Maj. Mark A. Smith and Sfc. Melvin C. McIntire, sued the U.S. government in September 1985

---

ligence, might have survived or whose fate should have been known by the Vietnamese. Other lists put 135 cases in this category, called "last-known-alive" or "discrepancy cases." Not even the National League of Families of American Prisoners and Missing in Southeast Asia, for years among the most fervent adherents of the idea that living Americans were left in captivity after 1973, had ever put out figures resembling those in the Morris document.

for allegedly covering up evidence that "in excess of 200" Americans might still be held prisoner in Indochina, newspapers and television and radio stations around the country flocked to publicize their charges. Among their appearances were interviews on *60 Minutes* and *The Phil Donahue Show,* both broadcast nationally. As with the forged photo and the Stephen Morris document, coverage was much sparser when the story began to fall apart. When Smith, after promising to hand over photos and other documents to a Senate committee "within a week," subsequently failed to appear and then ducked a Senate subpoena rather than turn over his "evidence," it was hardly reported at all. (Eventually, after the subpoena was finally served by U.S. marshals, he did turn over some material. Rather than being the irrefutable proof he had claimed, however, Smith's documents contained "no worthwhile information," a committee spokesman said.) Nor did national television programs or other major news outlets rush to report on the Defense Department's answer to Smith's and McIntire's charges—which showed, among other things, that their information was based entirely on hearsay, some of it from a refugee whose activities in Thailand were reported to include "attempting to bribe Thai officials, posing as a U.S. government official, threatening refugees to only turn over POW/MIA information to him. . . . Also, he is wanted in the U.S. for defrauding other refugees."

While credulously reporting one exposé after another and then all but ignoring later disclosures disproving them, journalists also helped perpetuate a remarkable misimpression of how many MIAs there actually were. For many years, the commonly repeated statistic was that more than 2,000 Americans were missing in Vietnam. In October 1995, for example, the *Washington Post* reported that "since the beginning of the war, 2,184 were considered to be missing in action"; a couple of months later, another *Post* article declared that "the list of servicemen still officially missing from the war stands at 2,162." Similar numbers appeared in nearly every article on the subject. In fact, there were not 2,000-plus men "officially missing" in the 1990s. Or ever. The true number was much lower, and always had been.

When U.S. military involvement in Vietnam ended in January 1973, the number of men listed as missing in action was approximately 1,330 (no precise number exists because lists prepared by the services and those compiled by the Defense Intelligence Agency were not identical). Four-fifths of the missing men were airmen. Of the MIA cases, 118 were classed as "non-hostile"—men who had disappeared for reasons not due to enemy action. The great majority of these were aircraft accidents.

After 591 U.S. prisoners were returned in February and March 1973, the DIA compiled a corrected list of 1,303 men who had been classed as MIA (1,238) or POW (65) but who were neither freed in the exchange nor included on the Vietnamese list of those who had died while in captivity. On the basis of information provided by returning POWs, the DIA concluded that about 100 of the 1,303 were "probably dead"; 70 were officially declared killed before a lawsuit by some MIA families suspended status changes for the next four years. That left, at most, 1,200-plus missing men. Why, then, was it almost universally reported twenty years later that nearly twice that number were missing—creating "the anomalous situation of having more Americans considered unaccounted for today than we had immediately after the war," as Senate investigators commented in 1993?

The reason was a peculiar Defense Department decision sometime in the late 1970s to lump together the wartime MIA list with another list of men who were known to have died, but whose remains could not be retrieved to be sent home and buried. These were cases in which aircraft were seen to explode or crash with no parachutes deployed, or when a plane was known to have gone down at sea but the crew was never found, or when soldiers saw comrades killed but could not bring out the bodies. The official wartime casualty status for this group was KIA/BNR ("killed in action, body not recovered"). Immediately after the end of U.S. military involvement, the DIA showed a total of 1,118 men in this category; other lists showed slightly different figures. During the war, those casualties were never included in the "missing" or "unaccounted for" total. It would have been illogical to do so. The KIA/BNRs were not missing, except in the sense that no bodies had been shipped home; nor were they unaccounted for, in the usual sense of the term. In the vast majority of cases the services knew exactly what had happened to them, since the KIA/BNR status was assigned only in cases where evidence of death was virtually conclusive. Air Force policy required "evidence so strong and convincing as to overbear any possibility of survival." If there were any chance that a man had survived, no matter how remote, he was to be carried as missing in action. Army guidelines were equally restrictive, declaring that for a man to be declared killed, "the facts must be such that death is the only plausible alternative under the circumstances." Despite those demanding standards, there were a few mistakes. Several Navy airmen thought to have been killed eventually turned up in POW camps. In the vast majority of cases, though, there was no possible doubt that the men had died.

There was no doubt, either, that the true number must have been considerably higher than the 1,100-plus on the KIA/BNR list. Because the standard of proof was so high and because unit commanders tended to be highly optimistic in making casualty status determinations, many men were classed MIA even when there was quite strong evidence that they had died. A 1976 House of Representatives committee—the first of numerous congressional panels to investigate the MIA issue—reported that when its staff began to look at the missing-in-action cases one by one, investigators concluded that in 40 of the first 53 cases reviewed, missing servicemen could "justifiably" have been declared KIA to begin with.

The MIA list was inflated for other reasons, too—for example, if a plane went down with two crewmen aboard and only one parachute was seen, but no one knew which man had ejected. In such cases, both crewmen were carried as missing, even though it was known that only one could have survived. And while it was logical to keep men on the missing-in-action list in those cases where planes had simply disappeared and no information ever reached U.S. intelligence to suggest what had happened to pilots or crews, it was also logical that a certain percentage of those men must have died, since it was obviously impossible that the crews of *every* vanished aircraft had managed to eject and land safely.*

Thus, facts and logic all suggested that if 1,200 or so men were listed as missing immediately after the 1973 prisoner exchange, the number whose fate was really in doubt must be something lower—in all probability, much lower. But facts and logic had little to do with the MIA issue as it gradually took shape in the postwar years. The effort to account for lost American servicemen was quickly overtaken by myth, false reasoning, distorted history, and deliberate deception, and so was the strange arithmetic that, from about 1980 on, added more than 1,000 men who were known to be dead to the mythic list of the missing.

The Defense Department's decision to add the entire KIA/BNR list to the missing-in-action total mollified some families who could not or would not give up hope. But it also muddied the whole issue, as did the gradual change in official language that eventually blended the missing and the captured under the single label "POW/MIA." Originally, POW status was assigned only when there was some information that a man had survived and been taken prisoner; MIA meant, logically enough, that there

---

*According to a 1995 Defense Department report, there were 308 cases in which "the location and circumstances of loss are still unknown." Referred to as "off-the-scope" cases, these involved men who "were never heard from again after embarking on long-range ground or air reconnaissance missions or after their aircraft were last seen visually on radar heading toward a given target."

was no such information. When the two categories were effectively merged into one, that crucial distinction was lost.

In consequence, just as the government's mythical mathematics changed hundreds of men from dead to missing, its illogical language changed hundreds of the missing into possible prisoners, fostering the persistent fantasy of hidden prison camps in the Southeast Asian jungles, and the companion fantasy that somehow the government itself had engaged in a gigantic conspiracy to cover up the deliberate abandonment of hundreds of its own soldiers. The combination of misleading numbers and misleading terminology also led to the formulation of a U.S. policy that was presented for many years as a sacred trust but in fact was as unattainable as it was illogical: the demand for a "full accounting" for *all* the men on the list while insisting that none could be considered accounted for if, as a Defense Department official explained, "we do not have a live person or his identifiable remains."

The truth, though the U.S. government refused to say it out loud for nearly a quarter of a century, was that a complete accounting for every single MIA was simply not possible. In modern war, particularly war fought in the sky with high-performance aircraft, men are blown to atoms in midair, or crash into the sea, or are pulverized against remote mountainsides or pulped in tropical vegetation or buried so far down in the muck of canals that no one will ever find them. The men who vanished in Vietnam deserved to be remembered and mourned with the war's other casualties. But making them into a twenty-year national obsession seemed to serve no purpose except for those who, for emotional or ideological reasons, hoped to block any move toward a new relationship between the United States and Vietnam.

In the end, it took nearly twenty-three years for the U.S. government to acknowledge what had been obvious from the start: that in hundreds of cases, there was no possibility that bodies could be recovered, and no point in continuing attempts to do so. Late in 1995, the Pentagon quietly released a ten-page report declaring that after a new case-by-case review of every "unaccounted for" casualty, analysts had concluded that there were 567 cases in which, they believed, "no actions by any government will result in the recovery of remains." It wasn't stated in the report, but in the great majority of those cases the facts had been known ever since the men were lost. What took a quarter of a century was not discovering the truth but summoning the will to say it. During all that time, the culture of denial and distortion surrounding the entire MIA issue took on a life of its own, reflecting in strange and contorted ways the troubling legacy left by the war itself.

In addition to distorting the debate on postwar U.S. policy, the government's approach to the MIA issue also nourished the unrealistic hopes of families who, in a great many cases, would have been far better served by more candid official acknowledgment of the plain truth that their husbands, fathers, brothers, or sons were dead.

It was understandable that some relatives, especially parents, clung to any hope, however unrealistic, that their men might have survived. Perhaps because there was no victory that might have made their loss more bearable, and also perhaps because the entire Vietnam experience had worn away so much public trust in the government, many families were unwilling to accept the services' MIA accounting, even when the evidence would have seemed completely convincing to anyone else. One incident, reported in *The Missing Man*, a 1979 study published by the National Defense University, was a striking illustration not only of how powerful those illusory hopes could be, but also of how far the government was willing to bend under pressure from relatives, backed by the MIA families' organization and their friends in Congress. The author, Navy Capt. Douglas L. Clarke, was an aviator who had flown more than three hundred combat missions during three tours in Vietnam and whose wartime assignments also included eighteen months (during 1970-72) working on prisoner-of-war issues. This particular case, Clarke wrote, involved

> the family of a Navy pilot who was never carried in either an MIA or KIA status. His F-4 fighter developed engine difficulties immediately following a catapult launch from the aircraft carrier and disintegrated upon impact with the water a few hundred yards ahead of the ship. The aircraft had been airborne for seconds. The Radar Intercept Officer (RIO) in the rear cockpit managed to successfully eject and was recovered. The pilot was briefly and routinely reported as missing (*not* missing in action) while a search by ship and helicopter was conducted of the crash site. Within hours the status was changed to killed, as the search was unsuccessful. At the time of the incident the carrier was approximately 65 miles off the coast of North Vietnam.

It was hard to imagine a clearer case. But in spite of overwhelming evidence, the pilot's parents could not be convinced that their son was dead. Instead, they seized on discrepancies in different reports that gave conflicting times for the incident. Even though it was obvious that the inconsistencies arose from reporting errors and that in fact the F-4 was in the air for no more than "mere seconds" after leaving the carrier's flight deck,

> the parents of the dead pilot . . . deduced from the earliest time of the launch and the latest time of the accident reported in the various official and unofficial accounts of the incident that their son's aircraft *could* have been airborne for as long as 22 minutes, conceivably time to reach the North Vietnamese coast. *Despite being shown films of the launch, eyewitness reports, and talking with the surviving RIO, the squadron commanding officer, and an eyewitness, the parents could not be dissuaded* [emphasis added]. Although their son has never been listed as MIA, the distraught couple are members of the National League of Families and have appealed to the Congress to help secure an accounting of their son from the North Vietnamese. In all likelihood as a result of the persistent inquiries from the family, the pilot's name was added to the Joint Casualty Recovery Center's list of names for which the North Vietnamese would be asked to provide information.

This was an extreme example, obviously. But what it showed about the emotions (and political clout) of the MIA families represented a larger reality. Those who backed the parents' request, and the officials who granted it, may have felt they were only doing a harmless kindness to people who had suffered a terrible loss. But their gesture, if well intentioned, was not without consequences. For the bereaved parents, it blocked "the normal and healthy process of mourning," in Clarke's words. And in the wider arena of national policy, it meant that for more than twenty years, as successive U.S. presidents and a host of other public and private figures demanded a "full accounting" of all the missing men, they were demanding something the Vietnamese could not possibly give—information on a man who had died many years ago far out at sea, and whose own government had never considered him missing in action in the first place.

II

The fantasy of hundreds of lost Americans possibly surviving years after the war was nourished not only by families' wishful thinking but also by politicians, moviemakers and pulp novelists, and a bizarre assortment of thrill-seekers and hustlers—and by the American public, too, whose readiness to believe the myth, in the face of all logic and evidence, seemed to reflect a deeper inability to face the realities of America's experience in Vietnam.

The roots of the MIA myth lay all the way back in the war years, when the Nixon administration, having inherited an unpopular and frustrating war, decided that recovering American prisoners of war was one policy goal that might sustain public sympathy and support. For lack of any other inspiring objective, freeing the POWs came to be at the center of the administration's stated goals—repeated to the point, as the writer Jonathan Schell observed, that the president and others "began to speak as though the North Vietnamese had kidnapped four hundred Americans and the United States had gone to war to retrieve them." The POWs continued to be politically useful after their release. The heroes' welcome given to the 591 men freed in early 1973 was made into a kind of strange substitute for the victory parade Americans would never have. The prisoners' goal had been to survive and protect their honor under brutal torture; if the nation's goals hadn't been achieved in Vietnam, then the POWs' record of bravery and endurance would have to do. "We're giving the American people what they want and badly need—heroes," a former POW declared. "I feel it's our responsibility, our duty to help them where possible shed the idea this war was a waste, useless, as unpopular as it may have been." The logic was unclear, since the POWs' conduct in captivity, however brave, had no bearing on the wisdom or rightness of American policy. But just as their captivity had become a justification for fighting the war when other reasons evaporated, their feats of heroic endurance now served to vindicate an effort that otherwise seemed to have yielded no gain.

The great majority of returning POWs took on that role willingly. With almost no exceptions, they came home expressing exactly the kind of fervent patriotism and reflexive support for national policy that had come under scornful attack during the country's long, exhausting debate on the war. In later years, most continued to espouse the same views. In part, this reflected the values of the professional military culture from which most POWs came. (Unlike the young draftees who fought the ground war, the great majority of the POWs were professional officers, mainly career aviators.) Their attitude must have reflected, too, a powerful need not to believe that their ordeal had been for nothing. "In our minds," one of them said, "we had done what we intended to do, we had accomplished it and wanted to tell everybody else that job has been accomplished."

The story of these Americans' bravery and pride during their long captivity gave the country its only heroic legend from the Vietnam tragedy. And to the extent that the POWs, with the immense moral authority conferred by their sacrifice, could help shore up public patriotism and support for the policy, that also meant they were shoring up trust in the national leadership—a welcome development for President Nixon, who missed few chances to identify himself and his administration and policies with the prisoners, their heroic record, their message of loyalty and patriotism, and the logically questionable but emotionally compelling argument that their courage somehow meant the Vietnam War was not an unnecessary tragedy after all.

Presumably, in publicizing the POWs and their treatment to try to mobilize support for their leadership and policies during the war, President Nixon and his advisers did not intend to create a national movement based on the belief that their administration had carelessly or deliberately left hundreds of men in continued captivity after the U.S. pullout. But the postwar mythology flowed logically from the wartime publicity effort and the lionization of the returning prisoners in the spring of 1973. In orchestrating its wartime effort and in other dealings with POW/MIA relatives, U.S. authorities had dealt with all families in exactly the same way whether their men were considered MIA or POW. All families were oriented, for example, on how and where to write to prisoners. At the time, no doubt, this was a matter of trying not to seem less sensitive or concerned about one group of relatives than another. But, as Captain Clarke pointed out in his study, the practice of treating MIA and POW families exactly alike, however well-meant, "was bound to raise the expectations of the MIA families, and consequently make more painful the failure of these expectations to be realized."

The MIA relatives who had organized (with considerable government assistance and support) to promote the MIA issue during the war did not disappear after the U.S. effort ended. Their group remained active, with an agenda that inevitably came to reflect the perspective of those family members most reluctant to give up hope that their men might have survived. To the extent that some of those families would not or could not accept any outcome short of their men miraculously coming home alive (or a body that could be identified with no possible doubt), they were bound to come into conflict with their own government, since U.S. authorities obviously could never bring back men from the dead or recover bodies that had been lost or destroyed. In that conflict, the families' influence was greatly magnified by the prominence their sacrifice had been given during the wartime publicity effort. After years of declaring that getting lost Americans back was the nation's first priority, and after orchestrating all manner of activities by the POW/MIA families to dramatize that point, officials were hardly in a position to oppose demands from any MIA relatives, no matter how unrealistic. As a result, only months after the last POWs returned from Vietnam, a relatively small group of families was able to overturn the established legal process for resolving MIA cases—a process that had been used, without significant dissent, after previous wars.

At issue was a procedure known as "presumptive finding of death." That meant that when a service member had been missing in action for a year or more without any further information on his fate, the service secretary or his representative could rule that there was now a "reasonable presumption" that the person was dead, and change the casualty status accordingly. (The law did not *require* a finding of death after a year; it was left to the secretary to decide how long a "lapse of time without information" was needed.) In Vietnam, while the war went on, U.S. policy was *not* to make presumptive-death findings just because a certain amount of time had passed, on the grounds that intelligence about who had been captured was not reliable enough. Thus, in cases where there was no information, those who were declared MIA when they disappeared normally remained in that status.* Once the prisoners were freed in 1973, though, the services began to issue presumptive findings, on the assumption that it was now known who had been captured and who had not. The proceedings were halted just a few months later, however, after five family members went into federal court and obtained an injunction preventing any further casualty status changes unless they were requested by the next-of-kin.

The National League of Families of American Prisoners and Missing in Southeast Asia, meanwhile, began to take a position opposing presumptive findings altogether. *No* status changes should be made based only on the passage of time without any information, the league now argued; instead, a man should be declared dead only if new information was

---

*From time to time during the war, U.S. authorities did receive reports from the Vietnamese informing them of the deaths of American servicemen, either in captivity or when their planes were shot down or crashed. Instead of shifting those men from MIA to the KIA list, however, the U.S. adopted a policy of not changing casualty status on the basis of information from the Vietnamese. This was in part because of opposition from the families, but also because the administration desired to keep the maximum political and public-relations pressure on the North Vietnamese.

found. That meant, of course, that a certain number of cases could never be resolved, but would remain in limbo forever. The league's policy, to some extent, put the feelings and needs of MIA wives in heartbreaking conflict with those of other relatives. Parents or brothers or sisters who could not relinquish hope for missing men lost nothing if the men remained on MIA status forever; wives, on the other hand, would find themselves with their own lives permanently on hold, unable to remarry or start new lives without excruciating feelings of guilt or disloyalty. Though wives founded the league and made up its leadership during the war, parents played an increasingly important role from 1973 on, accounting in part for the league's increasingly bitter opposition to casualty status changes as well as its harder-edged attitudes on other matters.

The league's greater stridency in the postwar years also reflected another kind of shift in its membership. After the war, family members whose men had returned had no reason to remain active in the organization. Nor did wives or other relatives of those still missing who, for whatever reason, chose to accept their loss and go on with their lives. When those groups fell away, leadership of the MIA movement passed into the hands of those relatives who clung most passionately to the hope that their men might still be alive. The activists who inherited control of the League of Families after 1973 did not necessarily represent the views of all MIA family members, perhaps not even a majority. But because theirs was now the only voice speaking out, they appeared to speak for all relatives. Increasingly, the activists were able to frame public discussion of the issue and to claim the moral authority of a group that had suffered a grievous and special loss—even more special, in fact, because the heroic status given to the returning POWs was easily extended to embrace the missing, too. To the extent that the MIAs were not just another group of casualties but lost heroes, the mystery of their fate was even more compelling.

To sustain their hopes, the activist MIA relatives had to cling to the belief that significant numbers of missing Americans had survived and remained alive in captivity after the war. Preserving the league's wartime name—Families of American Prisoners and Missing—also preserved the idea that there were still prisoners awaiting freedom, not just men whose fate was unknown. Relatives understood that a given MIA might be dead. But they needed to believe that *some* might be alive, or else there was no hope at all. Hence their legal and political battle to block presumptive findings of death, which in the end remained suspended for more than four years.

The issue was much broader than casualty status changes, however. Inevitably, the logic of the league's position led it to oppose passionately *any* government action or policy or statement suggesting the contrary view—including the official stance that there was no reason to believe that any POWs had been left behind and "no credible evidence" that any missing U.S. servicemen remained alive in Indochina. For years, the league crusaded against that position, finally gaining a sympathetic response from the Reagan administration, which changed the formula to say that the possibility of surviving Americans could not be ruled out. That change was heralded by the league as a significant victory for its crusade; it was even more gratified when, under President Bush, the officially stated policy on MIAs was altered again to say that the government's efforts were based "on the assumption that some are still alive." That was almost as strong as the league's own syllogism, as stated in a position paper in 1992, "that Americans are known to have been left behind, in captivity, in Vietnam, Laos and Cambodia. In the absence of evidence to the contrary, it can only be assumed that these Americans remain alive in captivity today."

It was possible to reverse that reasoning, of course. If no evidence had emerged in two decades to confirm that there *were* surviving Americans, it could also mean that there weren't any. To someone not emotionally involved in the issue, indeed, that might appear the more likely possibility. But the idea that a significant number of living prisoners were still held in Indochina, though originating with a relatively small group of unreconciled MIA families, was soon embraced by a much wider circle of believers. Those supposed prisoners became immensely useful, for instance, to those who, for emotional or ideological reasons, opposed any U.S. aid to Vietnam or any other move toward reconciliation with our former enemy. Vietnamese cooperation in accounting for MIAs had been from the start the essential U.S. condition for restoring relations. If the premise was that there *were* living Americans, then as long as the Vietnamese didn't turn them over they were lying about the issue and welshing on their obligation, and thus no improvement in relations was possible. It was a simple formula, sparing everyone the trouble and inconvenience of assessing how helpful or obstructive the Vietnamese were actually being.

The notion of surviving prisoners also appealed to a remarkable array of self-proclaimed rescuers, some driven by fantasies of adventure and some, it seemed, by the prospect of profit. There was, at any rate, a great deal more effort devoted to fund-raising than to actual rescue attempts, although there were a few forays into Indochina—all unsuccessful. The appeals for funds were imaginative, to say the least. In July 1990, for example, an organization called Skyhook II Project sent out a mailing declaring that "reliable estimates now show that as many as 253 American prisoners of war yet remain to be rescued." Signed by a former New York congressman, John LeBoutillier, and accompanied by a separate note from actor Charlton Heston, the letter went on to give a colorful account of the prisoners' plight: "Starved and clad only in filthy rags, American soldiers and airmen are kept chained in tiny bamboo cages . . . made to work like animals pulling heavy plows . . . forced to toil from daybreak to nightfall in steaming tropic heat . . . kicked and beaten constantly just for their guards' amusement." But there was hope for these "poor, forgotten U.S. soldiers and airmen," the letter went on, if a "few thousand dollars" could be raised for anti-Communist rebel forces cooperating with Skyhook II. Just imagine, readers were urged:

> Late one evening, as prison-camp guards kick and flog a group of our boys along the trail back to their cages, the last few Communists in line might be swiftly and quietly dragged into the jungle.
>
> Then, a few seconds later, the bedraggled American P.O.W.'s they were guarding might also vanish suddenly from the rear of the plodding group. The Americans, of course, would now be in friendly hands. (We won't talk about the guards' fate.)
>
> In a matter of just a day or two, the rescued Americans would be smuggled across the border to our SKYHOOK II PROJECT in Thailand.

In the final act of this fantasy, of course, the rescued prisoners would tell their story to the world, exploding once and for all the official conspiracy, maintained for all those years by craven and deceitful U.S. officials, to cover up the cruel truth that Americans captured in the Vietnam War were still held prisoner. First, though, the money had to be raised. "If each of you who are getting this letter would send just $10, $15 or even $20, it would quickly add up to the thousands we need to launch our mission." Needless to say, Skyhook II never rescued any prisoners, though it did manage to collect nearly $2 million between 1985 and 1992. Almost 90 percent of the money, it turned out, was kept by the Response Development Corporation, the direct-mail company that organized the fundraising effort.

Similar appeals, and similar spending practices, characterized another organization called Operation Rescue, Inc., whose fund-raising letters kept breathlessly hinting that success was very near. "You may wake up tomorrow morning and hear that the first American POW has been rescued. We are that close," one of its mailings declared. Another proclaimed, "We are very, very close to freeing one of our valiant Americans." (It is conventional wisdom in the fund-raising field that appeals should give donors a vivid, concrete image of the results of their generosity—which helps explain the MIA organizations' constant promises of an imminent rescue. Another organization, Red McDaniel's American Defense Institute, took a slightly different approach, promising prospective donors that the freed prisoners would be told "of the vital role you played in their release." Donors were further told to "write a brief note on the enclosed donation card, which I will personally hand to the first man to regain his freedom.")

Operation Rescue's professional fund-raiser, a direct-marketing company in Vienna, Virginia, named Eberle & Associates, came up with inventive ways to make the message more dramatic. One memorandum prepared by the firm proposed sending out an appeal that would appear to be "a handwritten or hand printed letter on lined note paper written by firelight during an intelligence gathering mission either inside of Cambodia or Vietnam, or at least on the banks of the river which divides Thailand and Cambodia." Another variant was to be a message—also "handwritten, hand printed or typed on a portable typewriter"—ostensibly sent from aboard a ship Operation Rescue claimed to operate in the South China Sea. The letter that eventually went out asked readers to "excuse the handwriting. But I'm writing at a makeshift desk on the deck of the Akuna III. The China Sea is tossing and rolling." In fact, for years the ship never left its dock in Songkhla, in southern Thailand; the letter was written in Virginia.

Like Skyhook II, instead of using its contributions to look for missing Americans, Operation Rescue, headed by a former Air Force colonel named Jack Bailey, spent nearly ninety cents of every dollar it collected for additional fund-raising. Senate investigators who examined the group's federal tax returns found that from 1985 through 1990 it received $2,283,472 in contributions and spent $2,028,440 on fund-raising expenses—88.8 percent of all the contributions it had received. MIA fund-raising was so lucrative, the Senate Select Committee on POW/MIA Affairs reported, that some professional fund-raisers "actively sought out, and sometimes even created POW/MIA groups."

In early 1986, a fund-raising letter of a different sort reached the White House. Instead of $10 or $20, the letter sought a rather larger sum:

$4.2 million, in cash. In return, "evidence of live Americans and other allied POWs still being held in Southeast Asia," including a film showing prisoners in a jungle camp, would be turned over "at a location somewhere in a foreign country." Dated February 28, 1986, and addressed to "Dear President Reagan," the letter was signed by Mark Waple, a lawyer from Fayetteville, North Carolina, who was representing retired Maj. Mark A. Smith and former Sfc. Melvin C. McIntire in their suit charging the U.S. government with covering up information about Americans still held prisoner in Indochina.* The film was said to be in the hands of a man in Southeast Asia named "John Obassy" (named in an earlier letter) who, Waple wrote, demanded acceptance of his offer "not later than the 3rd of March, 1986."

Waple's collaborator in this remarkable proposition was Bill Hendon, at the time a Republican congressman from North Carolina. It was Hendon who was supposed to hand-deliver Waple's letter to President Reagan, and it was also Hendon, with two congressional colleagues, who was supposed to carry the money and receive the film from John Obassy after the payment had been handed over. Waple's letter listed a detailed set of conditions for the flight to pick up the "evidence." It was to be in a chartered commercial aircraft, with one pilot to be selected by ex-Major Smith; the other crew members could be from the military services, but must be under "deep civilian cover," Waple insisted, for this mission. The proposal was taken seriously enough that George Bush, then vice president, reportedly approached Texas billionaire H. Ross Perot and asked him to advance the money, promising (according to Perot) to reimburse him if the film turned out to be real. But eventually the plan was judged too far-fetched even for the Reagan White House, whose occupant had often expressed a strong interest in the MIA issue and who reportedly kept several MIA bracelets in his White House office. Bush's offer to Perot was rescinded and Waple's cloak-and-dagger plan was turned down. The $4.2 million film, like all the other evidence Smith promised, never turned up. "John Obassy" turned out to be a British resident of Thailand named Robin Gregson, who at the time was in jail in Singapore awaiting trial on charges of extortion and fraud.

If no lost American prisoners were found in Vietnam or Cambodia or Laos, there was no shortage of POWs on movie theater screens or in popular fiction—where, unlike in real life, their heroic rescuers were invari-

*See pages 110–11.

ably successful. It was to be expected, no doubt, that POW rescue missions in the jungles of Indochina would become material for popular entertainment. The subject seemed made to order for American audiences' tastes. In addition to an exotic setting and a clear, patriotic story line, the POW novel or movie also afforded ample opportunity for violent scenes, portraying sadistic tortures inflicted by diabolic Asian Communists on their prisoners and the righteous vengeance inflicted by the rescuers. The structure and fictional images of the POW rescue story fit perfectly into the lineage of American popular drama, too. The bloodthirsty Vietnamese prison guards were an updated model of villainous Japanese soldiers or American Indians in earlier generations of books and films; the rescue teams bursting out of the jungle exactly recreated the classic cowboy-film climax, when the cavalry thunders out of a cloud of dust on the horizon to save the imperiled settlers.

The POW stories also helped audiences rewrite history, reimposing earlier and more satisfying images on an event that had been, for most Americans, profoundly unsatisfying. As H. Bruce Franklin pointed out in his book *M.I.A., or Mythmaking In America*, the POW legend was presented in ways "which would restore the discredited vision of idealistic, courageous Americans heroically battling hordes of sadistic Oriental Communists."

What did seem odd, though, was how consistently the fictional versions of POW rescues demanded to be taken not as fiction, but as fact. One of the first rescue novels, *Mission M.I.A.*, by J. C. Pollock, was sent to reviewers at the end of 1981 along with a packet of publicity material claiming the author had access to "sensitive and highly classified information" proving that American prisoners captured by the Vietnamese were still being held. A publisher's press release, absurdly stamped with "SECRET—For Eyes Only" in red ink, began: "When the last acknowledged prisoners of war returned home from Vietnam in April, 1973, they were instructed by the Department of Defense not to reveal information about those they knew were still held captive by the Vietnamese Communists, according to J. C. Pollock."* The only information about Pollock's background was a vague statement that he had "worked with" the National

---

*A major inconvenience for the MIA movement is that when returning prisoners were debriefed, none could identify even a single man who was known to have been left behind when the others were released. The suggestion that this was merely a cover-up, as alleged here by Pollock or his publicist, is plainly preposterous: it is hard to see how even the most ardent conspiracy theorist could imagine that nearly six hundred men would obey orders to remain silent for twenty years about comrades left in captivity.

League of Families. But the publicity material fostered the impression that he was close to U.S. intelligence sources and to the organizers of official and unofficial rescue attempts.

Mission M.I.A. was the prototype for a slew of other rescue thrillers, all with identical plots: evidence surfaces that Americans captured in Vietnam are still held prisoner; cowardly or inexplicably evil U.S. officials try to prevent their rescue; the hero and a small group of buddies defy their own government, march into the jungle, and liberate the prisoners, splattering the landscape as they go with hundreds of Vietnamese corpses. So similar were these stories that a reader or moviegoer could probably leave one book or film in the middle and switch to another without noticing the difference. Similar or not, the POW rescue genre won big audiences for books such as the awful but highly popular *M.I.A. Hunter* paperback series and for films such as *Missing in Action* and *Uncommon Valor* and various others. Most successful, and the archetype of the genre, was the 1985 Sylvester Stallone movie *Rambo: First Blood Part II*.

Rambo was one of those movies that escaped the screen to become a genuine cultural event. No matter that its plot and leading character were cartoonlike and its depiction of battle even more so. Audiences loved it, clapping and cheering in their seats as the hero mowed down enemies by the truckload. Stallone's Rambo became an instantly recognizable figure, reproduced in comic books, "action dolls," and pinball-machine displays. There were even Rambo-grams—messages delivered by hired musclemen who came with cartridge belts worn over their bare chests. The name Rambo passed into the language as an internationally understood synonym for a certain kind of swaggering, lethally violent superhero. Despite its ludicrous unrealism, *Rambo* was enlisted in support of claims that there really were POWs still languishing in the Asian jungle. The makers of a 1985 television documentary on the MIAs interviewed Stallone, as if having acted in a movie made him an authority on the facts. "Mounting evidence" was accumulating that American prisoners were still held captive, the actor solemnly told the documentary's viewers; "the question is why."

Other Hollywood stars also enlisted in the MIA cause. Actor Cliff Robertson appeared in a commercial produced for an organization called Veterans of the Vietnam War, Inc., soliciting petitions to be sent to the White House. More than 125,000 viewers responded, but Senate investigators reported that "rather than delivering these petitions to the President of the United States, as promised, VVnW simply collected and stored the petitions, adding the names . . . to its mailing and phone lists to be used in additional fundraising solicitations." Another actor prominent in the MIA movement was Charlton Heston, who taped a telephone message to be played in fund-raising calls from John LeBoutillier's Skyhook II Project. "Many of our men are held behind," Heston declared on the tape. "They're still there to this day. Locked in bamboo cages in the jungle or in caves in the mountains. Some of our men are used as slaves, forced to drag plows in rice paddies. . . . We have to bring them home, all of them . . . . They're ours and they're heroes, real heroes."

While film and pulp-novel heroes blazed their way through the jungles to rescue camp after camp of fictional POWs, a different kind of fiction was being created in Southeast Asian refugee camps, on the streets of Bangkok and other cities and towns in Thailand, and elsewhere in the region. "The manufacture of fraudulent POW/MIA-related materials, including photographs, dog tags and other purported evidence of live Americans has become a cottage industry in certain parts of Southeast Asia," the Senate Select Committee on POW/MIA Affairs declared in its final report in early 1993. The flood of fabricated evidence, it added, was partly spurred "by well-intentioned private offers of large rewards for information leading to the return of live U.S. POWs." Army Lt. Col. Paul Mather, who spent fifteen years assigned to the services' Joint Casualty Resolution Center, recalled that its investigators in Thailand and refugee camps elsewhere in Asia were "bombarded with offers of alleged remains of American servicemen, usually in exchange for money, material assistance for resistance efforts, or for priority treatment in refugee resettlement." Once in circulation, fakes were often copied and widely distributed, so that many of the same bogus items reappeared regularly in the MIA market.

There were plenty of customers for the fake evidence, in spite of the fact that none of it had ever led anywhere. "It has become apparent," the Senate committee found

> that in both Southeast Asia and the United States, information that purports to demonstrate that POWs are alive is eagerly consumed by those who are eager to believe. Despite the fact that none of the information has ever resulted in the return of a live American, the demand for and hope resulting from such information appears to be as strong as ever. Unscrupulous individuals throughout Southeast Asia are aware of this, and the volume of false POW/MIA information continues to rise.

One "committed, but frustrated, activist," the report added, told investigators that seemingly "every cab-driver, vagrant and baggage handler in Thailand runs a POW scam."

It wasn't only Thai swindlers or Indochinese refugees who concocted phony evidence. Plenty of fakery could be traced back to American activists, too, among them retired Air Force Col. Jack Bailey, head of Operation Rescue, and Lt. Col. James "Bo" Gritz, a swaggering retired Army Special Forces officer who appears to have been the real-life model for various fictional heroes. Among other deceptions, Gritz on one occasion gave congressional investigators documents he claimed were newly recovered by his "agents" in Laos but which were subsequently found to be falsified records concerning a captured Army officer known to have died way back in 1961.

It seemed likely that most of the phony POW evidence was circulated in the hope of possible cash rewards or preferential treatment in the refugee resettlement program. There were other possible motives, however. Some of the fakery may have originated with schemes by various Lao resistance groups to win favor with U.S. officials or to discredit rival factions. There was speculation that some was even deliberate disinformation, planted by the Chinese or Vietnamese intelligence services to bog down U.S. intelligence and other agencies in useless and confusing false reports and to disrupt anti-Communist refugee organizations. The timing of some of the more sensational and highly publicized fakes raised a different possibility: that they were deliberately floated to derail steps toward a U.S.–Vietnamese rapprochement. Still another possible motive was suggested in the Senate Select Committee's final report: that false evidence was being promoted on the theory that any publicity for the issue was better than none, and that "dissemination and publication of any POW/MIA information, bogus or not, keeps the POW/MIA issue, and million-dollar fundraising operations, alive."

III

What was most striking about the flood of fiction and falsehood on the MIA issue was not that it existed, but how thoroughly it was allowed to displace the facts. For that, American political leaders and senior government officials bore much of the blame. Instead of speaking plainly about the subject, politicians of both parties bent over backward not to give the slightest offense to the vocal MIA families—the National League of

Families, in particular—and their supporters. For years, officials avoided what would have been the only truly honest statement of the facts: that the vast majority of MIAs had undoubtedly been killed at the time they disappeared; that it was virtually inconceivable that any were still alive; and that in hundreds of cases, it would never be known exactly how or where a man had died. In tiptoeing around those truths, U.S. officials were also remarkably timid in answering even the more outlandish claims advanced by MIA activists. Typically, when a new story appeared, higher-ranking officials grabbed headlines and television time with firm promises to investigate. When the claimed evidence was eventually shown to be false or nonexistent, as invariably happened, that news was delivered without fanfare by some lower-level spokesman or functionary.

It was understandable that no politician wanted to appear indifferent to the fate of lost American servicemen or to their relatives' grief. But from a fairly early date, the official response to the National League crossed the line from appropriate respect and sympathy into pandering. The progression of official policy statements from "there is no evidence" of surviving American captives to "the possibility cannot be ruled out" and later to "we assume some are still alive" did not occur because any new evidence had become available, or even because old evidence had been reexamined. The changing formulas simply represented a decision—rooted partly in emotion, no doubt, and partly in political calculation—not to challenge the league or its allies on how to define the MIA issue.

This was not just a matter of meaningless words. Ann Mills Griffiths, the league's long-time executive director, was not wrong in putting the change in official policy formulation at the very top of her list of the league's accomplishments. Accepting the activists' premise that living Americans were still held prisoner, or could be, dictated following their policy preferences, too: that recovery of MIAs was the American government's "highest priority" in U.S.-Vietnamese relations, the issue to which all others must be subordinated. Without satisfaction on the MIAs, no other issue could even be approached. But if the assumption was that Americans were still held, the only possible way to break the logjam was for the Vietnamese to return living prisoners. Many in the U.S. government understood that this demand could not possibly be met. But accepting anything less risked cries of betrayal from the MIA movement—a risk American presidents from Gerald Ford to Bill Clinton were extraordinarily reluctant to take.

The government did more than let the League of Families and its supporters frame the MIA issue. For many years it also gave the league a remarkable degree of control over MIA policy through a highly unusual arrangement in which Ann Mills Griffiths served, along with representatives of the State and Defense Departments, the National Security Council, and the Joint Chiefs of Staff, on the government's principal policy-making body on MIA matters, the Interagency Group on POW/MIA Affairs. In that capacity, Griffiths, the sister of a missing Navy officer shot down off North Vietnam in 1966, attended meetings, received classified intelligence briefings, and participated in overseas delegations—but without the accountability or responsibility to national policy she would have had if actually holding a government position. It is hard to think of any other private advocacy or pressure group that has ever had that kind of formal role in policy decisions.

Griffiths regularly used her official status to promote the league's views and policy agenda and to silence, to the extent possible, any official with a different perspective. One former senior Defense Department official recalls being instructed that all testimony to Congress, speeches, and other public statements had to be cleared with Griffiths. When they came back, he added, she had invariably edited out any passage she deemed inconsistent with league positions—in particular, any words hinting that the United States should improve relations with Vietnam. Griffiths also lobbied on the issue publicly, surfacing to be interviewed any time it appeared a further step toward U.S.-Vietnamese rapprochement might be imminent. On the eve of President Clinton's decision to lift the trade embargo against Vietnam, for example, Griffiths declared in a *Baltimore Sun* interview that such a policy change would be a "betrayal" of Clinton's promise to seek a full accounting for the missing. Griffiths's unusual status and the league's extraordinary access and influence on MIA policy reflected the special standing given MIA families because of their loss—a moral authority that was magnified to the extent that the government magnified the issue. But there also seemed to be a trade, implicit or explicit, involved in Griffiths's position. For the one issue on which she broke with many other activists was also the one that mattered most to government officials—the suggestion that MIA evidence had been covered up by an official conspiracy. On that single matter, Griffiths unfailingly sided with the government and against its critics in the MIA movement, insisting that there was no evidence of a conspiracy or cover-up and that it "violates common sense," as she once observed, to think that any government would spend so much money, time, and energy promoting public awareness on an issue it wanted to bury. (To the conspiracy theorists, this of course meant that Griffiths and the league were part of the conspiracy.) Whether there was an overt bargain or not, only Griffiths and those who worked with her knew. But it was hard to escape the impression of a deal: the government would legitimize the National League and its insistence that there were surviving POWs; Griffiths in return would legitimize the government's record on the MIAs—no small matter, in a climate where conspiracy theories were widely promoted and, it seemed, almost as widely believed.

The League of Families was not alone in promoting the MIA cause. Inside the government, it found allies among officials who for various strategic, ideological, or emotional reasons sought to obstruct any rapprochement between the United States and Vietnam. Outside the executive branch, the league's views won support from the major national veterans organizations and from a group of conservative Republicans in Congress, particularly in the Senate. Most prominent in the congressional group were Bob Smith of New Hampshire, who served as vice chairman of the Senate Select Committee, and Jesse Helms of North Carolina.* Another significant supporter of the MIA movement was H. Ross Perot, the quirky Texas billionaire and independent presidential candidate in the 1992 and 1996 elections. Perot's involvement with the POW families dated back to 1969, when he underwrote several highly publicized efforts to call attention to the prisoners and demand improvement in their treatment. After the war, Perot remained convinced that American prisoners were still being held. Unlike Griffiths, he often sided with the conspiracy theorists. As the *Washington Post* reported in a long investigative article on Perot during the 1992 campaign, his cover-up theory centered on the Central Intelligence Agency and George Bush, its one-time director. Their motive, Perot was reported to have told associates, was to conceal wartime CIA involvement in the Southeast Asia heroin trade.

The League of Families and its allies, even when they kept their distance from the more rabid MIA activists, could only benefit from the sensational news reports and movies and pulp thrillers that kept the image of abandoned prisoners before the public. And they had a cause that was politically unassailable. Who, after all, could oppose making the MIA search the

---

*In one of the more astounding misstatements ever made on the MIA issue, Helms once claimed in a Senate floor speech that the U.S. government "had requested the Vietnamese to return five thousand men" after the 1973 peace accords—twice as many as had ever been reported missing. Helms cited the *New York Times* as the source for his figure. The article he cited wasn't referring to American POWs at all, but to five thousand Vietnamese prisoners held by the Saigon government whose return was being demanded by the Communist side.

"highest national priority" or suggest that any limit might properly be put on the time, effort, and resources devoted to it? The result was an issue that seemed to have taken on eternal life. Under a policy adopted in the Reagan administration more than a dozen years after the last POWs returned, MIA matters were assigned a "priority one" rating for U.S. intelligence agencies, a category meant to cover intelligence information "vital to U.S. survival." Twenty years after the last American soldiers left Indochina, the government was spending at least $100 million a year on MIA activities, a great deal of it on repeatedly chasing down false leads that every objective observer knew were false to begin with.

No one could object to maintaining reasonable efforts to find out what had happened to missing U.S. servicemen or to attempting to identify and recover remains when possible. But there was room to question if anything was gained by continuing to declare that this accounting overrode all other needs, including the need of MIA families to mourn, accept, and escape their past. It seemed reasonable to ask, too, what good was served by prolonging the almost certainly false idea that American prisoners were still alive and held in Vietnam against their will.

Realism, though, had little chance against the accumulated mythology of two decades or against a lobby that had succeeded in making the MIA issue politically sacred. The continued unwillingness of political leaders to challenge the activists was demonstrated yet again in 1994, when the League of Families and its allies mobilized against Chuck Searcy, a Vietnam veteran and one-time newspaper publisher from Georgia who was being considered for a post in the Pentagon's POW/MIA office. (Searcy's sins, in the eyes of the MIA movement, were that he had demonstrated against the war after returning from his Army service there and that he had endorsed ending the U.S. trade embargo against Vietnam.) Rather than take on the MIA lobby, the White House withdrew the appointment, giving in to a movement that, as Searcy observed, wanted to keep the issue "churning indefinitely, regardless of the facts or a reasonable determination that no further information will become available. . . . In my opinion, that's a disservice to the POW/MIA families, to Vietnam veterans, and the broader interests of the people of America and Vietnam. Some people," Searcy added, "just don't want this issue to go away, ever."

Under a cool October sky streaked with abstract swirls of cloud, Col. Charles E. Shelton's five children finally told their father goodbye. An Air Force honor guard unfolded a large American flag and came to rigid attention, holding the flag stretched out horizontally at chest-height over the grass while the colonel's oldest son, the Rev. Charles Shelton, eulogized his father as a faithful husband, devoted parent, and a deeply moral warrior who chose to fly reconnaissance planes in the Vietnam War, rather than bombers, "because he didn't want to risk taking innocent life." Following Shelton to the microphone, Air Force chaplain Lt. Col. James Snyder intoned the Twenty-third Psalm and the Lord's Prayer and then read the famous airman's poem that begins, "I have slipped the surly bonds of Earth"—the same lines President Ronald Reagan read in his famous televised speech after the space shuttle Challenger exploded in 1986. After the reading, three volleys of rifle fire cracked in salute from the brow of a low hill overlooking Section 36 of Arlington National Cemetery. An Air Force bugler standing about fifty yards away between two rows of graves played Taps. Then a flight of four F-15 fighters, with a gap in the formation representing the "missing man," streaked over the treetops shading the rows of headstones and aisles of neatly trimmed grass. The jets thundered straight out of the low autumn sun, so their path overhead ran exactly parallel to the shadows on the ground.

With that ceremony, Charles Shelton—a man who had been missing for nearly thirty years—became, in an ambiguous way reflecting the country's divided memories, the very last American to be declared killed in the Vietnam War. (Even that statement is an ambiguity, in fact. Shelton, who was shot down just before noon on April 29, 1965, crashed and probably died in northeastern Laos, not in Vietnam itself.) The day Shelton's RF-101 was shot down—his thirty-third birthday—other pilots saw him parachute safely from the burning plane, and one reported seeing him alive and apparently uninjured on the ground, thirty to forty yards from his chute. But heavy clouds closed in soon afterward and rescue helicopters were unable to land. Some days after the crash, U.S.-controlled tribal guerrillas in the area reported that Shelton had been captured by enemy forces. Four weeks later, the Air Force listed him as a prisoner of war. He remained in that status for twenty-nine years, three months, and twenty-seven days—kept on the list "as a symbol," the Air Force said, after all other unaccounted-for Americans were declared dead in the early 1980s. A captain when he was shot down, Shelton was promoted to colonel while missing. On September 19, 1994, at the request of his children, the Air Force changed his status from the last POW to the last KIA. He would have been sixty-two years old.

Two weeks later, the five younger Sheltons, now middle-aged themselves, gathered with other family members, friends, and military representatives to hold a memorial service in the green peacefulness of Arlington National Cemetery. The rituals were those of remembrance and resolution, as at any memorial. But there was no escaping Vietnam and its contradictions. "We wanted to put this behind us," said John Shelton, a few hours after the ceremony. But in the next breath he was saying that even at graveside, he still felt troubled: "It still haunts me. He could well be alive right now." His sister Lea Ann said that even though all five children were in agreement on asking the Air Force to declare their father dead, the family was "never satisfied" with the U.S. government's efforts to investigate his disappearance, or that of other men lost in the war.

"I don't believe all those men are dead," she said. "I believe there are men over there who are alive."

Section 36, where Colonel Shelton's memorial was held, is a gentle slope of grass and low, shady trees in Arlington's northeast corner, not far from the main gate. The gravestones stand in straight, orderly rows, like soldiers in uniform. President William Howard Taft is buried nearby, and so is the assassinated civil rights leader Medgar Evers. The name on the stone where the Shelton family gathered reads: Dorothy Marian Shelton.

For twenty-five years after her husband disappeared, Marian Shelton clung to the hope that her husband and other missing Americans were still alive. She became a prominent activist in the National League of POW/MIA Families, campaigning ceaselessly for the missing-in-action cause. When the Defense Department undertook in the late 1970s to declare all remaining MIAs dead, Shelton was among those who went to court to contest the decision. It was largely as a result of her activities, apparently, that her husband was chosen as the one man to be kept, for symbolic reasons, in POW status. Repeatedly, during Marian Shelton's long vigil, rumors that Charles had survived—some of them highly colorful and detailed—nourished her hopes. But the family had no way of knowing what was true and what was false, or whom to trust. On October 4, 1990, "emotionally exhausted" from years of veering between hope and disappointment, Marian Shelton killed herself at her house in San Diego, California. The day the five Shelton children chose for their father's funeral was the fourth anniversary of her death. "I think of my mom," John Shelton said, "as a casualty of the Vietnam War."

Exhausted in their own way, the five Shelton children found, as Lea Ann put it, that after their mother died, "none of us was going to take up like momma did." They didn't want to deal any more with endless political arguments in which, it seemed, their father was missing in action all over again—made into a symbol, an abstraction, rather than the man they loved. They wanted his memory back for themselves. They wanted, above all, to stop wondering and to be free to mourn.

In a way, the Sheltons' experience was a metaphor for the whole history of the MIA issue, with its strange compound of myth, hope, sorrow, doubt, and moral confusion. With their mother, the children had heard the stories—dramatic, detailed accounts of Colonel Shelton's heroism in captivity, enduring torture, escaping, killing guards with his bare hands. The idea that he was not only alive but a hero made it doubly hard to doubt. But it was also hard not to see that the various advocates, sympathizers, adventurers, and self-proclaimed POW rescuers who clustered around the Sheltons and other MIA families could hardly be considered credible sources of information. The hopes they kept raising were just as constantly crushed.

In Colonel Shelton's case, the Air Force version was more prosaic than the rumors. The U.S. government was continuing to seek information about his fate, said an official fact sheet, but it also pointed out that no other prisoners ever reported encountering Shelton and that "a number of intelligence reports" indicate he did not survive. "The best available information concerning Colonel Shelton," the fact sheet concludes, "is that he was captured, detained, died, and buried in the Vieng Xai area of Laos."

Best available information, though, wasn't the same as knowing for sure. His father's funeral was supposed to help put the questions in the past, but as he sat by his mother's grave and listened, John Shelton said later that day, the words that formed in his mind were a prayer: "Dear God, please let us know, one way or the other."

For the Sheltons and other families similarly situated, one could only feel sorrow. It was harder to sympathize with those who cultivated the MIA mythology, fostering a national obsession that kept the wounds fresh. The producers and consumers of bogus evidence, the assorted swindlers and would-be soldiers of fortune who kept alive the fairy-tale of rescue missions, officials who promoted the myth to serve their own policy goals, and professional activists who perpetuated it to sustain their careers—all of them, in the end, succeeded only in blocking the normal passage from grief to healing among the very families they claimed to be supporting, while at the same time distorting national policy as well. Careless and gullible journalists shared responsibility for the damage. And so did the nation's political leaders, from presidents on down, who for years allowed the mythology to overwhelm logic and the facts until realism on the issue became virtually impossible.

Neither manipulation nor political flabbiness, however, could fully explain the strength of the myth. Its seemingly unbreakable hold on America's imagination long after the war suggested a metaphor that sounds farfetched but became increasingly hard to avoid: that it was not only men who were missing in action. It was some vital piece of America's vision of itself—trust, self-confidence, social order, belief in the benevolence and ordained success of American power—which had disappeared in the mountain mists and vine-tangled jungles of Vietnam, and which so many Americans wanted so desperately to get back. "The longing for recovery, retrieval, and reconciliation is so pervasive," wrote the critic Leo Cawley (who also served as a marine infantryman in Vietnam), "that it cannot be due merely to claims of some people, especially family members, that Vietnam is still holding MIAs in prison. It can only signify some deeper sense of loss associated with the war, a nostalgia for our short-lived global preeminence and for a national unity now wrecked. . . . We hated losing," Cawley continued, "and still hate the Vietnamese for it. Nobody knows how much."

That longing to recover something we lost—a loss so painful that we could not even see it for what it was, but had to disguise it in the mythical image of imaginary American prisoners—also reflected troubling traits of the society that embraced the MIA legend so uncritically for so long. Behind the legend, there could be sensed a society and a people grown so spoiled and self-indulgent that they demanded a simple, satisfying solution for every mystery, gratification for every need, a cure for every pain. The myth revealed a society so saturated in the imaginary violence of popular entertainment that it could no longer distinguish reality from fiction or recognize the real nature of modern war; a people choosing to blame others rather than accept responsibility for its mistakes; a country grown so childlike that it clung to any comforting fiction, no matter how implausible, instead of facing the uncertainties of the human condition and the painful truths of its own past.

6

LEARNING ABOUT THE WAR

*When we talk about Vietnam, we are seldom talking about the country of
that name or the situation of the people who live there. Usually we
are talking about ourselves. Probably we always were.*
—Joseph Lelyveld

*I learned that there probably wasn't so much government cover-ups and
conspiracy, mostly people trying to do the best they could. . . . It wasn't
Americans going in and blasting villages filled with women and children,
but kids following rules believing they were doing the right thing
by serving their country as their elders had done. It was a war
and sometimes things got out of hand. And how much did all those
hippie protesters actually know? How much could they have known?
It's twenty-five years later and we still haven't figured it out.*
—Diane Reyes

If even participants' memories were muddy ("Vietnam is one long
blur, sir," a retired colonel testified in the 1984 Westmoreland-CBS libel
trial), Vietnam was an even more confusing subject to Americans coming
of age after the war was over. To many, the war seemed like a messy and embarrassing family scandal that no one wanted to tell them the truth about,

but which they needed to understand because it was part of their past, too. "Vietnam seems to be another word for mistakes or dishonesty or whatever," Kevin T. Farrell, a twenty-two-year-old college student from Maryland, wrote in 1989, adding, "I really just want to know what happened and why."

More than twenty years after the war and the domestic turmoil associated with it, however, what happened and why, and what it meant, were still matters of sharp dispute. Not only did Americans still disagree on the broad questions—whether Vietnam was a tragic mistake or a "noble cause," or whether the war was fought in morally justified ways; there were also disagreements on many concrete issues of fact, including (to mention only a few of many possible examples): What was the impact and effectiveness of U.S. air power as it was employed in Vietnam? How did American opinion on the war evolve, how was it influenced by the antiwar movement and by press and television coverage, how accurate or faulty was the media's representation of the war, and how did public attitudes affect policymakers' decisions? To what extent did direction from civilian officials in Washington hamper military operations? Were U.S. forces "winning" or "losing" during the period of escalation (1965–1967)—and what was a valid means of measuring military success, anyway?

The cloud of emotion, confusion, and controversy surrounding nearly every issue of the war left the public with a remarkably muddled sense of what had really happened. Reflecting the country's jumbled thoughts, a 1979 opinion poll conducted for the Veterans Administration found that a majority of Americans simultaneously agreed with two conflicting conclusions: while nearly two-thirds "strongly" or "somewhat" agreed with the statement that "the trouble in Vietnam was that our troops were asked to fight in a war we could never win," almost three-quarters also agreed with the contradictory view that "our troops were asked to fight in a war which our leaders in Washington would not let them win."

For all the furor it aroused on American campuses, Vietnam was virtually invisible in course catalogs during the war. Only a tiny handful of universities taught Vietnamese history or culture or language, or anything at all about the war's origins. In general, as one writer commented, Vietnam remained "a giant black hole in American academia" through the 1960s and beyond—possibly, historian Marilyn Young suggested tartly, because in the academic universe of the time, "everyone thought they knew all there was to know about the subject." It was only when the war burst into the popular culture in the 1980s, suddenly becoming visible in movies, television programs, and books, that it also emerged as a fashionable subject on many college and university campuses. More than two hundred colleges offered television courses designed around the Public Broadcasting System's thirteen-part documentary series *Vietnam—A Television History,* first aired in 1983. Several years later, a packaged high-school course called "The Lessons of the Vietnam War" was ordered by nine hundred teachers in the first few months after its release. "As far as the students are concerned, it is about time," proclaimed the introduction to an accompanying teacher's manual. "For them, the Vietnam War is 'hot.' Movies, TV shows, paperbacks, even comic books on the War have been doing a booming business."

But the many unresolved questions of fact and interpretation continued to confound teachers and students alike. Instead of tackling the difficult, complicated story of what actually happened in Vietnam, many instructors took the easier route of teaching what amounted to courses in 1960s nostalgia, inviting veterans and war protesters to share their reminiscences with students. (Some "taught" the war by having students dress up in camouflage and camp out in the woods for a couple of days.) Students in such courses may have learned something about the experience of American soldiers, or about the American experience of frustration, disillusion, and moral confusion. But they learned almost nothing about why the war started, or about the opposing Vietnamese sides, or about the events that gave the conflict its shape before the United States became involved. The war that curious young Americans learned about often seemed to be one that happened mainly in Americans' minds, connected only tenuously with the war that actually happened on the other side of the Pacific Ocean among fifty million Vietnamese, Lao, and Cambodians.

The thirty-five or so students who showed up for my first class in Vietnam in the fall of 1983 were a mix of traditional college-age undergraduates and night-school students, most in their middle or late twenties, working full-time and attending school at night. The Vietnam Veterans Memorial had been dedicated less than a year earlier, breaking the country's long silence on the war. (At least one student was led to my course, a few years later, as the explicit and direct result of the memorial. Her interest in the war was sparked, she told me, when during an internship at a local cable TV station she worked on a documentary about the memorial and its wall of names.)

In that first class, curious about what had drawn these students to enroll and wondering what they wanted from the course, I asked each of them to write a short note explaining why they were there and what they hoped to learn. From the responses, I learned that there were three Vietnam veterans in the class, and several others who had served in the military during the war but were stationed elsewhere. Others had relatives who served in Vietnam, or remembered participating in demonstrations. A nurse wrote that she had occasionally encountered patients "labeled as suffering from 'Vietnam psychosis'" and wondered why Vietnam, but not other wars, had a disease named for it. Another student wrote that his "sense of suspense and intrigue" about the war dated from his draft physical at Fort Holabird in Baltimore in the fall of 1972! (He was not drafted.)

In subsequent years, teaching on the war at various local universities, I asked for similar notes from each class. Among the several hundred responses I received over the years, there were sharp reminders of not just the confusion but the pain associated with Vietnam. One quiet young woman wrote, "My feeling is that the American public was plied with so many lies that I am now trying to figure out what was truth and what the lies were. . . . I also have a brother who was killed there." Another woman's note said, "My husband was hurt in Vietnam. I'd like to know why. Also my brother is still not the same after Vietnam." And one year I had in the class a young man named Dinh who wrote only a single sentence: "My prime objective in this course is to obtain as much information as I can about my country." Not all the notes were that poignant, of course. But whether they had such personal associations with the war or not, my students—virtually without exception—seemed to share a kind of urgent, personal curiosity about the subject, a sense that the truth about the war was elusive, even perhaps deliberately kept from them. "My father served two tours of duty there," one girl wrote, "but I really do not know anything about U.S. goals or how the United States got involved. Since the war happened in my lifetime and had a pretty deep effect on my life, I'd like to learn more about it than the generalities I pick up from people who don't know much more than I did." Another student commented that Vietnam "is so often discussed and argued . . . and yet it seems that nobody really knows what happened."

Other teachers discovered similar feelings. Pamela Steinle, teaching in the American Studies program at California State University–Fullerton, found that her students' most urgent question about Vietnam was why Americans were there at all. "The Vietnam War era seems to be kept like a secret," one wrote. A high-school teacher in Somerville, Massachusetts, wrote about her students that "one common characteristic is the feeling that they have been left out of a terrible and well-kept secret." Some, she added, even believed that "the government doesn't want that history taught." That sense of missing truth—a suspicion that the real story of the war has for mysterious reasons remained secret, out of reach—appeared to cut across all lines of age and experience. Adult students, even veterans, with first-hand memories of the era expressed that feeling as intensely as undergraduates who were still toddlers when the war ended.

The continuing debate over Vietnam didn't provide much enlightenment for young Americans who wondered exactly what had happened there. All she ever heard about the war while she was growing up, one student told me, was "emotion and opinion, no facts." Emotion and opinion certainly overwhelmed facts and dispassionate research as Americans continued to argue about the war and its meaning. On many disputed issues, the intensity of argument has hardly lessened with time. Indeed, as competing mythologies have overtaken memories of the actual events, some of those debates—on the reporting of the war and its impact, for example—seem to have become even more partisan and emotional and polarized, not less, over the years. More often than not, as new information became available, it was pressed into the service of opinions already formed. "By and large," commented the historian William Turley, "the people who were arguing position A during the war are still arguing it; those who held position B still hold it. Very few have significantly changed their minds."

If most Americans clung to the opinions they had started out with, a few were clear-eyed enough to see that none of the partisan mythologies could really explain Vietnam and its terrible ambiguities. I prized a final paper written for one of my classes by a thirty-four-year-old hospital technician named Diane Reyes, who was a teenager when the war ended and nearly twenty years later felt a nagging need "to know what happened and why." At the end of the course, she wrote, she had learned

> that there probably wasn't so much government cover-ups and conspiracy, mostly people trying to do the best they could. There was more to it than a bunch of old men sending off young men to die. It wasn't Americans going in and blasting villages filled with women and children, but kids following rules believing they were doing the right thing by serving their country as their elders had done. It was a war and sometimes things

got out of hand. And how much did all those hippie protesters actually know? How much could they have known? It's twenty-five years later and we still haven't figured it out. . . .

Did the media affect public opinion? Certainly they did, but may have done so unknowingly. How could they know the full ramifications of what they would present? They were showing what they saw, maybe they didn't see any further. . . . Of course people can be changed by what they see, like with Rodney King,* you know it happens a lot but when you actually see it, you feel responsible and you want it to stop. . . .

What was life like for Vietnamese women? What about the ones who cohorted with American men, how were they persecuted? Are they still? What problems were unique to women? What was it like for Vietnamese families who split, some Viet Cong, some South Vietnamese? Was it like the Civil War in the U.S.? Were the families able to reunite at all? What about the generation of Vietnamese in their 30s? They were children in the war, how are they faring now? . . .

I've discussed the war with a co-worker who is a vet, there is always a good deal of reluctance on his part to do so. He is defensive, angry about his return home reception. When I asked about his medals, he said, "I didn't blow up any women or children, I saved three guys."

One could go through a whole library of books by the experts, I thought when I read Reyes's paper, without finding many passages that stated the issues as clearly, or were as successful in escaping the competing myths that still surrounded the war.

The shelf of books on Vietnam, scant during the war, grew dramatically after it ended. In the ten years following 1975, by one estimate, the number of published works on Vietnam doubled every year. Vietnam courses proliferated along with the books. A 1986 survey found more than four hundred courses offered on American campuses dealing with "Vietnam era events"—including, as well as the war itself, other subjects such as the civil rights and women's movements and the counterculture of the 1960s. The number of courses undoubtedly continued to grow in the subsequent decade. But in a field where knowledge remained "incomplete and profoundly confused," as historian Ronald H. Spector noted, and where

---

*Reyes's paper was written in the spring of 1993, less than a year after the acquittal of four Los Angeles police officers in the Rodney King brutality case and the ensuing riot.

the facts were in chronic danger of being smothered by emotion and partisan mythology, more courses didn't necessarily mean more true understanding or knowledge of the war.

For one thing, teachers were hardly immune to the ideological passions still surrounding the subject. The designer of "The Lessons of the Vietnam War"—which by 1996 had been used in 2,500 high schools and 500 colleges—wrote approvingly of instructors who taught the subject as a way of "insulating" students "from cold war propaganda and militaristic appeals." (He also worried that the lessons of Vietnam might be resisted by "those males who embrace the egoistic, aggressive, and achievement-driven adult role models of the 1980s.") A Massachusetts high-school instructor—the same one whose students thought the government was keeping the history of the war from them—wrote in a professional journal about a classroom exercise in which a few students were designated as "landlords" or "overseers" while most of the class played the role of "peasant-workers." Usually, she reported, "the peasant-workers elect to overthrow the feudal landlords and seize control of the land. In evaluating this exercise," she added, "students find it easy to connect with the collectivist spirit behind Vietnam's indigenous nationalist movements." In the same journal, a college instructor wrote that he spent the first day of his class on Vietnam War literature explaining to his students that his opinions about the war had not cooled since his days as "an outspoken opponent of the war in Vietnam, involved in sit-ins, teach-ins, marches, letter-writing campaigns, call-ins, being teargassed, severely beaten, and threatened with death." (After several more paragraphs in the same vein, this instructor added, "I also explain that I have no hidden agenda, that the course is not a forum for my antiwar views.")

No doubt, courses taught by former peace activists or sympathizers gave students some glimmering of the moral issues and passions of the era. But one was entitled to wonder how they might deal with the great complexities and ambiguities presented by the *facts* of the conflict—just as one would also wonder about instructors committed to the view that U.S. policy was justified and correct, and that only defeatist or perhaps disloyal political forces at home kept U.S. military and political leaders from achieving success. Students were not always swayed by their instructors' ideology, of course. Perry Oldham, a Vietnam veteran, used novels and memoirs of the war in his classes at an Oklahoma high school, hoping his students would "share my own visceral rejection of war and violence in general as a means of solving disputes." The effort was unsuccessful. "My attempts to deglamorize the war for these youngsters failed," he reported. Instead, his students were attracted to the battle scenes—the more violent, the better—until Oldham came to feel he was offering "the literary equivalent of computer games about blowing up continents or one of those 'combat' games in which persons wearing tiger-stripe fatigues pay a fee to chase each other around with guns loaded with colored paint." After a couple of years, Oldham stopped giving the course.

Many instructors—often in an explicit effort to present the "other side" of the issue—invited veterans to speak or even co-teach classes on the war. Local veterans groups and national organizations such as the Vietnam Veterans of America and the Vietnam Veterans Leadership Project promoted these appearances, partly to help teach about the war but also to improve the veterans' image by showing students that not all veterans came home as "drunks, dopers, murderers and rapists." Vets in the classroom didn't hide the subjects of post-traumatic stress, drug and alcohol use, and other problems, said a Vietnam Veterans of America spokesman, "but at the same time, we tell students that their doctor, banker, lawyer, insurance salesman, and postman are all likely to be Vietnam vets."

Almost invariably, students primed by movies and television scenes of Vietnam combat (and knowing virtually nothing else of the war) found these in-the-flesh meetings with former soldiers fascinating. "They are the ones who know what really went on," said one Maryland tenth-grader. Former soldiers could speak knowledgeably and often compellingly about their own experiences, of course. But having served in the war did not make them authorities on its larger history or circumstances, or on U.S. policy or strategy. "A case probably can be made for the idea that a veteran who experienced the war in Southeast Asia may understand it better than a professor who experienced it mainly on television," wrote Ronald Spector, who was a marine officer in Vietnam. But the veterans' perspective had its limits, too. Spector's fellow marines in Vietnam, he recalled,

> did not seem to clearly distinguish between the people of Okinawa, from which our unit had deployed, and the people of South Vietnam. They were not only "gooks," they were the same gooks. . . . Like Oliver Wendell Holmes's soldier of the Civil War, the Vietnam combatant was involved "in a cause which he little understands, in a plan of campaign of which he has no notion, under tactics of which he does not see the use." This may make him a transcendently noble figure, as Holmes believed, or a

tragic victim of senseless mass murder, but few would argue that it makes him a historian.

Along with partisan distortions, a graver problem in many Vietnam courses was an American-centered perspective on the subject. With almost no significant exceptions, the movies, TV programs, and novels from which students (and teachers) got most of their impressions of the war showed it as an entirely *American* event. In those representations of the war, whether in print or on small or large screens, the war in Vietnam is typically treated as a piece of American history, in which Vietnam and the Vietnamese are no more than background scenery for a story whose main actors and terms of reference are all American. If Vietnamese characters appear at all, it is nearly always as stock Hollywood stereotypes: as sadistic, fanatic enemy or as mysterious, exotic lover.

For that matter, even the American experience is shown through very narrow lenses. What is usually represented, to the exclusion of all other aspects of the war, is the experience of American soldiers—almost always infantrymen, although a large majority of Americans in Vietnam actually served in support units. Even combat air units, which played an important part in the war, are rarely shown. Occasionally, some other image of the American experience appears; of antiwar demonstrators, for example. But the experience and perspective of the Vietnamese, on either side, remained almost entirely invisible. This vision of the war nourished the fallacy that events always occurred for American, not Vietnamese reasons. That in turn led to the further fallacy that only different American decisions were needed for the conflict to have had a different outcome, as if Vietnamese history or circumstances or the qualities and traditions and strengths of the opposing Vietnamese sides were of no importance at all.

The American-centered perspective prevailed not only in popular culture but in the scholarly world as well. American scholars were far more likely to be experts on U.S. politics and policymaking than on Vietnamese history or society; and the documentary records so beloved of academic historians were much more complete and accessible on decisions in Washington than on the actions, perceptions, and decisions of our Vietnamese allies and enemies. As a result, on the academic bookshelf hardly less than in the popular literature, American personalities, calculations, decisions, and actions are typically shown as crucial, while the Vietnamese on both sides and their historical, political, and cultural environment remain shadowy and unexamined.

In this respect, postwar scholarship and popular entertainment recreated the cultural blindness of the wartime era, when, generally speaking, neither the American public, its scholars, its government, nor its military leaders knew even the most basic facts about Vietnam, or thought it necessary to know any. During the war and long afterward, U.S. officials tended to complain that the Vietnamese were mysterious. They behaved in ways that were "indirect and, by American standards, devious or baffling," Henry Kissinger wrote in his memoirs, as if it were their fault that we understood them so poorly (and as if Henry Kissinger, of all people, were entitled to gripe at someone else for being devious!). The truth, as the historian Loren Baritz noted, was that it wasn't "the strangeness of the land or the inscrutability of its people" that caused problems for American policymakers, but our unwillingness to learn about them: "Our difficulty was not with the peculiarities of the Vietnamese. Our problem was us, not them."

In the absence of systematic research, it was hard to know how solid or superficial most Vietnam courses on U.S. campuses really were. Some (but not many) were taught by recognized experts on Vietnam; some by scholars who specialized in other Asian societies or in military history or in U.S. history or government or foreign relations; and some, no doubt, by instructors who seemed to believe, as one commentator noted, that "just having lived through the 1960s" qualified them to teach on the war. The most popular course on Vietnam taught anywhere, by all accounts, was given in the religious studies department, not history or political science, at the University of California at Santa Barbara. Taught by a professor of religion, Walter Capps, and drawing up to nine hundred students each time it was offered, the course focused not on events in Vietnam but on Americans who had to choose whether to serve, and the consequences of that decision. Most of Capps's classes were not lectures but "encounter sessions," as one journalist called them, "at which individuals whose lives were shaped by the era—mainly vets—unpack their anger, fears and dreams."

Some instructors did try to explain to their students that the Vietnamese background was important, too. But a good many did not, or gave only the most superficial attention to the Vietnamese dimension of the story. Course descriptions and instructors' comments collected in the mid-1980s for a survey by the Project on the Vietnam Generation showed a heavy emphasis on teaching about the experience of American soldiers, exactly mirroring the focus of popular novels and movies. A teacher in Montana reported that he assigned his students to make lists of GI slang and military terminology while another, at an Ohio college, split his class "into five 20-student 'companies' or platoons: Alpha, Bravo, Charlie, Delta and Echo."*

Underlying the American-centered vision of Vietnam was a traditional American self-centeredness. We are not a people who are well educated about other countries; nor do we easily make the effort to imagine historical experiences other than our own. "When we talk about Vietnam," the journalist Joseph Lelyveld once wrote, "we are seldom talking about the country of that name or the situation of the people who live there. Usually we are talking about ourselves." ("Probably we always were," he added, "which is one conspicuous reason our leaders found it so hard to shape a strategy that fit us and our chosen terrain.") Not surprisingly, talk of Vietnam on the campuses was mainly about ourselves, too. Whenever he asked his students to consider the Vietnamese and their response to events, Penn State University historian William J. Duiker once remarked, the usual response was a blank stare. "They still cannot grasp," Duiker said, "that the war had something to do with other people."

Nor was it easy for Americans to accept the reality of their own country's failure in Vietnam. Hence the noticeable tendency for Americans' postwar discussions of the war to take place largely in the conditional tense. Instead of seeking to clarify and reflect on what *did* happen, the post-1975 debate tended to get stuck in an endless chain of "what-ifs," hypothesizing different U.S. tactics or policy choices that might have changed the result. Once in a while this approach could be illuminating. Most of the time, though, it seemed an exercise in escapism or scapegoating (escapegoating, perhaps?) whose real purpose, it seemed, was not to help explain the war but to provide comfort through constructing an alternative history in which our side wins. Meanwhile, the war that actually took place often seemed to have disappeared entirely from the American consciousness. The national memory was of an event that occurred chiefly in our own imaginations: a painful *American* experience of frustration, defeat, disillusion, and moral confusion. Quite literally, the word Vietnam ceased to mean a real country on the far side of the Pacific Ocean with its own history and traditions and circumstances and became instead, just as Kevin Farrell wrote, "another word for mistakes or dishonesty or whatever."

---

*At a conference in 1992, I heard a presentation by an instructor, a combat-wounded veteran, who not only required all his students to assume the identities of soldiers in a platoon, but from time to time, picked out a student or two and told them they had been killed or wounded in action.

But ignorance of Vietnam and its history was not the whole story. For a new generation of Americans, the chief obstacle to understanding the war may not have been, after all, the "incomplete and profoundly confused" knowledge (as Ronald Spector called it) of the historical facts, but another gap: the unbridgeable gulf separating their experience and consciousness from that of Americans before Vietnam. For those born during and after the war, the United States of Dwight Eisenhower and John F. Kennedy was as foreign as any distant Asian nation. No one growing up in the cramped, contentious, cynical society of the 1980s and 1990s could fully imagine a time when America's resources seemed limitless and its power seemed certain to prevail. Nor was there any path back to that earlier consciousness. "We're not going to have another Vietnam now because we've already had Vietnam," Don Oberdorfer, one of America's wisest and most respected journalists, once remarked, meaning that America would never again be unaware of the risks and uncertainties of stepping into another country's violence.

It was also true that the United States could never again be the same country it was before Vietnam, no matter how often its presidents or other leaders tried to evoke nostalgic visions of a more trusting and unified past. "Vietnam Vietnam Vietnam, we've all been there," Michael Herr wrote in the closing lines of his book *Dispatches*. Nearly a quarter of a century after the war that was true, in a sense, even for Americans who were children during the war, or not yet born.

7

THE NEW AMERICANS

Inside I was sad
feeling myself on a desert
knowing my customs will die with me.
—Tran Thi Nga

This is my home. This is definitely my home.
—Lydia Trang

While Americans struggled with their memories of the war, a million Indochinese immigrants in the United States were writing a new chapter in a very old American story.

"I have freedom for myself, to work, to live, freedom to do everything," said one man who started off in America as a farm laborer, eventually achieved modest success as a businessman, and felt that "everything is very smooth for us in America." But, like millions of immigrants before him, he also found in American freedom a kind of loneliness: "We have all the material comforts, very good. But the joy and sentiment are not like we had in Vietnam. There . . . we had many relatives and friends to come to see us at home. Here in America, I only know what goes on in my home; my neighbor knows only what goes on in his home. . . . I still remember the small road, the trees in the village where I grew up. Vietnam is forever in my mind."

Unlike most events in social history, the Vietnamese migration to America could be traced back to an exact place and time—almost, indeed, to a precise week. Before the 1970s, only a few thousand Vietnamese lived in the United States. Then came the spring of 1975, when the U.S.-backed South Vietnamese army suddenly disintegrated in a series of panicky retreats that yielded most of the country to the North Vietnamese in only five weeks. By mid-April, Communist divisions were closing in on Saigon, but their approach sparked no spirit of resistance in the demoralized South Vietnamese capital. Instead, the city became obsessed with escape. Senior government officials, civil servants, military officers, ordinary soldiers, and countless others with some official or unofficial link to the U.S. effort now desperately sought American help to leave the country and avoid the bloody Communist reprisals they all were certain awaited them.

The evacuation effort started slowly, in part because of obstructions raised by Ambassador Graham A. Martin, who for days stubbornly refused to acknowledge that South Vietnam was lost. By April 21, only about 3,000 Vietnamese, some authorized and some not, had made it onto evacuation flights. That night, South Vietnam's President Nguyen Van Thieu tearfully resigned. The next day, a larger refugee airlift finally got under way. In the seven days remaining before Communist artillery fire closed the airport, approximately 35,000 Vietnamese were flown out of the country in American transport planes. Another 5,500 Vietnamese, along with the remaining Americans in Saigon, were lifted out by helicopter in the final evacuation, which began on the afternoon of April 29 and ended at dawn the next morning, just a few hours before South Vietnam's last president, Duong Van Minh, surrendered the capital to Communist troops.

Scores of thousands of other refugees, meanwhile, were afloat on the South China Sea, heading toward the U.S. evacuation ships waiting off the coast. They came in a vast flotilla of military and civilian vessels: destroyers, landing craft, supply vessels, patrol boats, barges, tugs, rusty freighters, fishing trawlers, even an old Saigon River ferry that a group of refugees had purchased for the equivalent of about $66,000. U.S. ships along the coast picked up nearly 60,000 refugees, taking them either to the huge U.S. naval base at Subic Bay in the Philippines or fifteen hundred miles farther east to Guam, the closest U.S. territory. Another 20,000 Vietnamese headed for the Philippines aboard a bedraggled fleet of thirty-two vessels belonging to the defeated South Vietnamese navy.

Despite the fears and confusion of the evacuation, those earliest refugees from Indochina were also, relatively speaking, the luckiest, if anyone going into permanent exile can be called lucky. Even those who escaped by sea were rescued after only hours or at most a few days of acute danger and hardship. More important, the doors to their new home were open. With virtually no exceptions, all of the approximately 125,000 Vietnamese who left in the 1975 air- and sealifts were all resettled in the United States, most of them relatively quickly. For most of the hundreds of thousands of refugees who would follow them, the journey to America would be far longer, harder, and more dangerous.

Lydia Trang's journey, for example. . . .

The most extraordinary thing about Lydia's story, as she told it one fall afternoon in a quiet college classroom in a leafy Maryland suburb, was that it was not extraordinary at all. With only minor changes in detail, the same story could have been told by almost any of the more than three-quarters of a million Vietnamese who, over a period lasting nearly fifteen years, escaped their troubled country by sea.

In 1978, the year Lydia was thirteen (and still called by her Vietnamese name, Bang Hue Trang), the Communist authorities began imposing their system more tightly on South Vietnamese society. Part of her family's land was confiscated, along with many of their household possessions. Lydia's private Chinese-language school was ordered to switch to the Vietnamese language and a heavily ideological Communist curriculum. Meanwhile, her draft-age brothers faced possible conscription for an increasingly violent border conflict with Cambodia. When her brothers began speaking of escape, their father was against it. He thought the risk of being caught and sent to a labor camp was too great. But eventually, he left it to his children to decide for themselves. Of the eight children, four chose to leave: an older sister, then thirty; a sixteen-year-old brother; and the two youngest in the family, Lydia and her younger brother, then ten.

Just before Christmas 1978, the escape group gathered in Rach Gia, a coastal town in the western Mekong delta. There were about four hundred people altogether, Lydia remembered, most of them, like her family, relatively wealthy and of Chinese descent. Each had paid somewhere between $4,000 and $5,000 for the journey. The final assembly point was a stretch of beach outside the town, where the trip organizers had bribed the local Communist security officials to look the other way. Each refugee was allowed to bring only one small piece of luggage.

Their first embarkation almost ended in disaster. A driving rainstorm soaked the refugees and whipped up waves that almost overturned the ninety-foot boat, top-heavy with its terrified cargo of four hundred screaming passengers. Ten minutes after they got under way, the engine quit. Somehow the crew got the drifting craft back into the shelter of land. The bribed Communist guards gave them five days to fix the engine, but refused to let the passengers come ashore. A few gave up and slipped off to return home; at one point, Lydia and her younger brother wanted to give up too, but the crew wouldn't let them off. Two days after New Year's Day 1979, five days after their failed first attempt, the boat and its passengers headed out again into the Gulf of Thailand.

Shortly after dark on the fourth day at sea, out of fresh water and nearly out of food, the boat reached an island off the Malaysian coast. The crew wanted to go a little farther, but the passengers had had enough. Reluctantly the crew turned toward shore, but stopped too far out for the passengers to wade to the beach. Those who could swim helped the rest. Soaked, scared, not sure where they were, the refugees waited for the local authorities, or someone, to find them. When Malaysian naval police arrived, though, the first thing they did was order the refugees back into their boat. "We don't want you here," one told them. Instead of complying, the crewmen unloaded all the remaining luggage and, with axes and saws, began demolishing the boat.

The next day, the Malaysians took them to another island and then, three days after that, to a local jail. Eventually, a week after coming ashore, they were loaded onto boats and taken to Pulau Bidong, a formerly uninhabited island where, starting in 1978, the Malaysians had sent thousands of the Vietnamese whom the world was beginning to call by a new term: boat people. By the time the group from Lydia's boat arrived, though the Bidong camp had only been established for a few months, the island was already teeming with more than forty-two thousand refugees, crammed into an area no larger than a modest-sized American farm.

The camp was a foul place, full of rats and a thick stench of human waste and rotting garbage. Lady Borton, an American medical relief worker who arrived there about the time Lydia and her sister and brothers left, recorded her first glimpse from the dock, after arriving by trawler from the mainland: "a flux of people all with straight black hair. Behind them, blue plastic huts overlapped one another like the shards of a kaleidoscope. Bidong Mountain rose above the people and their shanties, bare and forbidding, its orange slopes stripped of foliage and bristling with stumps."

During Lydia's first month there, overwhelmed relief agencies could only get enough supplies to the island to give the refugees one meal a day. For a pail of fresh water, people stood in line for twelve hours, under a stifling sun. Human rats abounded, as well as the animal variety; every night there were robberies, as those who were stronger and more ruthless preyed on those who were weak and defenseless. Months of squalor and idleness and traumatic memories of the sea drove some people genuinely mad; there was also an eerie outbreak of feigned insanity, after several mentally ill people were accepted for resettlement in Switzerland.

Grim as it was, almost none of the Vietnamese who arrived there would have willingly left the island to go back to Vietnam. However long it took, they were prepared to endure the camp until some other country, somewhere, agreed to take them in. It might resemble a prison, but the refugees saw it differently. Pulau Bidong, one man declared, was "one border of the free world."

While the Trangs waited on Pulau Bidong, the tide of boat refugees continued to swell, at times reaching more than 50,000 a month. Altogether, in 1978 and 1979 more than 300,000 came ashore in various Southeast Asian countries. No one knows how many others died on the way, drowned or murdered by pirates who regularly preyed on refugee boats approaching the coast of Thailand. Sometimes, commercial ships rescued refugees from disabled or sinking boats. But many shipping companies ordered their captains not to pick up refugees, fearing that they would not be able to land them at the next port, or anywhere. (This fear was not wholly unfounded. One family taken aboard an Italian oil tanker in 1976 ended up staying on the ship for two and a half months, journeying to Singapore, Saudi Arabia, Madagascar, South Africa, Angola, Spain, and North Africa before they were finally allowed to get off in Italy.) Although some captains disregarded the order, many obeyed it. Some vessels stopped to give food and water to refugee boats, but frequently, refugees reported, ship after ship steamed by without stopping at all.

Unlike their countrymen who had left in 1975, the new refugees faced only more hardship and uncertainty even after surviving their journeys from Vietnam. None of Vietnam's neighbors was willing to give permanent refuge to the arrivals. The countries of the region were reluctant even to allow temporary shelter (first asylum, in the jargon of international refugee agencies) for fear no other country would take the refugees off their hands. Their fears led to policies that at times became heartless. Malaysia and Thailand, the two leading first-asylum destinations, periodically turned refugee boats away. In the first six months of 1979 alone, Malaysian authorities towed 267 boats with more than 40,000 passengers back out to sea, according to official statistics released by the home affairs minister. Similar cases occurred in Thailand, which was already an unwilling host to some 100,000 refugees from Laos and was suddenly inundated in 1979—just as the boat refugee crisis was reaching its peak—by several hundred thousand additional refugees from Cambodia. In June, at around the same time officials on the Thai coast were attempting to force Vietnamese refugee boats back to sea, Thai soldiers along the Cambodian border marched some forty thousand Khmer refugees at gunpoint back into Cambodia along a heavily mined trail at a place called Preah Vihear, causing many casualties.

Such extreme acts were the exception, not the rule. However reluctantly, the Thai and Malaysian governments and others in the region did give haven to most of the arriving refugees, albeit under a policy known as "humane deterrence," one of those political euphemisms that belongs in the same class as such terms as "reeducation" and "final solution." It meant that conditions in refugee camps were deliberately kept as grim as world opinion would allow, to discourage other refugees from coming. No one could justify marching helpless men, women, and children into minefields or shoving them out into a hostile sea. But Thailand, Malaysia, and their neighbors faced a genuine dilemma. If they were too hospitable, the rest of the world would not feel pressured to find new homes for the boat people—who would keep coming only to become permanent wards of the first-asylum countries, which had no part in causing the crisis. Thai and Malaysian leaders saw no reason why their humanitarianism should be punished by being stuck with hundreds of thousands of people they had not asked to come and did not want. The refugees flooding his country "were conceived by U.S. policies during the 1970-75 war," Thailand's Prime Minister Kriangsak Chamanand told the British writer William Shawcross, "and were delivered by Vietnam. Why should they be left on our doorstep?"

In response to the crisis, the United States accepted 167,000 new refugees between mid-1979 and mid-1980—including Lydia Trang and her brothers and sister, who were accepted after waiting almost exactly one year in the Pulau Bidong camp. (Had they come a few years later, the Trangs might have been stuck on the island indefinitely, since they had no relatives abroad and no past association with the American effort during the war. In 1979, though, U.S. policy still regarded anyone fleeing Vietnam as eligible for resettlement.) Other countries also increased their quotas, with

France, Canada, and Australia taking the largest numbers. But the resettlement countries had a dilemma, too: letting in more refugees was also an invitation for still more dissatisfied Vietnamese to flee. Despite the dangers and the grim conditions in the camps, a quarter of a million more boat people arrived between 1980 and 1984. As the years passed and the dilemma remained insoluble, the rest of the world grew weary of the issue. As early as 1982, one observer commented that "the problem appears to seem stale to all but the refugees themselves." A few years later, in the annual survey compiled by the U.S. Committee for Refugees, another analyst wrote, "Increasingly, refugees are presented not as people in need of help, but as people who constitute a threat to the order of things; they do not *have* problems, they *are* the problem."

The boat people weren't the only Indochinese seeking to escape the wreckage of war and find new lives in the United States. Between 1976 and 1993, more than 190,000 refugees arrived from Laos. A large number of them were Hmong, the ethnic group that had been the backbone of the U.S.-directed "secret army" that fought the Vietnamese Communists for more than ten years, at devastating cost, in the misty valleys and gnarled mountains of northern Laos. Another 130,000 reached the United States from Cambodia, where one-fifth of the population had died in the war or under the murderous rule of the Khmer Rouge, the most brutal and fanatical of the Indochinese Communist revolutionaries.

In Vietnam, after a halting beginning, emigration procedures instituted in 1979 permitted increasing numbers of Vietnamese to exit legally, instead of joining the risky exodus by sea. Among those approved for emigration under the Orderly Departure Program, as it was called, were Amerasian children fathered by American servicemen or civilians during the war and Vietnamese seeking to join family members in the United States. From the mid-1980s on, there was also a widening flow of former prisoners released after years in what were euphemistically called re-education camps. Many of those prisoners might have been released years earlier. As early as 1982, Vietnam's Communist leaders had offered to free all those still being held and send them immediately to the United States. But U.S. officials inexplicably cold-shouldered the proposal for more than two years, even when it was repeated publicly by senior Vietnamese officials up to and including Prime Minister Pham Van Dong. America's failure to respond meant more years of confinement for thousands of prisoners, most of whom had been officials or soldiers in the U.S.-backed Saigon regime. Eventually, though, a trickle of freed re-education prisoners, with their families, joined the flow of emigrés. By 1994, a total of 112,000 former prisoners and family members had reached the United States.

Among the Indochinese immigrants, different groups fared differently as they tried to find a place in American life. In general, the Vietnamese, coming from a more commercial and cosmopolitan culture, had less difficulty assimilating. Most successful of all, if success is measured by employment and income, was the first wave of Vietnamese who came in 1975. Compared with later arrivals, many more of the 1975 refugees came from the South Vietnamese elite, with education, job experience, and skills that helped them fit into American society. Many also had wartime relationships with Americans (often, that was how they joined the evacuation in the first place) who became helpful contacts when they reached the United States. The adjustment wasn't easy, even with those advantages. But within four years of their arrival, according to official statistics, the first wave of Vietnamese were employed and had incomes at roughly the same levels as the rest of the U.S. population.

Those who had the toughest time in America, by most accounts, were the Hmong. Coming from a remote, isolated region of one of the least-developed nations on earth, the Hmongs' traditions of hunting, farming, polygamy, clan loyalties, and spirit worship were disastrously ill-matched with American culture, particularly in the rough, high-crime areas of big cities where many were placed by refugee agencies. From time to time, whole communities of resettled Hmong families would disappear from city neighborhoods overnight, often without a word to the American agencies that were supposed to assist them, and take to the road in caravans of shabby old cars, like depression-era migrants from the Dust Bowl, searching vainly for someplace on the American landscape that would feel less hostile and strange.

While struggling to adjust to a new and often bewildering land, immigrants from all three Indochinese countries also struggled with demons from their past. Often, just as they had during the war, they kept silent about their suffering. But the invisible wounds left by years of violence, fear, flight, and loss were slow to heal. Sometimes they were even fatal, or so it seemed: around the country, mysterious cases were reported of dozens of Southeast Asian refugees—mostly men, mostly in their twenties or thirties—dying at night, in their sleep, without any evident cause. About half the victims were Hmong, the rest from other groups. Scientists at the federal Centers for Disease Control found that many of them had the same minor heart abnormality, but clinical evidence did not explain why it became fatal. Stress, researchers guessed, was the most likely culprit. A Hmong health specialist had a different explanation. In America, it was impossible for the Hmong to sustain many of their rituals and traditions, he told the journalist Marc Kaufman, "and many people think the ancestors are angry." And when ancestors are angry, the Hmong believe, they can do very harmful things. "This makes people very, very worried. Could they be so worried that it kills them? It could be."

Equally haunting and mysterious were cases of nearly 150 middle-aged Cambodian women in California, survivors of the Khmer Rouge terror, who had no identifiable eye disease but could no longer see. "The ones who were worst afflicted could see nothing at all," the writer Alec Wilkinson reported in a 1994 article for *The New Yorker* magazine. "Those whose vision was clearest could make out shadows, and some could count fingers on hands held a few feet from their faces. All had been victims of the Khmer Rouge, but none had known any of the others or been aware when she lost her sight that anyone else had the same problem." Some of the things that had happened to them in Cambodia—disease, infection, starvation, torture—might have led to blindness. But they would either have recovered their sight in America or else would have had eye problems that could be diagnosed, since all diseases causing blindness are detectable. These women had none. Doctors' tests found nothing wrong with their eyes. In some cases, after being examined, the women had been turned down for disability benefits because, even if they couldn't see, test results showed they were not blind.

If there was no physical explanation, the reason had to lie in their minds, related somehow to the terrible experiences they had undergone. It was as if, after seeing people clubbed or sliced or stabbed to death for trivial infractions of Khmer Rouge rules, or watching their own children taken away from them, or looking so often in terror at their guards to see if their own executions were imminent, the women's eyes had simply refused to absorb any more.

The past also burdened the thousands of immigrants who had worn the uniform of the defeated South Vietnamese army. In the United States, even as Americans gradually gave recognition and honor to their own veterans, the former Vietnamese soldiers remained almost entirely invisible, remembered, if at all, only for the tragic shambles of South Vietnam's collapse in 1975. Few Americans knew, or cared, about the years of endurance preceding that disaster, or realized the enormous sacrifice that had been paid: more than 200,000 South Vietnamese soldiers killed, nearly four times the number of American deaths. In Vietnam, after 1975, no one could publicly honor those who had died for the losing side. In an act of vengeance against their defeated enemies, the Communists bulldozed dozens of military cemeteries, obliterating the grave markers that had borne the names of the dead or, often, the single word "Unknown." In a sense, South Vietnam's dead had been bulldozed under in the United States, too, forgotten by all except the families who mourned them and their comrades who, in Vietnamese fashion, nursed their memories and feelings silently and alone.

Many former soldiers sustained their pride and spirits by clinging to the dream that someday the regime they had fought for might be restored. At holiday festivals and other gatherings, veterans kept alive the symbols of their lost nation, singing the South Vietnamese anthem and saluting the Republic of Vietnam flag, with its three horizontal red stripes on a saffron yellow field. Some imagined coming out of exile to recapture their homeland from its Communist rulers; others were more realistic. "The flag is a great symbol, and it has deep meaning in my heart," said Phan Nhat Nam, a veteran living in California, "but it does not have any other meaning. The Republic of Vietnam has vanished. These people want the war to continue, but the war no longer exists."

Among the Vietnamese exiles, some remained so wholly identified with the war that, if it didn't exist, it could be said that they didn't fully exist, either—including Nam himself, who spent fourteen years in re-education camps after the war and didn't reach the United States until 1994. The author of a series of books reflecting the South Vietnamese experience in the war, Nam felt his life had truly ended with South Vietnam's defeat, he told a reporter; "At that moment, I realized that I was dead. In my mind, I had died in the war. And in my mind, I have been dead from that moment until today."

If some refugees remained trapped in a sorrowful past, there were many more who, like millions of immigrants before them, quietly set about mastering English, finding new livelihoods, and constructing new lives in their new country. Over time, Indochinese Americans moved into the American mainstream. Names like Nguyen, Tran, and Pham grew more familiar, joining other American names inherited from earlier immigrants on graduation lists and office directories and business-page articles. Newcomers continued to arrive from Vietnam, Cambodia, and Laos at the rate of forty to fifty thousand a year, but with many of their countrymen now solidly established in the United States, there were more guides to teach new arrivals how to manage among the inscrutable Americans.

Meanwhile, the long saga of the boat people was at last coming to an end. After a last major crisis in 1988 and 1989, when more than 120,000 boat refugees came ashore, the flow subsided. Escapes fell off in part because life in Vietnam improved and also because an increasing number of Vietnamese who wanted to leave and could obtain visas to other countries were able to do so legally. In 1992, for the first time in over fifteen years, the seas around Vietnam were virtually empty of refugee boats. During the entire year, only 41 boat people landed in the region, while 80,000 emigrated legally to the United States. But camps in Hong Kong and Southeast Asia still housed thousands of Vietnamese who had been turned down by all the resettlement countries but still refused to return to Vietnam. The term often used for these refugees was a suggestive one: residue, as if they were some vile or toxic substance.

By international agreement, all Vietnamese in first-asylum countries who had not been resettled were supposed to be returned to Vietnam, voluntarily or not, by the end of 1995. Many did give up hope and go home, but others resisted, sometimes violently. When the deadline passed, nearly forty thousand boat people were still sitting in the camps, still refusing repatriation in the stubborn hope that some country, somewhere, would let them in. About half were in Hong Kong; most of the rest were distributed, in roughly equal numbers, among Indonesia, Malaysia, and Thailand. These refugees by now had been in the camps for years; some had been born there. A large number were children and teenagers who were not even born in 1975, when the first boat refugees headed out to sea.

Among the Vietnamese in the United States, too, a new generation had grown up in the two decades since the first refugees arrived. Few families escaped tension between their old and new cultures. Parents lamented that America taught their children to disobey; children felt stifled by parents who expected the lifelong submission required under Confucian codes of behavior. Even without direct conflict, there was a kind of sadness for parents whose children no longer fully belonged to Vietnam or its traditions. In a poem written in the style of a *truyen*, a traditional Vietnamese verse narrative, one woman wrote about celebrating the Tet festival, with its special meals, after coming to the United States:

How silly I felt each noontime
alone in my house
surrounded by little saucers of food,
no one to share them with
no neighbors around me celebrating.

I'd asked my children to take time off
the way I had.
They said, "What for?
So we can sit around the table
and stare at each other?"

I said I did this not for them
but for our ancestors.
Inside I was sad
feeling myself on a desert
*knowing my customs will die with me.**

The gap between Vietnamese parents and their American-born children was nothing new. It was part of a story that had been a piece of America's history from the beginning, as successive groups of immigrants arrived and struggled to find their own form of American identity. Like other immigrants before them, even while embracing their new home, the first generation of Vietnamese, Cambodians, and Lao could not entirely escape sadness for the traditions and spiritual roots they had left behind. For most, the sorrow was balanced by the greater hope and freedom they and their children found in their new country.

More than most other immigrants, this particular group of new Americans also came with memories seared by violent and tragic events. In human fashion, some were haunted, some numbed, while a few somehow distilled their experiences into a more fully developed compassion and humanity. Lydia Trang was one of those. Sixteen years after coming to the United States, she was teaching English to other immigrant children in Montgomery County, Maryland, and studying for a master's degree in counseling, though she was already doing plenty of counseling without the degree. "Sometimes I feel like their mother," she said about her students, with a cheerful little giggle. "I understand them because I went through the

*©1986 by Wendy Wilder Larsen and Tran Thi Nga. Reprinted by permission.

same things they are going through." She felt especially close, she added, to those who had come to the United States, as she did, without their parents.

Her own mother and father were now in America too, though it had taken Lydia and her brothers and sister thirteen years to bring them over. Like Lydia, the other Trang children had become solidly established in middle-class America. The older sister who brought them to the United States was working for a publishing company; one brother was a computer operator for the National Aeronautics and Space Agency; the other had earned a graduate engineering degree at the Johns Hopkins University and was now employed at the National Institutes of Health.

Among the four of them, Lydia thought, she was the one who most often thought about their journey from Vietnam—naturally enough, since a classroom full of immigrant children reminded her every day of her own experience. But the past, she said, didn't haunt her: "In order to have the life I have right now, I had to go through that." Nor did she have any doubts about belonging to her new country, which she had endured so much to reach. "This is my home," she said, echoing the many millions of immigrants who had come before her. Lydia paused, then repeated firmly: "This is definitely my home."

8
GHOSTS

"If we found a way to tell them news of a victory, would they be happier?"
"Come on! Even if we could, what would be the point?
People in hell don't give a damn about wars."
—Bao Ninh, *The Sorrow of War*

I

William Broyles Jr. went to Vietnam as a twenty-five-year-old Marine lieutenant in 1969, the same year two other Americans made the first landing on the moon. "Those astronauts," Broyles reflected in his memoir *Brothers in Arms*, "were the first men to leave the earth for another celestial body, but they knew more about the moon than we knew about Vietnam." Broyles and his platoon felt like strangers on their own planet, fighting in an alien place for elusive reasons among people whose lives, history, beliefs, and feelings remained hidden. Like the terrifying tunnel where he once hunted an unseen Communist soldier, the whole country became "a darkness we could neither penetrate nor understand."

Fifteen years later, still hoping to find some answers, Broyles returned to Vietnam, hoping particularly to understand why his country's enemy had been so tenacious, and why the American effort had failed despite overwhelming advantages in wealth, resources, technology, and destructive power. In Vietnam, he revisited old battlefields, met old enemies who had survived ("You know," one Communist general told him, not without sympathy, "your mistake was not in your tactics or even in your strategy. You simply should not have gotten into this war in the first place"), and mourned over the graves of those who had died. If Broyles did not escape sorrow or find the solutions to all his mysteries, he came away at least with some sense of having made peace with the past. "I had gone back to Vietnam with the war still raging in my head," he wrote, but once back at his old combat base, he found no war, only empty fields and the sound of the wind rustling quietly in ripe rice plants. Finally, the war was only a memory.

As gradually thawing relations between the United States and Vietnam made travel easier, a slowly growing trickle of other American veterans made the same journey. Some went to help build clinics or schools, some went to establish contact with Vietnamese who shared professional or cultural interests, some went only to revisit old battlefields and mourn their youth and the dead—on both sides. Like Broyles, they did not escape all sorrow. But a surprising number found that going back to Vietnam did somehow ease troubled memories.

Returning with a group of other veterans of the Eleventh Armored Cavalry Regiment left Gordon Livingston "filled with a terrible sadness that I could not define." But Livingston, now a Maryland psychiatrist, also wrote that the trip "helped most of us, I think, to experience Vietnam as a place rather than a war, to see the people friendly and unafraid. Perhaps that's as much closure as we're entitled to. We can't bring back the dead, ours or theirs. We seem to be forgiven by those who remember us at all. We might as well forgive ourselves and come home at last, each with whatever separate peace he is able to attain." Martha Green, a former army nurse from Massachusetts who traveled to Vietnam in early 1990, found that going back and meeting Vietnamese in peacetime helped "replace all the negative in my mind with positive. . . . These people don't have freedom," Green added, "but they do have peace. I finally feel at peace. Going there put the ghosts to rest."

One of the other veterans traveling with Green, a former marine sharpshooter named Ronald Szpond, had been haunted for nearly twenty-five years by guilt over the enemy soldiers he had killed during the war. When their escorts took the group to My Lai, Szpond carried away a single marigold from the memorial garden there. Later, outside the former U.S. base at Chu Lai where he had served, Szpond climbed to a hilltop memorial for Vietnamese war dead, put the marigold down, and said a prayer. Soon, he said later, he felt a weight lifting from him: "I felt I was forgiven."

In part, going back to Vietnam helped veterans put the war behind them simply by letting them see that it was over. The scenery they remembered—charred timbers that had once been farmers' houses, sandbagged bunkers and sprawling coils of concertina wire, little hills of expended shell cases heaped untidily alongside blackened gunpits—was no longer there. In its place was a landscape of orchards, shimmering fields of ripe rice, peaceful villages, gleaming-eyed children on the swaying backs of water buffaloes that plodded stolidly beside muddy canals. "You'd think there would be *something* left, some faint imprint," the novelist Tim O'Brien thought after returning to the place in Quang Ngai province the Army had called LZ Gator. The base had seemed "huge and imposing and permanent" when O'Brien first saw it as a young soldier in the 198th Infantry Brigade. But when he returned twenty-five years later, nothing was left. The LZ (landing zone) was "utterly and forever erased from the earth. Nothing here but ghosts and wind." Armed with military terrain maps and a compass and a stack of old after-action reports he had retrieved from military archives, O'Brien eventually located the exact spot of his own worst combat nightmares, and found himself "looking out on a wide and very lovely field of rice. The sunlight gives it some gold and yellow," he wrote. "There is no wind at all. Before us is how peace would be defined in a dictionary for the speechless."

Even Long Binh, once the biggest U.S. military base in the world, had vanished into the past. Ten years after the war, almost no trace remained of the sprawling, bustling place that had been the Army's logistical and administrative headquarters, housing thirty thousand U.S. soldiers and civilian contractors in a vast complex of offices, warehouses, bars, bowling alleys, swimming pools, and golf driving ranges. "One wanders through the fields of weeds that once were Long Binh," a visitor wrote in 1985, "searching for some remnant of a lost civilization, a helmet or bowling pin or pop-top beer can. But there are none." Instead, he found only two young Vietnamese soldiers tending a herd of cows in the deserted fields. Asked if they knew the place's history, one remembered being told Americans once lived there—but he said it in skeptical tones, "much as a Montana rancher might note that dinosaurs might once have lived on his land."

Another veteran who found his way back to Vietnam, twenty years after he almost died there, was John Phillip Baca. Drafted into the Army after a troubled youth of poverty and petty crime, Baca ended up in an infantry unit in Phuoc Long Province, north of Saigon near the Cambodian border. On February 10, 1970, in one of the numberless, nameless battles of that war, Baca became a hero when he slammed down his helmet over a live enemy grenade and smothered the blast with his body, saving eight men. His act earned him many months in military hospitals, where he nearly died from his wounds. It also earned him the Medal of Honor, the nation's highest award for heroism in battle.

Sometimes, Baca told a reporter long afterward, the medal made him "feel blessed to do something more for humanity. . . . But sometimes I curse the medal," he added, "how it raises you above who you are, an imaginary person." Like many other veterans, especially those who had endured the most harrowing combat, Baca did not easily fit into peacetime America. He bounced around the country, bought a boat with another vet and fished and crabbed in the Chesapeake Bay, spent months alone in a trailer in Nova Scotia, then settled in a nine-by-twelve-foot garden shed on the western Maryland farm of Art James, one of the men he had saved in Vietnam.

In 1990, Baca and James went back and helped build a clinic in northern Vietnam. "When the Vietnamese people found out about me," Baca said, "they put flowers on my wounds."

The Vietnamese, after what their new rulers chose to call their country's "liberation," had their darkness, too. The revolutionaries who had shown such tenacity and skill in war proved bumbling and inept as peacetime leaders. Outmoded Marxist-Leninist doctrines, combined with blundering management and widespread corruption, made the first decade of Communist rule in reunified Vietnam an almost unmitigated disaster. No less a figure than Prime Minister Pham Van Dong admitted, in a 1981 conversation with the author Stanley Karnow, "Yes, we defeated the United States. But now we are plagued by problems. We do not have enough to eat. We are a poor, underdeveloped nation. *Vous savez*, waging a war is simple, but running a country is very difficult."

Disenchantment was rife, even among those who had been most dedicated to the struggle. Duong Quynh Hoa, a physician and long-time revolutionary who had served as deputy health minister in the underground Communist government during the war, told Karnow over dinner in her Saigon home, "I've been a Communist all my life. But now, for the first time, I have seen the realities of Communism. It is failure—mismanagement, corruption, privilege, repression. My ideals are gone." A European journalist—a fervent supporter of the revolution before 1975 who had wept with joy at the Communist triumph and written an admiring book on the early months of their rule—wrote about his disillusion on returning in 1985:

> I felt once again like crying, this time out of despair at the sight of all that has not been done, all that has been wasted, all that has gone astray. People are still divided. There is no peace, and hundreds of young Vietnamese still are killed and maimed on the battlefields of Cambodia. There is no justice, unless justice means to turn a society upside down and to replace one dictatorship with another. The quality of life has worsened: poverty, inefficiency and corruption are rampant. . . . The revolution has broken all its promises.

Promising national reconciliation, the Communists instead locked scores of thousands of their defeated enemies in remote concentration camps for what was euphemistically called re-education. Catholic and Buddhist leaders were imprisoned, too, as were other dissidents, including many who had been revolutionary sympathizers during the war.

Also treated as enemies were the one and a half million Vietnamese of Chinese ancestry. The prosperous Chinese in the South (who like ethnic Chinese in other Southeast Asian countries had largely controlled South Vietnam's commercial business) were the first target, but after Vietnam's conflict with China deepened in 1979, the authorities also turned on Chinese who had lived their whole lives in the North and who were, by and large, dutiful citizens of the Communist state. Even Chinese who had been long-time, active revolutionaries were not spared. Veteran cadres were arrested and charged with being Chinese spies, or were sent to China. Hundreds of thousands of other ethnic Chinese, after being robbed of their wealth and possessions by official and unofficial extortionists, fled into exile on dangerous, rickety boats. Though ostensibly they were escaping, in effect they were being expelled.

If the promise of reconciliation was broken, so was the promise of peace. Vietnam's invasion of neighboring Cambodia, launched on Christmas Day 1978, did not produce the quick victory the leadership hoped for but led instead to a seemingly endless campaign against guerrillas of the fanatical Khmer Rouge (Red Khmer) and a brief but destructive clash with Chinese forces to the north. The war in Cambodia and continuing tension with China kept the country on a war footing, but without the compelling goal of national unification that had sustained the revolutionary mystique during the decades of struggle against France, the United States, and the U.S.-backed South Vietnamese government.

Overriding all other issues was a deep economic crisis. Communist leaders approached the postwar economy, one Vietnamese recalled years afterward, with a blind confidence that "after defeating the French, the United States, and China, they could do anything. . . . It was very simple. Mobilize the people in peacetime as they mobilized people in war. But it turned out not to be so simple." The liberators' initial postwar five-year plan for reshaping Vietnam's economy—a traditional Stalinist blueprint, calling for wholesale nationalization of land and forced-march industrial development—was an utter, disastrous failure. Economic growth between 1976 and 1980 was a dismal 0.4 percent a year, lagging far behind the growth in population, which increased at slightly more than 2 percent annually.

Planners' heavy-handed directives and unrealistic assumptions combined to produce catastrophic results in the countryside. Farmers were frequently ordered to plant crops unsuitable for their land, recalled a former Communist cadre from the coastal resort of Vung Tau. "Also," he continued, "they had to sell their produce to the government at the official price. In return, the government was supposed to sell them fertilizer and tools at the official price. But the reality was that there were never enough supplies. So they had to go to the black market and buy what they needed at black market prices. In the end they had less and less to eat. After the harvest they wouldn't have anything left for themselves." The same thing happened to the region's fishermen. While being forced to sell their catch at the official price, they had to pay black market prices for fuel and nets.

Many of those peasants and fishermen had supported the revolution, risking their lives during the war to hide guerrillas or smuggle food and arms to Communist soldiers. But that support was rapidly squandered by the government's policies and the resulting hardships. Disillusioned fishermen were taking their boats and disappearing overseas, bribing or on occasion even killing security agents who were sent out on the boats to prevent escapes. The exodus further crippled the vital fishing industry.

Sinking food production created near-famine conditions by the late 1970s. The food ration for city- and town-dwellers in 1978 was nearly one-quarter less than during the hardest years of the war. "The most ordinary goods, like soap or needles or envelopes, cannot be found in Hanoi," Karnow found in his 1981 visit; at the time, the grain ration for most Vietnamese was about thirty pounds a month, five pounds less than the min-

imum diet recommended by the World Health Organization. Fish, traditionally the main protein source, was hard to find, partly because fishermen had no fuel and partly because so many boats had slipped away in the
exodus of hundreds of thousands of boat people from villages up and
down the coast.

By the time Vietnam's rulers staged huge public ceremonies to celebrate the tenth anniversary of their victory, it was no longer possible to
conceal—even from themselves—how poorly their leadership had repaid
the enormous sacrifices that had given their revolution its victory. They had
not even achieved true peace. Six years after invading Cambodia, Vietnamese soldiers were still bleeding and dying there, and with a million men
under arms, military budgets consumed one-third to one-half of the national budget. The party and national policy remained in the fossilized grip
of aging leaders who seemed to have exhausted all their creative force in
the great struggles of the past. In 1985, the average age of the 116 Central
Committee members was reported to be sixty-nine. A sizeable majority of
the thirteen Politburo members had been associated with the party since
1930, the date of its founding, or shortly thereafter.

Limited reform policies instituted between 1979 and 1982 brought
some temporary relief from the economic crisis, but then faltered. On the
eve of the anniversary, a visiting journalist reported from Hanoi, "Beggars
crowd around hotels and restaurants. Raggedly garbed cyclo drivers huddle
under tarpaulins in their carts during the chilly night. . . . Throughout the
northern provinces, where few Westerners are allowed, thousands of people still live on the streets. Almost 20 percent of the work force is unem-
ployed and must get by on odd jobs." Those with jobs were scarcely better
off. A single chicken cost as much as a civil servant's monthly salary; a dozen
eggs cost two weeks' wages; a tube of Colgate toothpaste sold for the equivalent of three months' pay. The rice supply per person, international econ-
omists calculated, was lower than in India or Bangladesh. One-tenth of
Vietnamese children, it was reported, died of gastroenteritis caused by mal-
nutrition.

Prices continued to shoot up, with the inflation rate reaching 500
percent by early 1986. Pork and rice prices tripled within a few months; res-
idential electricity rates doubled; bus fares increased tenfold. By January
1986, rationing was reinstated for most basic commodities. Largely because of energy shortages, industry was operating at a scant 40 percent of
capacity in southern Vietnam and at only 20 percent in the North.

It was certainly true, as Vietnamese officials repeated ad nauseam, that wartime destruction and the postwar U.S. trade embargo contributed to Vietnam's woes. But a full decade after the end of the war, those excuses sounded increasingly hollow. Within the Communist Party leadership as well as in the public at large, more and more people found the cause of their difficulties in the bungling and the "self-defeating policy," as one Vietnamese called it, of their own ruling party and its officials and the small group of steely old men at the top whose revolutionary dream, once so powerful, now seemed so tattered and threadbare.

Amid the general misery, mismanagement and corruption and abuses of power flourished. So did cynicism, shredding the wartime spirit of unity and shared sacrifice much as millions of buried U.S. bombs and artillery rounds, detonating long after the war, still tore apart the land itself. If it was possible to imagine former American commanders lying awake many years later and asking themselves in the dark, *How did we lose?*, it was equally possible to imagine the Vietnamese Communists whispering into the silence of their own nights, *What did we fight for?*

II

In opening its doors to returning American veterans, as well as other visitors—even a handful of Vietnamese Americans—Vietnam was signaling its hope for a new relationship with its old enemy.

As far back as 1977, the Hanoi leadership had sought to normalize relations with the United States. The following year, after Vietnam dropped its long-standing demand for billions of dollars in U.S. funds to "heal the wounds of war,"* negotiations between Vietnamese and American officials came to the brink of an agreement—so close that State Department planners dredged up photographs and dusty blueprints of the old prewar U.S. consulate in Hanoi and began laying out a new floor plan. The deal fell through, however, virtually at the last moment and largely as the

---

*This demand traced back to the failed January 1973 peace agreement between North Vietnam and the United States, which pledged U.S. aid for postwar reconstruction. (At American insistence, the word "reparations" was not used.) Four days after the Paris agreement took effect, President Nixon sent a secret message to North Vietnamese Prime Minister Pham Van Dong declaring that the reconstruction aid would be given "without any political conditions" and that an "appropriate" aid program, in the U.S. view, would "fall in the range of 3.25 billion dollars . . . over five years." The United States subsequently refused to send any aid on the grounds that North Vietnam was violating other provisions of the peace agreement.

result of maneuvering by Carter administration officials who believed U.S. strategic interests lay in closer relations with China, not Vietnam.

The Chinese, though they had given aid and public support to the Vietnamese Communists during the war, now regarded Vietnam as an ally, even a surrogate, of the Soviet Union, China's most feared enemy. (As one China-watcher put it, the Chinese felt that "the Russian bear has had a cub.") Accordingly, officials in Washington feared, closer U.S. relations with Vietnam would be received badly in Beijing. After sharp internal debate, President Carter sided with the pro-China faction, whose most prominent member was his national security adviser, Zbigniew Brzezinski. In October 1978, Carter put the normalization agreement with Hanoi on hold, not anticipating, presumably, that relations would remain frozen for nearly seventeen more years.

On Christmas Day 1978, two months after Carter's decision and following many months of escalating border clashes, the Vietnamese invaded Cambodia, quickly occupied Phnom Penh, and established a pro-Vietnamese puppet government in place of the fanatical Khmer Rouge regime, which had drenched Cambodia in blood during its three and a half years in power. Despite the bloody record of the Khmer Rouge and despite clear evidence that the Cambodians were chiefly responsible for provoking the conflict, the Vietnamese reaped no international thanks for driving out the murderers. Instead, Vietnam became something close to a pariah state.

Less than a month after Vietnamese forces occupied the Cambodian capital, the United States welcomed China's leader Deng Xiaoping on a triumphal visit to celebrate the resumption of full U.S.-Chinese diplomatic ties. During his visit, Deng, whose government was the most prominent ally and supporter of the Khmer Rouge, denounced the invasion and bluntly warned, in public, that China would have to teach the Vietnamese "some necessary lessons." Within weeks, eighty-five thousand Chinese troops plunged across the Vietnamese border. The sixteen days of fighting that followed left four Vietnamese province capitals in ruins and thousands dead or wounded on both sides.

To the Vietnamese, it seemed obvious that the Chinese offensive, coming so quickly after Deng's U.S. trip, had been carried out with Washington's blessing. The United States made no criticism of China but called on Vietnam to withdraw its troops from Cambodia and—in what struck many observers as a policy of breathtaking cynicism—became tacit supporters, for nearly a decade, of the Khmer Rouge, despite their murderous regime. The United States government continued to recognize the ousted butchers as the legitimate occupants of Cambodia's seat in the United Nations; it gave recognition and eventually small amounts of aid to a "coalition" in which the Khmer Rouge were the dominant partner; it acquiesced in refugee relief operations that were deliberately set up to supply the Khmer Rouge resistance as well. Washington would not even give support to an international movement to try the top Khmer Rouge leaders for crimes against humanity.

During the 1980s, the Hanoi leadership repeatedly signaled its hope for better relations with the United States. But Washington continued to ostracize Vietnam, even after Hanoi pledged to withdraw all Vietnamese troops from Cambodia by the fall of 1989. The withdrawal was carried out on schedule, even while Vietnam's client government in Phnom Penh continued to face armed resistance from the Khmer Rouge and their smaller partners. Following their pullout, the Vietnamese renewed their call for normalization with the United States but were rebuffed by U.S. leaders, who now insisted that a settlement among the Cambodian factions, not just a Vietnamese withdrawal, had to come before relations could be resumed. Hanoi, understandably, felt that the Americans had moved the goalposts, and that they were unreasonably being held responsible for a settlement among groups they did not control. Through all of these events, U.S. leaders continued to insist that Vietnam was still not giving sufficient cooperation in accounting for lost U.S. servicemen, even though the Vietnamese authorities declared they were doing everything they possibly could to be helpful in the search.

The first break in the logjam did not come until April 1991, eighteen months after the Vietnamese withdrawal from Cambodia was completed, when the Bush administration presented Vietnamese officials with what became known as the "road map" plan. Under that proposal, the United States offered better relations in return for progress on a peace agreement in Cambodia, continued cooperation on the search for missing Americans, and the release of any remaining political prisoners held in Vietnamese re-education camps. As evidence of their hope for quick progress, the Hanoi authorities almost immediately agreed to let the U.S. Defense Department establish a full-time MIA office in Hanoi to arrange and oversee crash-site searches and other investigative efforts. Subsequently, the Vietnamese also agreed to comb military and government archives throughout the country and turn over to the United States any information that might help clear up MIA cases.

As the searches continued, American officials generally expressed complete satisfaction with the cooperation they received from the Vietnamese side. An official Defense Department report in late 1994 declared that Vietnamese cooperation had been "good to excellent" in carrying out searches and in arranging investigations of MIA cases in Laos. In addition, the Vietnamese were showing "increased cooperation" in going back through wartime records, the Pentagon added. The only area in which Vietnamese efforts were still judged inadequate was in locating bodies that had been moved, for some reason, from wartime burial sites. The Vietnamese also moved to resolve the issue of former South Vietnamese soldiers and officials and other prisoners held in re-education camps, most of whom had already been freed by 1991. In the spring of 1992, the Vietnamese government announced that all remaining re-education prisoners had been released. That didn't mean there were no more political prisoners at all. But it did mean no one was still imprisoned for activities or affiliations during the war. More than forty thousand former detainees and their families were resettled in the United States between 1989 and 1992.

Despite these efforts to meet U.S. demands, the pace of normalization remained glacial. It took a full year after the "road map" for the United States to announce that its seventeen-year economic embargo would be eased to allow "humanitarian transactions" with Vietnam, such as shipments of food, clothing, and health and educational materials. There was also gradual relaxation of restrictions on travel, telephone communications, and relief agency activities. In December 1992, the outgoing Bush administration further eased the embargo to permit U.S. companies to open offices and negotiate contracts or carry out feasibility studies in anticipation of full economic ties.

When President Clinton took office the following month, it was widely predicted that he would move swiftly to lift the embargo altogether and normalize relations—a step by now strongly advocated by U.S. businessmen anxious to begin investing and trading with Vietnam and worried that they would be left hopelessly behind European and Japanese investors if the embargo remained in force for much longer. Many American entrepreneurs, indeed, felt that U.S. policy was hurting them more than it was hurting the Vietnamese. "If the embargo's purpose was to punish Vietnam," declared an expert at the University of Hawaii's East-West Center, "it didn't work. It punished U.S. companies."

Early in Clinton's administration, his own secretary of state, Warren Christopher, observed that there were "strong business incentives" for the United States to end restrictions on trade with Vietnam. For that reason and others, though normalization still had enemies, by now it also appeared to have fairly broad support across the political spectrum. Less than two months after Clinton took office, the Democratic chairman and the ranking Republican member of the Senate Foreign Relations Committee joined in urging the new president to end the embargo, drop U.S. opposition to international bank loans to Vietnam, and establish a diplomatic liaison office in Hanoi. But Clinton, chronically indecisive and no doubt feeling politically vulnerable because of the draft controversy in his own past, was slow to act. His first significant step came in July 1993, nearly six months after his inauguration, when he abandoned a long-standing U.S. policy of blocking International Monetary Fund loans to Vietnam. Several months after that, he further eased the embargo to allow U.S. firms to participate in internationally financed development projects.

Finally, in February 1994, Clinton lifted the embargo. But he then let another seventeen months go by before his announcement, on July 11, 1995, that the United States and Vietnam would establish full diplomatic ties. No doubt intending to illustrate that normalization was also supported by Americans who had served there, the president's stage managers carefully placed two of the Senate's best-known veterans—Republican John McCain of Arizona and Democrat John Kerry of Massachusetts—directly behind Clinton, in full view of the cameras, as he announced his decision in the East Room of the White House. Also at the ceremony were past and present military and politically prominent veterans, including Sen. Bob Kerrey of Nebraska, who won the Medal of Honor while serving in Vietnam, and Florida Congressman Pete Peterson, who like McCain was a former POW. "We can now move on to common ground," Clinton declared at the close of his short speech announcing normalization. "Whatever divided us before, let us consign to the past." But Clinton seemed aware, wrote the columnist Mary McGrory, that after so long, there was really nothing more to be said about Vietnam. Still defensive about his own past, unable as always to convey any conviction about his choices, the president, McGrory wrote, now spoke "with an air of glumness and relief."

Clinton's words did seem an uncomfortable straddle across the great divide that still separated his country and generation. "Whatever we may think about the political decisions of the Vietnam era," he said, "the brave Americans who fought and died there had noble motives. They fought for the freedom and the independence of the Vietnamese people. Today the Vietnamese are independent" (the president's speechwriters apparently having thought it tactless to mention that the government whose independence Americans fought to protect had been defeated and overthrown by the Vietnamese we had fought against) and, the president went on, he believed normalizing relations "will help to extend the reach of freedom in Vietnam, and in so doing enable these fine veterans . . . to keep working for that freedom."

The president's logic may have been tortured and his decision so long delayed that it came with a sense of anticlimax. But the lack of drama mirrored the national reaction. Predictably, MIA activists denounced Clinton's action, insisting that the Vietnamese still had not come clean about missing Americans who might have survived. Many Vietnamese Americans also opposed the decision (though there were also many who quietly supported it). Some U.S. veterans responded bitterly—or others did on their behalf. "It's like none of those 58,000 names on the wall meant anything," said a woman whose husband had both legs blown off during the war. A Navy veteran told a reporter on the day of Clinton's announcement: "I guess Uncle Sam can go in there and make some money now. That's what this is all about." But most Americans seemed to agree, though without much passion, that the time had finally come to turn the page on the war and resume ties, at last, with the country where so many American men and illusions had died a quarter-century before. If some veterans were bitter, many others no doubt felt, as one of them wrote a few days after Clinton's announcement, that recognizing Vietnam did not "dishonor the memory of our fallen or missing comrades. It is to recognize the truth. The war is over."

Even Clinton's Republican opponents mounted no unified or concentrated attack on his decision, thanks largely to Senator McCain, whose gold-plated credentials both as a conservative Republican stalwart and as a war hero helped immeasurably to shield the president from criticism. McCain, despite having been savagely tortured while a prisoner in North Vietnam, had advocated normalization for several years, a stance in keeping with his steely personal determination not to let his prison-camp ordeal dominate the rest of his life. To McCain, the reasons for restoring relations with Hanoi were not sentimental but hard-headed and pragmatic. The U.S. national interest required that Asia should not fall under the economic or military dominance of any single power, McCain declared in a *Washington Post* article some weeks before Clinton's announcement. China's ambitions and its "growing economic and military might" could well become America's number-one international security problem, McCain went on. "It is, therefore, absolutely in our national security interests," he concluded, "to have an economically viable Vietnam strong enough to resist, in concert with its neighbors, the heavy-handed tactics of its great power neighbor."

If McCain was aware of the stunning irony imbedded in this reasoning, he gave no hint in his article. Nor did most of the other commentators who made the same geopolitical argument. But if the rationale for recognizing Vietnam was to contain China, as McCain and many others contended, then the country's long ordeal in Vietnam, and his own, had arisen from a colossal, devastating mistake. Fear of China was the paramount reason for U.S. intervention in Indochina, from the mid-1950s on. To U.S. policymakers of that era, the Vietnamese Communists were surrogates for Chinese power, which, if not stopped, would plunge past the borders of Indochina to engulf the rest of Southeast Asia, and beyond. Lyndon B. Johnson, then vice president and later the man who sent a half-million U.S. troops to Vietnam, warned President Kennedy in a 1961 memorandum:

> The battle against Communism must be joined in Southeast Asia with strength and determination to achieve success there—or the United States, inevitably, must surrender the Pacific and take up our defenses on our own shores. Asian Communism is compromised and contained by the maintenance of free nations on the subcontinent. Without this inhibitory influence, the island outposts—Philippines, Japan, Taiwan—have no security and the vast Pacific becomes a Red Sea.

Johnson's memo reflected the conventional thinking of the time. But its logic was thoroughly disproven by everything that followed America's failure. The Vietnamese Communists' victory in 1975, though humiliating and painful for the United States, brought about none of the dire consequences the domino theorists had predicted. After the war, nearly all of the supposed domino nations of Southeast Asia, far from tottering, entered an era of sustained economic success and political stability. Except in the Philippines, local Communist insurgencies all but vanished in the region. Far from advancing China's interests in Asia, Vietnam "proved to be China's most bitter foe and rival," wrote Nayan Chanda, one of the most knowledgeable of all Indochina experts. Seen from Beijing, the postwar strategic landscape was China's worst nightmare: "a strong, reunified Vietnam challenging China from the south in cahoots with China's bitter enemy in the north. . . . More than the United States," Chanda concluded, "it was China who lost the Vietnam war."

If U.S. leaders in the 1960s had had a clearer vision of the Asian realities, they might have seen Vietnam's war more clearly for what it was: a local struggle for mastery of Indochina, rather than a proxy struggle between major adversaries with all of Southeast Asia, or even the entire Pacific region, at stake. And seeing that, the American leadership might also have more accurately seen how limited U.S. interests were in Vietnam— interests that did not even come close to justifying the enormous cost of our doomed effort there. Instead, the United States based its decisions on a narrow and faulty perception that blotted out the complex particulars of Vietnamese politics and history. Through American lenses, Vietnam appeared only as a battleground for competing superpowers—a square on a chessboard, without distinctive shape or other features of its own.

More than any other single factor, it was that blindness that brought the American effort to its disastrous conclusion. Having never really looked at Vietnam for what it was, U.S. leaders never saw, until far too late, either the true nature of our enemy or the fatal weaknesses of the regime and society we tried, and failed, to save. Twenty years after that failure, American strategists' belated vision of a strong Communist Vietnam as a valuable "counterweight" to Communist China compounded the irony of those earlier miscalculations. But, as U.S. Secretary of State Warren Christopher—quoting an aphorism of the late Supreme Court Justice Felix Frankfurter—told Vietnamese leaders in Hanoi after ceremonies opening the new U.S. embassy there, "Wisdom comes so rarely, you should not complain when it is tardy."

III

The Vietnam that welcomed the American secretary of state in the summer of 1995 was still poor but a different, and more hopeful, place than it had been a decade earlier. On its borders, a shaky peace held in Cambodia, where a 1991 peace agreement had led to United Nations–supervised elections and installation of a new government in September 1993. To the north, the Vietnamese—in the transformed international climate left by the disappearance of the Soviet Union—had achieved a wary coexistence with China, in place of the harsh hostility of the past. Inside the country, meanwhile, a far-reaching reform policy called *doi moi* ("ren-

ovation"), similar in many respects to the successful economic reform policies undertaken under Deng Xiaoping's leadership in China, had gone a
long way toward unshackling Vietnam's economy from the paralytic grip
of orthodox Marxist central planning. Bringing with it a burst of entrepre-
neurship and an unevenly distributed but significant burst of prosperity,
doi moi had also inevitably begun to weaken the Communist Party's control of people's private affairs, of art and literature, and even of political life
and the news media.

Doi moi's principal author was the veteran Communist Nguyen
Van Linh, often called Vietnam's Gorbachev. In a way, though, Linh's story
was even more remarkable than Gorbachev's. Mikhail Gorbachev came out
of the generation that grew up in the Soviet Union after its great ordeals of
revolution, repression, slave-labor industrialization, and war. Linh, by contrast, belonged to Vietnam's revolutionary generation; his entire life, indeed, was bound up with the revolution and its dangers and the extraordinary discipline forged in long years of struggle, hardship, and sacrifice.

Born in Hanoi in 1915, Linh endured a dozen years in French prisons—his first sentence coming before he was fifteen years old—and another thirty years of repression and war, all of them, despite his northern
origins, in the contested South. It was exactly the same background that
forged the hardened, rigid, old-line Leninist leaders who, to the country's
sorrow, dominated the first postwar years. Yet Linh, somehow, emerged
from the fires of war and the closed, tightly controlled world of the revolutionary inner circle with more liberal, flexible views—unorthodox enough,
in fact, that his old-guard comrades attacked him for right-wing ideas and,
in 1982, kicked him out of the Politburo. Four years later, however, with
the country and its economy in such a shambles that even the party leaders could no longer defend their policies, the seventy-one-year-old Linh,
who had been quietly reinstated in mid-1985, was chosen by the Sixth
Party Congress to become the new secretary-general of the Vietnamese
Communist Party.

Like Deng Xiaoping in China (though neither man might welcome the comparison) Linh unhesitatingly put pragmatism ahead of Marxist dogma. "Socialism," he once said, "is prosperity." Under doi moi, the
leadership sharply reduced the authority of central planners, encouraged
private businesses, and set out to strengthen ties with the capitalist world
and attract foreign investors. Though the U.S. embargo kept Americans on
the sidelines, entrepreneurs from Western Europe and Japan found their
way to Vietnam in steadily increasing numbers.

Like other Communist reformers, Linh and his colleagues had to overcome powerful resistance among entrenched party bureaucrats and lower-level officials. Among other tactics, they sought to mobilize grassroots discontent against the encrusted power structure. An officially inspired campaign of self-criticism (*kiem thao*) and a policy of relatively free debate (*coi mo*—"open attitude") unleashed a torrent of complaints. One Saigon newspaper received thirteen thousand letters in a single weekend. Most public criticisms had to do with economic conditions, but complaints about abusive, inept, or corrupt officials ran a close second. Similar charges appeared regularly in a new column in the Communist Party's daily newspaper, *Nhan Dan*. The column was signed with the initials N. V. L.—the same as Linh's. Most Vietnamese correctly assumed their new party leader was the author, though Linh once archly told an interviewer that the initials stood for "Noi Va Lam," which means "Speak and Act." (Linh was less coy in a 1987 meeting with Vietnamese writers and artists, where he not only acknowledged the column as his but also remarked that some unnamed critics were not happy with him for comments that "blacken the regime.")

Under Linh and Do Muoi, who succeeded him as secretary-general in 1991, Vietnam's battered economy began to recover. Private businesses thrived, especially in Saigon—only rarely called by its new official name, Ho Chi Minh City. With capitalism, glitzy Western commercialism and pop culture also flourished, in ever more ironic contrast with an increasingly threadbare Marxist ideology and the official myths of revolutionary sacrifice and glory. Rather than the Communists' tradition of austerity, cooperation, and shared suffering, Saigon suggested exactly the opposite. ("Remind me," an American banker in Saigon asked wryly, "who won this war?") Unemployment, crime, and prostitution mushroomed, and with them official corruption, drug use, and AIDS. In 1995, 183,000 addicts were officially registered with the same government that had claimed, ten years earlier, that drug addiction had been wiped out. By other estimates, the true number of addicts was at least 500,000.

On Saigon's crowded streets, hustlers, hawkers, prostitutes, destitute war veterans, and homeless children mingled under splashy, colorful advertisements for credit cards and video recorders. Commercial billboards overshadowed the old black-and-white photographs of Ho Chi Minh and the revolutionary slogans lettered on fading streetcorner banners. Dealmakers met over expensive imported scotch and brandy in glossy hotel bars or at the pricey Song Be golf club outside the city; youthful crowds in the latest American-style fashions crowded into nightclubs where deafening rock music pounded from loudspeakers into hot, smoky nights; automobile showrooms displayed luxury cars at outlandish prices (a Mercedes-Benz sedan on offer for $420,000, for example) while not far away, some of the city's thousands of amputees pushed themselves along on crude carts made of boards and roller-skate wheels.

The new wealth generated by foreign and local entrepreneurs and the accompanying pop-culture boom nourished a trendy, pleasure-seeking (not to say decadent) youth culture amid Saigon's new privileged class. Openly scornful of the old revolutionary pieties, these children of a new commercial elite lived by the watchword phrase *song voi*—"living quickly." The "king" of youthful high society was said to be a French Vietnamese named Ly Hong Tan, who became even more notorious after police raided a lavish karaoke birthday party he threw for himself in the luxurious Century Saigon Hotel. According to the Saigon press, Tan had rented an entire floor for his party, where numerous guests stripped off their clothes and indulged in drugs and sex. Among those arrested, besides Tan, were several prominent entertainers.

If some Vietnamese were getting rich, though, the number living in poverty was also growing. Official statistics in 1994 showed wealthy Vietnamese, calculated to be 7 to 10 percent of the population, had, on average, incomes forty times higher than those in the bottom 30 percent. Unemployment remained high: the official estimate was 15 percent, with a far higher percentage working at casual or part-time jobs because no full-time employment was available.

Seven hundred miles to the north, Hanoi remained less frenetic and more puritan than its wilder southern cousin. But there, too, old symbols and styles had undergone an unsettling change. In the National Economics University, instead of Marxist tracts, a visitor found faculty members using the American board game Monopoly as a teaching aid. A sidestreet cafe called the Green Bamboo became a hangout for long-haired young European and American travelers "who look exactly like the hippies of 20 years ago," one travel writer noted, "only now they are called backpackers and may be entering Harvard Business School next semester." At other bars, foreign customers could sit with Vietnamese hostesses over beers at five dollars a glass, listening to the pounding beat of heavy-metal rock music.

Presiding over this sometimes surreal landscape was a leadership that was, as the *Boston Globe*'s Paul Quinn-Judge observed in a particularly perceptive dispatch from Hanoi, "both obsessed with change and terrified by it"—eager for development and greater prosperity, but fearful that their own power might be swept away along with the old rules and structures of their system. Meanwhile, the leadership itself quickly moved to cash in on the new rules, illustrating, as Quinn-Judge tartly observed, "one of the rules of post-Communist development in the former socialist world: Ideology dies, but the ruling class remains. And the old elite usually becomes quite rich by using its power and prestige to give itself a head start in the world of commerce." Exactly as in South Vietnam before the revolution, close family members of national leaders made a visible bonanza out of their connections: prominent among the newly rich were said to be the son-in-law of party leader Do Muoi and the wife of Prime Minister Vo Van Kiet. Bribery and graft pervaded the system—by some reports, on a scale approaching the legendary corruption of Indonesia or the Philippines.

Amid these contradictions, Western memories of the war, cycled through American popular culture and then reexported to Vietnam, reappeared as props for a kind of bizarre, rock-video fantasy of the past. At a popular cafe called Apocalypse Now, the sound-track voice of actor Robin Williams boomed out the old Armed Forces Radio greeting from the sound system: "GOOOOOD MOOOORNNINNG, VEE-YET-NAMMMM!" Meanwhile, images of Vietnam reappeared in the West as new, exotic icons for Western travelers and consumers. "If you want to enjoy a fabulous Asian country before high-tech development overwhelms it," one tourism consultant burbled in a glossy travel magazine, "this is precisely the moment to head for Viet Nam." A fashion spread in the "Style" pages of the *New York Times Magazine* used photos of village and street scenes in Vietnam ("one of the rare places where one can still experience true glamour") to publicize "the new Indo-chic clothes" which, according to the paper's fashion experts, had "intoxicated . . . the foot soldiers of style." The photos showed peasants, shopkeepers, a mother and daughter at a Hanoi temple, a farm girl tending a flock of ducks, and two other willowy young women in a ricefield. The captions promoted such items as a simple black dress ($1,610 at New York's Chanel Boutique), peasant-style linen jacket and pants ($840 at Bergdorf Goodman), a farm girl's jacket in "periwinkle blue" raw silk ($1,460, by Richard Tyler), and a woman's vest and sarong ($1,096, by Ralph Lauren). If any of the magazine's caption writers were aware that even the lowest of these prices represented four or five years' income for the average Vietnamese worker, they evidently did not consider that fact worth mentioning.

It all didn't seem to have much to do with socialism or Ho Chi

Minh or Vietnam's tradition of heroic nationalism. No doubt, some of those who had struggled and sacrificed during the war found it hard to reconcile the new Vietnam with their wartime visions. Not all the old revolutionaries felt that way, however. Karl Marx never said people had to be poor, remarked the eighty-three-year-old Tran Van Giau, revered as one of Ho Chi Minh's oldest and closest associates. Economic reform did bring with it some adverse side effects, Giau acknowledged in a conversation with *National Geographic* writer Tracy Dahlby, but, he went on, "poverty is always more threatening to society than wealth." Even so, Dahlby asked, wasn't he bothered by the garish commercial advertisements and Saigon's proliferating disco scene? Giau gave him a sharp look. He didn't know about Dahlby's young days, the old Marxist theoretician and underground revolutionary replied quizzically, but "even I used to go dancing when I was 18!"

With economic change, inevitably, fresh political winds began to blow. In the more liberal climate following the Sixth Party Congress, the government announced in July 1987 the release of 6,685 political prisoners from re-education camps. Another 6,404 were freed early in 1988 in time for Tet, the traditional lunar new year festival. Meanwhile, both within the Communist Party hierarchy and without, more and more Vietnamese began to speak out for greater democracy and freedom. Often, Linh seemed receptive. At a remarkable session of the Vietnam Writers and Artists Association in Hanoi in the fall of 1987, Linh listened with apparent sympathy as one participant after another urged an end to restrictions and censorship and the Leninist concept of making art serve as propaganda for the Communist Party's policies and goals. Centralized party control and bureaucracy, the writer Nguyen Khac Vien told the meeting, had hurt the arts even more than they had hurt the economy: "The people have been told how many kilos of rice to eat each month; the poets have been told how many poems to write each month. Everything is decided from above—how to write, how to think. It is forbidden for writers to create or think for themselves. In this situation, human beings lose their nature and become like machines."

Nguyen Quang Sang, a writer whose own works had been restricted for many years, told Linh bluntly that party officials had a history of "condemning the best works and praising the bad ones. It should surprise no one," Sang added, "that the worst work flourished and the good works disappeared." And the critic Nguyen Dan Manh declared: "The arts are like birds. Birds in cages sing badly. But leaders are afraid that if they let the birds go free they will be uncontrollable. Good leaders can let the birds fly free and sing their best songs."

Linh, for his part, seemed to endorse artistic freedom—though he also appeared to link it to political aims of his own. "I have heard some comrades say that artists and writers have been restricted in writing and are often afraid of writing something unclear that is 'not in line,' 'anti-Party,' or 'against Party policy,'" he told the meeting. "I am aware of this and I understand you. . . . I think that we have to push away the darkness in just the way that we have to weed a rice field so that the rice grows strong. The good man and good works need room to grow—we must push away bad people and bad works to make way for them. Our challenge today is to dare to expose bad men and bad works"—meaning, presumably, the lower level cadres and bureaucrats who were frustrating Linh's reform policies.

The loosening of official controls released a burst of films, novels, plays, poems, and short stories that spotlighted Vietnam's economic and moral crisis with merciless frankness. Visiting Saigon in the spring of 1988, *New York Times* reporter Barbara Crossette found "a bitter sense of political abandonment and betrayal" reflected in the new wave of literature and film. Among other examples, she described a documentary called *Kindness* (which, Crossette was told, aired on Hanoi television only after Linh himself intervened). The film showed images of privileged officials juxtaposed with searing scenes of poverty: "people in a people's republic collapsing of hunger in the street, people working as beasts of burden." In Saigon, Crossette saw an experimental play, written by a young cameraman who had come south from Hanoi to work in a "more dynamic" atmosphere, savagely mocking one aspect of contemporary Vietnamese life after another, to enthusiastic applause and laughter from the audience. In the play, Crossette recounted, a robber keeps hijacking a script from a penniless writer, forcing him at gunpoint to rewrite scenes that have displeased influential people. Finally, the play has become so bad that the writer asks his persecutor how he will persuade anyone to stay in the theater. "At the intermission," the robber replies, "we announce that if the audience goes home, they will find things even worse there."

Along with artistic protest, the new, more liberal climate also brought a new openness in Vietnamese political life. In the National Assembly, where a number of nonparty members had been approved as candidates in the April 1987 election, issues and policies were now more freely debated than ever in the past. Increasingly, public debate burst out of the boundaries the Communist authorities hoped to place on free discussion.

Calls for greater democracy along with economic reform began to surface more and more frequently. One important platform for pro-democracy statements was a group of veterans of the Southern revolution, among them Tran Van Giau and Gen. Tran Van Tra, deputy commander of the victorious Ho Chi Minh Campaign at the end of the war. With the moral authority of their own former service to the revolution, members of this group—the Club of Former Resistance Fighters, which eventually claimed a membership of four thousand veterans—sought to function as a kind of loyal opposition, supporting Linh's reforms but going far beyond the Communist leaders' policies on political liberalization.*

A number of the nonparty, nongovernmental associations known as "mass organizations" also became forums for advocating political reform. "Why has our country come to this dark moment?" asked Nguyen Huu Tho, wartime president of the National Liberation Front and the Provisional Revolutionary Government of South Vietnam, in a remarkably forceful 1989 speech to the Fatherland Front, the associations' umbrella organization. "It is not because our people are lazy, unskilled, inactive, or uninventive. . . . The root causes of failure are the weight of our conservative bureaucratic system, the lack of democracy on the part of the government, and struggle on the part of the people. . . . The conditions exist for struggle, but the people dare not move."

Declaring that Vietnam's "biggest weakness is that we have no real democracy," Tho challenged the basic Leninist principle that the Communist Party should have sole authority over national policy. Nonparty institutions, such as the courts and the various "front" organizations that were intended (like the wartime Liberation Front) to represent a broader spectrum of the population, should strive for genuine independence, Tho asserted—and that meant challenging the Communist authorities. "Do not be deluded that the conservatives will automatically hand democracy over to the people, or that the people will automatically carry out reforms," he said. "These things depend on struggle, including struggle in the mass organizations such as the National Assembly, the Fatherland Front, and others. . . . Democracy will not come as a gift, but must be obtained by struggle."

Two years later, on the eve of the party's Seventh Congress, an unpublished but widely circulated commentary by the dissident intellectual Hoang Minh Chinh attacked in scathing terms the party's policies, officials,

---

*The government periodically detained leaders of this group and in 1990 replaced it with a more pliant, official organization of Southern veterans.

and its constitutionally guaranteed absolute power. The party's monolithic power was the reason Vietnam lacked democracy, Chinh wrote; its officials at all levels were guilty of using that power "to abuse their authority, obtain special privileges, engage in corruption, suppress the people, practice deception, and manifest false virtue," and their "outmoded" policies were heading in a direction "contrary to the dominant course of the world . . . [where] the socialist model is now actually falling apart before the eyes of all mankind." The fall of Communism in Eastern Europe, he added, wasn't caused by "imperialist capitalism's attacks from outside. . . . It was caused by a hidden cancer in the body of socialism that grew and exploded."

Party leaders clung to the view that Vietnam must evolve toward "Marxist democracy, not capitalist democracy." But in the context of economic reform and a raw but thriving free-market system, it grew less and less clear what Marxism meant, or what relevance it might still have for any Vietnamese, whether they belonged to the party or not. Increasingly, the word *Communist* appeared to refer only to the name of the ruling party, not to any set of beliefs or principles. The party press and official speeches and resolutions were still laced with phrases from the old Marxist vocabulary, but they seemed more and more empty of meaning. It was as if someone had gone through the dictionary and erased all the definitions, leaving only the words.

"I don't care if you want to call this system Communism or capitalism, just so long as the people are getting rich," one official said. Phan Dinh Dieu, a mathematician and one of a group of prominent intellectuals urging greater openness in Vietnamese political life, called Communism an "irrelevant" ideology that was no longer believed even by most party members and should be abandoned. The party retained some public goodwill because it had achieved national independence, Dieu told an interviewer in 1992, but it would "wither and die" if it tried to maintain an outmoded system of one-party rule.

If the myths and slogans of the past were losing their power in all sectors of Vietnamese society, by many accounts they had become almost entirely meaningless to the young, who had grown up amid the poverty and disillusion of postwar Communist rule with only dim memories, or none at all, of the heroic wartime victory. The writer Nguyen Manh Tuan, whose novel *Loving and Living* portrayed four young Vietnamese losing their idealism as they discover the realities of their society, seemed to be describing an entire generation as lost and morally adrift. Young people in Vietnam, Tuan remarked in a 1988 interview, "have nothing to believe in."

The party's response to the growing demands for democracy was erratic. Though policies in general were more liberal, from time to time writers' works were still banned and religious and political dissidents and human-rights campaigners still faced persecution or imprisonment for their activities. The novelist Duong Thu Huong, whose devastating portrayals of venal and oppressive party officials won her a wide and devoted public following, was expelled from the Communist Party in 1990 and imprisoned for seven months the following year on charges of attempting to smuggle "reactionary documents" (that is, her own writings) out of the country. The charge was eventually dropped and Huong was freed, but her works remained unavailable—not officially banned, but not approved for publication or sale, which had the same effect.

In late 1991, Nguyen Dan Que, a physician who was the first person in Vietnam to join the human rights organization Amnesty International, was tried in a Saigon court for "subversive activities" and for denigrating "the leading role of the Communist Party in the liberation struggle." Que, who had already spent ten years in prison from 1978 to 1988, was given a twenty-year sentence on the new charges. In another case, eight Vietnamese who attempted to circulate a newsletter on press-freedom issues were arrested, held without trial from November 1990 to March 1993, and then suddenly tried and convicted of "subversion."

Other writers, intellectuals, and religious leaders were periodically arrested and tried on similar charges. The summer of 1995 saw another wave of repression, including the arrest of the seventy-five-year-old Hoang Minh Chinh, who subsequently received a twelve-month prison sentence. Also targeted were several leading members of the Club of Former Resistance Fighters, the organization of former southern revolutionaries that had become a focal point for criticism of the regime. When police arrived to arrest Nguyen Ho, one of the founders of the club, Ho reportedly handed them the text of his latest essay, in which he tartly commented that Vietnam's Communist leaders were rapidly establishing friendly relations with "former enemies of the people" such as the Americans, the French, the Japanese, and the Chinese. Why, Ho asked, could not Vietnam's Communist Party "reconcile with its own Vietnamese brothers whom it has oppressed and victimized? Are dollars the condition for reconciliation? . . . If that is the truth, then it is a great sadness and shame for the unfortunate people of Vietnam. However, I hope that is never the truth."

Ho, who had already been detained on two earlier occasions, in-

formed the officers who came to arrest him that he would rather kill himself than be imprisoned again—at which, Human Rights Watch reported,
the policemen "left to consult their superiors." Unexpectedly, his defiance
was successful, at least for the moment; instead of taking him to prison, the
authorities left Ho at his Saigon home, though under police surveillance.

Even with periodic crackdowns, policies toward dissent were erratic. While some dissidents were being tried and imprisoned, others were
being freed, among them long-time prisoners such as the poet Nguyen Chi
Thien, the Catholic priest Joseph Le Thanh Que, and the writer Doan Quoc
Sy. For many Vietnamese, the air seemed genuinely freer than in any past
period of Communist rule. "It is more breathable," said Trinh Con Son, the
singer and poet whose songs about divided families, grieving lovers, and
the sorrows of war had made him one of the best-known dissidents in
wartime South Vietnam. Despite his record of opposition to the Saigon
government, which regularly and futilely banned his songs as "defeatist,"
Son had been banished by the Communists to a remote village for four
years after the war, and since then had written only love songs, avoiding
political subjects. There were still "forbidden zones" for artists, Son told
Henry Kamm of the *New York Times* in 1993, but there was not an obvious
or explicit climate of repression; "today, the dictatorship is imperceptible."

A mid-1995 survey by the New York–based organization Human
Rights Watch agreed that there were "areas of gradual improvement" in
Vietnam:

> Restrictions on everyday life for most citizens have eased noticeably as the
> market economy takes root. Travel within the country is easier. Surveil-
> lance by Vietnam's extensive network of monitors, from neighbors to
> plainclothes police, has become less intrusive in the lives of most people,
> although those whom the government regards as "reactionary" are still
> placed on tight watch. The regularly scheduled worship services of many
> major religions now proceed unhindered, although the government con-
> tinues to exercise control over virtually all other aspects of religion, from
> ordination of clergy to approval of sermons.

Like other observers, the authors of the Human Rights Watch report found the Vietnamese political atmosphere full of contradictory currents. The extent of political freedoms and the effects of national policy
varied widely from place to place, depending on local leaders and conditions. Censorship persisted, but so did "a lively black market in forbidden

literature." A growing number of civic associations, formed to promote action on such matters as the environment, public health, or social problems such as prostitution, became forums for discussion—often vigorously critical—of government policies. But the authorities did not hesitate to crush those organizations it considered dangerous.

Similar conflicting impulses were apparent in the developing field of law. The very process of writing laws was a step away from arbitrary rule: instead of simply being told what to do by Communist Party bureaucrats, people could now turn to a legal system to resolve disputes and manage the details of civil life. There was no way to create laws without at the same time establishing legal rights; defining a crime, obviously, also defines what is *not* a crime. But in many areas, the new laws were written to protect the Communist Party's power, including its control of ideas. The criminal code's list of crimes against national security included offenses such as "anti-socialist propaganda" and "undermining the policy of unity"; the 1993 law on publishing strictly prohibited publication of any works "distorting history, rejecting revolutionary achievements [or] discrediting . . . national heroes."

Amid all these ambiguities, there was no way to predict how Vietnamese political life would evolve as a new century approached: whether the Communist Party would cling to its constitutionally guaranteed supremacy or give way to a new, pluralistic system. What did seem certain was that just as in the rest of the Communist world, Vietnam's leaders would face challenges in direct, paradoxical proportion to their success in bringing the country out of its economic morass. Greater economic freedom and material prosperity would inevitably give rise to greater demands for political freedoms as well. And while "the current generation of Vietnamese leaders may not have to face that dilemma," observed the scholar William J. Duiker, "the next one undoubtedly will."

IV

The last myths to weaken were those surrounding the war. Shedding outdated Marxist dogma was one thing; relinquishing the epic legend of Vietnam's victories over France and the United States was something else. The legend was sacred: the war and its suffering could only be remembered as glorious, not tragic.

In a poem in the early 1980s called "White Circle" (the image is of the traditional band of white cloth worn around the head as a sign of mourning) the poet Pham Tien Duat wrote about "the expected silence after the war" that locked away memories of personal loss or sorrow. The poem's next line, "There is no greater loss than death," caused Duat "much difficulty," he said laconically during a 1993 visit to the United States. Notes supplied by his Vietnamese translator explained that the "difficulty" included a ten-year expulsion from the Communist Party for suggesting that death was more important than the revolution or its goals. The full poem, as Duat read it to an American audience during his U.S. visit, seems an expression of purely private sorrow, with no political message at all:

> The smoke of bombs rises to the sky
> and makes a black circle.
> On the ground, white circles are made.

> My friend and I go on in silence;
> the expected silence [i.e., about suffering and loss]
> after the war.

> There is no greater loss than death.
> The white mourning headband
> takes the shape of a zero
> and inside that white circle,
> inside the head of my friend,
> the war goes on. *

Yet the authorities' harsh response showed that even those seemingly non-political lines were considered to tarnish the heroic memory of the war—the memory Vietnam's leaders were determined to preserve.

For years, the official vision of the war prevailed, at least on the surface. Foreigners regularly reported, in wonder and at times with something approaching envy, the impression that the Vietnamese had successfully done what Americans could not: reconciled with their past. "I was constantly amazed at how unmarked they seemed by the experience . . . the scars all seemed to have healed," William Broyles Jr. wrote about the Viet-

---

*During the war, Duat was a military journalist whose accounts of ordinary soldiers' lives won him a considerable popular following. By the time of his U.S. visit, he had been reinstated in the Communist Party and was editor of the Hanoi literary magazine *Van Nge*.

namese veterans he met during his 1984 visit. Compared with American veterans, those former Vietnamese soldiers seemed so free of doubt, confusion, and guilt that Broyles wondered "if they looked into their selves, in our Western self-infatuated way, at all. . . . They were sustained then, and are now, by simple ideas, believed without question."

Other foreign visitors came away with similar impressions. One journalist commented in a 1994 dispatch from Hanoi that the "American war" had become, for the Vietnamese, "little more than a blip on the screen" of their long history of turmoil and violence. A travel writer, speaking of Vietnamese under the age of thirty but by implication including the rest of the population as well, marveled at their "genuine friendliness" toward American visitors and added breezily that "it takes only hours to become aware that the American war is as distant and unimportant to them as World War I is to the average American."

Those reactions, and others like them, almost certainly reflected something more than the Vietnamese effort to perpetuate the official patriotic mythology of the war, though that was part of it. The idea that Vietnamese veterans and civilians really bore no permanent scars from the war also echoed long-time *American* myths about the Vietnamese, and about Asians in general. The condescension was unconscious, no doubt, but to believe that the Vietnamese had so easily buried their own experiences—or that they were satisfied by "simple ideas," or that a foreigner could truly fathom the war's impact in a few hours—came disturbingly close to believing that they didn't quite fully share human feelings. It recalled old clichés about the cheapness of life in Asia, reflected in Gen. William Westmoreland's notorious wartime comment that the Vietnamese didn't value human life in the same way Americans did.

In fact, the war wasn't buried as deeply as many foreigners supposed. Nor was it plausible that it would be. The war had cost, by most estimates, between one-and-a-half and two million Vietnamese lives. In its aftermath, another million had emigrated. Hundreds of thousands, both soldiers and civilians, had been wounded. North and South, nearly every man over the age of forty had served, on one side or the other. And their service, unlike the one-year tour experienced by nearly all U.S. soldiers, usually involved many years of combat. More than 300,000 veterans were permanently disabled by their wounds.

During those years, millions of acres of farmland and forest were poisoned, countless villages obliterated, families torn apart, and lives disrupted on a scale that left virtually no family untouched. It was simply not possible that such deep wounds would be so quickly healed, or so easily forgotten, whatever gauze of mythic glory was wrapped around them. Tragic memories remained just beneath the surface, like the tons of buried shrapnel and the litter of unexploded shells, bombs, and mines lying hidden and still deadly in Vietnam's earth.

Like the Americans, the Vietnamese had their share of soldiers who were mentally maimed by the war. Thousands were living out their lives in mental hospitals—often, squalid cages where underfed, emaciated patients huddled in rags on filthy floors, clawed at each other in bloody fights, and spent their nights screaming out old terrors. Additional thousands of mentally ill veterans were living with relatives or receiving treatment at regular hospitals, Vietnamese officials acknowledged.

While bearing their physical and mental scars, war veterans also bore, along with the rest of their countrymen, the terrible economic hardships of the postwar period. The same authorities who so jealously guarded the heroic legend of the war were hardly generous in their treatment of the returned heroes. Only about one-fifth of war veterans were receiving any form of pension, their official association reported in 1994. The million or more who were veterans of the vanquished South Vietnamese forces, of course, received no benefits of any kind.

Among the many families whose walls displayed the red-bordered death certificate issued for those killed in the war, many knew no more than the bare fact lettered on the documents: that their son or husband or father had died for the country. They were not told where or how their men had been killed or where the remains might be found. It was as if they had simply been vaporized by the war. Some had been hastily buried in remote battle sites by comrades who were later killed themselves. Others were bull-dozed into unmarked mass graves by American troops (some of whom, quite possibly, later joined the loud chorus of veterans condemning the Vietnamese for failing to account for every last missing American). Still others were never buried at all but were lost forever in thick jungle or flooded ricefields or muddy canals, or so pulverized by bombs or shellfire that nothing remained for burial.

Altogether, by Vietnamese estimates, approximately 300,000 soldiers were still missing long after the war. So were many civilians, among them Prime Minister Vo Van Kiet's first wife and two children, killed by U.S. fire in 1966. Even when remains were found, as they sometimes were, there was seldom any way to identify them, since Vietnam had neither the sophisticated equipment nor the kind of records (dental charts, for example) that forensic specialists need. "We can tell if bones are animal or human, but that is about it," one searcher admitted.

For the families of the missing, the chance of locating a particular grave or body was infinitesimal. Still, thousands tried to do what they could, placing newspaper advertisements with faded photos in the hope of catching some former comrade's eye, or traveling to former war zones with yellowing copies of the death notifications received from military authorities years before, which might have had some vague mention of a date or place. Some relatives even consulted psychics. Most, though, had to reconcile themselves to the reality that their missing men would never be found and that the traditional ceremonies of proper burial and paying respects to the dead could not be observed.

Without those rituals, Vietnamese tradition taught that the dead could not rest but would be condemned to spend eternity as restless ghosts wandering the earth, unable to depart for the next world. Like memories of the war itself, the ghosts of lost soldiers haunted the country's soul, sighing and moaning, as a disillusioned veteran named Kien sees them in his dreams in Bao Ninh's novel *The Sorrow of War*, "whispering as they floated around like pale vapors, shredded with bullet-holes." The ghosts in Kien's dreams—from a place with so many unburied corpses it was called the Jungle of Screaming Souls—seemed to represent his own restless memories, too: "They moved into his sleep as though they were mirrors surrounding him."

Coiled within Vietnam's sorrow, like a hidden spring, was the forbidden thought: *What had all the sacrifice been for? And was it worth it?*

Many, perhaps most, hid their doubts, not only because it was dangerous to express them but also because the truth might be too painful. "Was it worth what we sacrificed?" asked one elderly man, a veteran of the French war. Holding a picture of his lost son, one among the hundreds of thousands who vanished while fighting the Americans, the old soldier paused, considered the question, then went on: "I don't want to say." When Anh-Huong Thi Tu, a forty-three-year-old Vietnamese American from Virginia, went back to visit her homeland in 1993, she sensed that people felt "cheated and hollow" at a victory that had brought only more hardship and sacrifice. But, Tu wrote, even among her own relatives in Hanoi, no one wanted to speak about their wartime experiences. When she asked for details about their lives during the war, Tu recalled, "typically, people would change the subject, as if everyone wanted to forget that whole chapter. My theory is that their wartime sacrifices and losses were so immense that in order to carry on with their lives today, psychologically, northern Vietnamese cannot afford to reflect on those grim years. What would they find in looking back?"

But even the power of the state and its official myths could not keep such thoughts silenced forever. Twenty years after the war, writers and artists were beginning to show it in a different light: not glorious, but unheroic, cruel, and tragic, full of terror and crushed illusions. "The future lied to us," reflects the veteran Kien in *The Sorrow of War*, who—like his creator—spent so long at war that when peace finally came, he and his comrades "were more amazed than happy. . . . War had been their whole world. So many lives, so many fates. The end of the fighting was like the deflation of an entire landscape, with fields, mountains, and rivers collapsing in on themselves." His generation, Kien recalls, "threw itself into the war enthusiastically, making its own blood flow, and causing the blood of others to flow in torrents." But those who survived found the peace "painful, bitter, and sad. . . . Justice may have won, but cruelty, death, and inhuman violence have also won."

In one of the novel's memorable passages, another soldier, a military truck driver who has been removing corpses from the Jungle of Screaming Souls, tells Kien about his conversations with the ghosts:

> "Not a night goes by without them waking me up to have a talk [the driver says]. It terrifies me. All kinds of ghosts, new soldiers, old soldiers, soldiers from the 10th Division, the 2nd Division, the 320th Mobile Forces, 559th Corps, sometimes women, and every now and again some southern souls, from Saigon." The driver spoke as though it were common knowledge.
> "Meet any old friends?"
> "Sure! Even some from my old village. Guys from my first unit. Once I met a cousin who died way back in sixty-five."
> "Do you speak to them?"
> "Yes, but . . . well, differently. The way you speak in hell. There are no sounds, no words. It's hard to describe. It's like when you're dreaming. . . ."
> "If we found a way to tell them news of a victory, would they be happier?" Kien asked.
> "Come on! Even if we could, what would be the point? People in hell don't give a damn about wars."

Eventually, Kien asks, "But isn't peace better than war?" The driver answers bitterly: "This kind of peace? In this kind of peace it seems people have unmasked themselves and revealed their true, horrible selves. So much blood, so many lives were sacrificed—for what?" At the end of their conversation, he tells Kien, "When we're demobbed I'll stop driving. I'll carry my guitar everywhere and be a singer. Sing and tell stories. 'Gentlemen, brothers and sisters, please listen to my painful story, then I'll sing you a horror song of our times.'"

Similar in spirit was Duong Thu Huong's *Novel Without a Name*, one of the "reactionary" works she had been accused of trying to smuggle abroad. Like Kien in *The Sorrow of War*, Huong's protagonist, Quan, is also a North Vietnamese soldier who has spent years in combat but can no longer believe in the official patriotic myths of his country's glorious struggle or that the party leaders truly represent the "people" in whose name the revolution, with all its sacrifice, has been waged. Huong's characters speak scathingly about the cant, corruption, and selfishness of Communist officials. "Little despots . . . ignoramuses who never even learned the most basic morals," one furious villager tells Quan. "They study their Marxism-Leninism, and then come and pillage our vegetable gardens and rice fields with Marx's blessing."

In another passage toward the end of the book, as Quan and his detachment are poised for the final victory over the Saigon forces, another soldier named Kha stuns Quan with the question, "Do the people really exist? . . . I've thought a lot," Kha continues. "I also listen to everything that's said. You see, the people, they do exist from time to time, but they're only a shadow. When they need rice, the people are the buffalo that pulls the plow. When they need soldiers, they cover the people with armor, put guns in the people's hands. When all is said and done, at the festivals, when it comes time for the banquets, they put the people on an altar, and feed them incense and ashes. But the real food, that's always for them."

After listening to that extraordinary diatribe, Quan is shattered. "I was cold. . . . A cold more intense than all the rainy seasons on the Truong Son mountain range, than all the water and jungle fog. It was as if the cold of all those years had suddenly frozen my heart. . . . Deep down inside, I cursed Kha and yet, inexplicably, I knew he was right."

Surprisingly, *The Sorrow of War* was published in Vietnam, though Bao Ninh was sharply attacked in official publications for his outlook on the war. *Novel Without a Name* was not published, although pirated English-language copies did circulate.

While wrestling with their own memories, some Vietnamese made space in their remembrance for American ghosts, too.

Visiting the central Vietnamese city of Da Nang with a group of American poets in 1990, Bill Ehrhart was given a poem called "A Vietnamese Bidding Farewell to the Remains of an American." Speaking to a dead U.S. soldier, the poem begins:

Was your plane on fire, or did you die
of bullet wounds, or fall down exhausted?
Just so you died in the forest, alone.

Only the two of us, a woodcutter and his wife,
dug this grave for you, burned joss sticks,
prayed for you to rest in peace.

And the writer Larry Rottmann, a former infantryman, told of encountering another Vietnamese who took time to pay respect to a dead enemy:

"The airplane crashed into my rice paddy on the night of December 21st, 1972,"
says the old farmer from Vinh.
"It fell like a star out of the heavens,
and knocked me and my wife right out of our bed!

"The army soldiers who came running said it was a fighting jet,
and that the driver was still inside.
But after the terrible burning was over,
it looked only like a huge lump of charcoal in my field.

"My wife was afraid of the plane, and wouldn't go near.
But I knew its hurting days were finished,
and since the American had no one to say prayers over him,
I built a small altar on the wreckage.

"Each week, I still burn some joss for that young man
who died all alone so far from his ancestors.
Many times the local cadres have ordered me to stop doing that,
but they are all too young to know about important things." *

---

*©1993 by Larry Rottmann. Reprinted by permission.

EPILOGUE

Eleven years and a few days after the Vietnam Veterans Memorial was dedicated, the sky over Washington was gray and chilly, with low clouds the color of ashes. Piles of brown leaves covered the spongy ground and made little whispering noises on the paved walks. Jets swooshed low overhead, descending across the gray Potomac toward Washington's National Airport.

Until I stood in front of it again, I hadn't remembered the exact way the names are arranged on the wall. They're inscribed chronologically by the date of death, but they don't start at one end and finish at the other. Instead, they begin at the center, where the two wings come together to form a shallow V. The names run from there to the far right panel, then resume at the far left and continue back toward the middle, so the list ends where it began, closing a circle of sorrow, with the names of the last dead adjoining those of the first.

One of the names on that last panel, about halfway up, is Lt. Col. Burr Willey's.

Willey was a lanky, soft-spoken Virginian who was killed a couple of hundred feet from me in the very first battle I saw in Vietnam. He was there that spring day in 1972 as an adviser with the Republic of Vietnam's Twenty-first Division—one of Saigon's worst, led by a commander whose incompetence and thievery stood out even in an army where corruption and poor leadership were not the exception, but the rule. I was too new then to know about the Twenty-first Division or to appreciate how hard it must have been, in that last sour year of an unsuccessful war that most Americans already wanted only to forget, for Colonel Willey to still find any worthwhile purpose in what he was doing. Later, whenever I remembered Willey, I hoped that he did still somehow feel it was worth it, that he hadn't died on that nameless stretch of roadside north of Saigon believing it was pointless to be there at all.

Along the base of the wall that November afternoon there were little tokens of remembrance. Flags, bunches of flowers, photos, notes—the kinds of things people had been leaving at the wall for years, messages of love and sorrow to the dead. Leaning against one panel was a brand-new book, with an inscription inside the cover: "For the Echos of 2/7, Dec. 10 65, Love you forever." A few yards away was a bouquet of red and white silk carnations, tied with a red-white-and-blue ribbon. Pinned to the ribbon was this note, dated Veterans Day even though it must have been placed there a few days later:

> *Nov. 11 1993*
> *Veterans Day*
> *To my son & brother Pfc. John D. Slesh Jr. You are gone but not forgotten after 25 yrs. May 8 1967 Viet Nam. May God keep you in his love and care until we all meet in Heaven. Sadly missed by Mom and M. Sgt. Thomas Slesh, your brother Danna and Tonya & J. D., your sister Barbara McCarthy and Chuck. May you Rest in Peace. May the Perpetual Light shine upon you.*
> *We love you. Mom.*

I found Pfc. John Daniel Slesh Jr.'s name on the wall, and later in one of the alphabetical directories placed on stands near the wall to help people find specific names. His home town was Washington, Pennsylvania, and he had died one month and twenty-four days after his twenty-first birthday.

Back the other way—exactly at the center of the V again, though I didn't notice that right away—there was a small flag with a paper heart, cut out by hand like a child's valentine, pinned to it. I knelt down to read what was written on it: "Love from your brothers. Ulster County Vets. Donated by Jim O'Byrne."

I started to stand up and then noticed another note, on a tiny scrap of paper lying flat on the low ledge of black marble that runs along the base of the wall. It was no more than an inch long, torn from the corner of a larger sheet as if to mark someone's page in a book. It had been carefully placed exactly at the left edge of the crease where the two wings meet, under the names of the very last dead and the carved date 1975—as if whoever put it there had walked along and read all 58,183 names, in order, and then bent down to leave his message at the very end.

The note was written in pencil. It said only, "I'm sorry."

BIBLIOGRAPHICAL ESSAY

Since this book ranges over so many subjects, a comprehensive bibliography would, almost certainly, be longer than the book itself. One could compile hundreds, perhaps thousands, of titles on any one of several themes: the experience of Vietnam veterans, for example, or the political and cultural aftermath of the 1960s. Even a list meant to be representative, rather than comprehensive, of the published literature on these and other subjects would be so unwieldy as to exhaust most readers' patience, not to mention my own.

Accordingly, this essay is not intended either to cover all works in the field or to select a representative sample. The opening section discusses a small number of works that helped shape the content and spirit of this book as a whole. The following chapter-by-chapter sections list the major sources for each chapter or for broad subject areas within each chapter. These sections also give citations for specific facts, quotations, or interpretations that were not attributed in the text. Lastly, for each chapter, some additional works are listed for readers who may be interested in further exploring the subject.

General Sources

Any approach to the subject of Vietnam's aftermath must begin with Myra MacPherson's groundbreaking book *Long Time Passing: Vietnam and the Haunted Generation* (Garden City, N.Y.: Doubleday, 1984). MacPherson, who like many others "sat out" the war in numb confusion, set out at the end of the 1970s to interview veterans, former war protesters, and members of "that vast army who . . . were simply swept up by the times." From that material, MacPherson (who was "continually amazed" at how many of her subjects said they had never spoken about these things before) documented Vietnam's legacy of division, disillusion, sorrow, anger, and moral confusion. Her book, among the first to break the long national silence on the war, remains one of the most moving and important works on the Vietnam bookshelf.

From the vast number of memoirs and personal accounts produced in the twenty years since the war, two deserve mention here: William Broyles Jr., *Brothers in Arms: A Journey from War to Peace* (New York: Knopf, 1986) and W. D. Ehrhart, *Passing Time* (Jefferson, N.C.: McFarland, 1989).

Broyles, a marine lieutenant in Vietnam in 1969–70, went back fifteen years later, one of the first in a growing trickle of American veterans revisiting their old battleground. He did not solve all his mysteries or lay to rest all his ghosts. But his book, beautifully written and full of an overwhelming sadness, brings back with great force why Vietnam and its wasted sacrifice were so troubling to the American spirit.

Ehrhart, who also served in the Marine Corps in Vietnam and was badly wounded there, returned to the United States to discover, as did many other veterans, that he felt like a stranger among his own countrymen. ("It ain't my country any more. Maybe it never was," he told a friend.) Even though many veterans will disagree with Ehrhart's vehement condemnation of U.S. policy, most will find their own emotions and experiences mirrored in this memoir—above all, the desolating sense that their country did not understand or care about them, and that their hardship and sacrifice had been unrecognized, unappreciated, and useless.

Those men who fought in Vietnam as young officers trained at the nation's service academies represent an especially poignant part of the Vietnam experience, because they stood at the exact meeting place of old and new loyalties, beliefs, traditions, and values. Sent to fight in an unsuccessful and unpopular war, many young lieutenants and captains from West Point or the Naval Academy found themselves on the front line in a kind of war within their own culture, too—a war between old-fashioned patriotism and a new culture of disillusion and protest; between conventional codes of discipline, duty, and authority and new styles of personal freedom, rebelliousness, and "doing your own thing"; between ancient and new ideas of courage and manliness. Even though they were hardly representative of their society or their contemporaries, those officers' experiences illuminate the conflicts of the era somewhat as flares illuminate a battlefield at night, deepening the shadows and brightening the lit-up surfaces, so that the contrasts show with particular sharpness.

Two fine works that light up the terrain of this book are Robert Timberg, *The Nightingale's Song* (New York: Simon & Schuster, 1995) and Rick Atkinson, *The Long Gray Line* (Boston: Houghton Mifflin, 1989).

Timberg, a Naval Academy graduate who served as a marine officer in Vietnam and subsequently became a Washington correspondent for the *Baltimore Sun*, writes about five Annapolis graduates who were marked by Vietnam and whose lives later intersected in Ronald Reagan's Washington and, in particular, the Iran-Contra affair. Atkinson, a talented *Washington Post* reporter, focuses on West Point's class of 1966, which arrived at the academy in the calm, peaceful summer of 1962 and graduated four years later into the twin storms of Vietnam and the gathering cultural upheaval at home. Thirty 1966 graduates died in Vietnam, the highest toll of any West Point class.

Significant works focusing on the opposite side of the generational divide include James Fallows's celebrated essay "What Did You Do in the Class War, Daddy?" First published in *The Washington Monthly* in October 1975, the article has been widely reprinted, among many other places in Grace Sevy, ed., *The American Experience in Vietnam: A Reader* (Norman, Okla.: University of Oklahoma Press, 1989).

David Maraniss, *First in His Class: A Biography of Bill Clinton* (New York: Simon & Schuster, 1995) deals, obviously, with many other issues besides Vietnam. But Maraniss's close and careful examination of Clinton's draft record and his anguish over the war, while unsparing of Clinton's later evasions on the subject, also forcefully reminds readers of the difficult and morally agonizing choices that Clinton, and millions of other young men in his generation, had to make.

The mythical history of the 1960s portrays a generation split between those who fought the war and those who demonstrated against it. Paul Lyons, *New Left, New Right and the Legacy of the Sixties* (Philadelphia: Temple University Press, 1996) is a useful reminder that most young Americans did neither, but, as Lyons writes, "cultivated their own gardens, dated, played sports, married, pursued careers, worried about insurance," and, by and large, avoided the passions and moral turmoil of the era.

Chapter 1: The Wall

Relics at the wall are described in MacPherson, *Long Time Passing*; William Broyles Jr., "A Ritual for Saying Goodbye," *U.S. News & World Report*, Nov. 10, 1986; Michael Norman's introduction in Sal Lopes, ed., *The Wall: Images and Offerings from the Vietnam Veterans Memorial* (New York: Collins, 1987); Laura Palmer, *Shrapnel in the Heart: Letters and Remembrances from the Vietnam Veterans Memorial* (New York: Random House, 1987). Disputes over the wall's design are in Atkinson, *Long Gray Line*, 449–480; also Timberg, *Nightingale*, 306–317. W. D. Erhart's lines are from "The Invasion of Grenada," in Ehrhart, ed., *Carrying the Darkness* (New York: Avon Books, 1985); "the right memorial for that war" is from John Douglas Marshall, *Reconciliation Road* (Syracuse, N.Y.: Syracuse University Press, 1993), 202.

The baby boomer survey is reported in William Greider, "The Rolling Stone Survey," and "Hell No, We Won't Go!" *Rolling Stone*, Apr. 7, 1988, reprinted in William Dudley and David Bender, eds., *The Vietnam War: Opposing Viewpoints* (San Diego, Calif.: Greenhaven Press, 2nd ed., 1990).

Quotes about Secretary McNamara are from David Von Drehle, "McNamara's War Over the War," *Washington Post*, Apr. 24, 1995. Neil Sheehan's observations are from Sheehan, *A Bright Shining Lie: John Paul Vann and America in Vietnam* (New York: Random House, 1988), 285, 287. "The good guys against the bad guys" is from Loren Baritz, *Backfire: A History of How American Culture Led Us Into Vietnam and Made Us Fight the Way We Did* (New York: William Morrow, 1985), 283.

"We want to give ourselves absolution" is from Joseph Lelyveld, "The Enduring Legacy," *New York Times Magazine*, Mar. 31, 1985.

Chapter 2: The Veterans

Major sources for this chapter include MacPherson, *Long Time Passing*; Broyles, *Brothers in Arms*; Keith Walker, *A Piece of My Heart: The Stories of Twenty-Six American Women Who Served in Vietnam* (Novato, Calif.: Presidio, 1985); and Richard A. Kulka et al., *Trauma and the Vietnam War Generation: Report of Findings from the National Vietnam Veterans Readjustment Study* (New York: Brunner/Mazel, 1990).

Material on veterans' experience is also drawn from Marlene Cimons, "War Experiences Haunt Many Vietnam Veterans," *Los Angeles Times*, Apr. 28, 1985; and Larry Heinemann, "Syndrome: Making One's Way, Again, through Vietnam," *Harper's Magazine*, July 1991. Dale Wilson's letter and the account of his antiamnesty demonstration in North Carolina are from the *Statesville Record & Landmark*, Feb. 12 and 21, 1977.

On Vietnam literature, sources include C.D.B. Bryan, "Barely Suppressed Screams: Getting a Bead on Vietnam War Literature," *Harper's Magazine*, June 1984; Jack Fuller, "The War in Words," *Chicago Tribune Magazine*, Sept. 19, 1982; Michiko Kakutani, "Novelists and Vietnam: The War Goes On," *New York Times Book Review*, Apr. 15, 1984.

Reactions to the Iran hostages' return are from Ron Zaczek, *Farewell, Darkness* (Annapolis, Md.: Naval Institute Press, 1994); Walker, *Piece of My Heart*; Kim Willenson, *The Bad War: An Oral History of the Vietnam War* (New York: New American Library, 1987). "The stereotype has been shattered" is from Joseph Ferrandino, "The Impact of the War on a Generation of Americans," paper delivered at an Asia Society conference, "The Vietnam Experience in American Literature," New York, May 7–9, 1985.

Material on women veterans is from Walker, *Piece of My Heart*; Kulka, *Trauma*; Peter Perl, "A Matter of Honor," *Washington Post Magazine*, Oct. 25, 1992; Carol Lynn Mithers, "Missing in Action: Women Warriors in Vietnam," in John Carlos Rowe and Rick Berg, eds., *The Vietnam War and American Culture* (New York: Columbia University Press, 1991); David M. Berman, "Interviews with Two Vietnam Veterans: Welcome Home," *Vietnam Generation*, summer-fall 1989; Joan A. Furey, "Women Vietnam Veterans: A Comparison of Studies," *Journal of Psychosocial Nursing*, Mar. 1, 1991; Laura Palmer, "The Nurses of Vietnam, Still Wounded," *New York Times Magazine*, Nov. 7, 1993.

Bill Sullivan's comment at the Naval Academy reunion is in the *Baltimore Sun*, Sept. 27, 1993. "Vietnam veterans more alienated" is from Veterans Administration, *Myths and Realities: A Study of Attitudes toward Vietnam Era Veterans* (Washington, D.C.: Senate Veterans Affairs Committee, July 1980). Incident at Georgetown Law School is in Timberg, *Nightingale*, 180–181. Letters to Bob Greene are in Greene, *Homecoming: When the Soldiers Returned from Vietnam* (New York: G. P. Putnam, 1989).

Additional Material

On the experience of African American soldiers, see Wallace Terry, *Bloods: An Oral History of the War by Black Veterans* (New York: Ballantine, 1992), and Horace Coleman, *In the Grass* (Woodbridge, Conn.: Viet Nam Generation and Burning Cities Press, 1995), a collection of wonderfully sardonic poems by an African American veteran.

Sarah Hansel et al., eds., *Soldier's Heart* (Lutherville, Md.: Sidran Press, 1995) is an extraordinary collection of writings by soldiers suffering from PTSD (posttraumatic stress disorder). Included are selections by veterans of World War II, Korea, Vietnam, Lebanon, and the Persian Gulf War. Also see Arthur Egendorf et al., *Legacies of War: Comparative Adjustment of Veterans and Their Peers* (New York: Center for Policy Research, 1981) and Egendorf, *Healing from the War: Trauma and Transformation After Vietnam* (Boston: Houghton Mifflin, 1985).

Veterans' attitudes about many aspects of the Vietnam War are explored in Ellen Frey-Wouters and Robert Laufer, *The Legacy of a War: The American Soldier in Vietnam* (Armonk, N.Y.: M. E. Sharpe, 1986). Postwar veterans' issues are examined in Wilbur J. Scott, *Politics of Readjustment: Vietnam Veterans Since the War* (New York: Aldine de Gruyter, 1993).

Poetry, fiction, and memoirs reflecting the Vietnam veterans' experience fill a shelf far longer than can be adequately summarized here. Two collections edited by W. D. Ehrhart, *Carrying the Darkness: The Poetry of the Vietnam War* and *Unaccustomed Mercy: Soldier-Poets of the Vietnam War* (both from Lubbock, Tex.: Texas Tech University Press, 1989) offer a sampling of poems by both well-known and obscure poets. Two memorable prose collections are Tim O'Brien, *The Things They Carried* (Boston: Houghton Mifflin/Seymour Lawrence, 1990), and William E. Merritt's short, sharp-edged sketches in *Where the Rivers Ran Backward* (Athens: University of Georgia Press, 1989).

Among the many novels, Wayne Karlin, *Lost Armies* (New York: Henry Holt, 1988) and Allen Glick, *Winters Coming, Winters Gone* (New York: Pinnacle Books, 1985) both deserved more attention than they received.

Notable memoirs include Lewis B. Puller, *Fortunate Son* (New York: Grove Weidenfeld, 1991); Lynda Van Devanter, *Home Before Morning* (New York: Beaufort Books, 1983); Robert Mason, *Chickenhawk: Back in the World* (New York: Viking, 1993); and Frederick Downs, *Aftermath: A Soldier's Return from Vietnam* (New York: Norton, 1984).

Several prominent veteran authors are among the subjects in Eric James Schroeder, *Vietnam, We've All Been There: Interviews with American Writers* (Westport, Conn.: Praeger, 1992).

Chapter 3: The Generation

Principal sources for this chapter include MacPherson, *Long Time Passing*; Fallows, "What Did You Do?"; Lyons, *New Left, New Right*; Christian G. Appy, *Working-Class War* (Chapel Hill: University of North Carolina Press, 1993).

Material on the Vietnam draft and the composition of the post-Vietnam all-volunteer force is from Lawrence M. Baskir and William A. Strauss, *Chance and Circumstance: The Draft, The War, and the Vietnam Generation* (New York: Knopf, 1978); D. Michael Shafer, "The Vietnam-Era Draft: Who Went, Who Didn't, and Why It Matters," in Shafer, ed., *The Legacy: The Vietnam War in the American Imagination* (Boston: Beacon Press, 1990); James Fallows, *National Defense* (New York: Random House, 1981); U.S. Department of Defense, Office of the Assistant Secretary for Force Management Policy, *Population Representation in the Military Services: Fiscal Year 1994*, Dec. 1995.

"I'm bitter" is from Robert Coles, *The Middle Americans* (Boston: Little, Brown, 1971), quoted in Appy, *Working-Class War*, 42–43. Material on Harvard in World War II is from *Harvard University Alumni Gazette*, summer 1994, and John T. Bethell, "Harvard and the Arts of War," *Harvard Magazine*, Sept.–Oct. 1995. McCain's comment is in Timberg, *Nightingale*, 234–235.

Webb's comment on Calley is in *Nightingale*, 185. Material on athletes and the draft is from Baskir and Strauss, *Chance and Circumstance*, 48–49. The summary of Clinton's draft record is based mainly on Maraniss, *First in His Class*, 165–205. Phil Gramm's comments are from Richard L. Berke, "Tough Texan: Phil Gramm," *New York Times Magazine*, Feb. 19, 1995; *Washington Post*, Feb. 19, 1995; *Baltimore Sun*, Feb. 24, 1995.

The incidence of campus protests is reported in David W. Levy, *The Debate over Vietnam* (Baltimore: Johns Hopkins University Press, 1991), 104. Material on prosecutions of draft evaders is from Baskir and Strauss, *Chance and Circumstance*, 11–12, 82. "A wall ten miles high" is in Timberg, *Nightingale*, 91. "Basic American good guy" is from Samuel G. Freedman, "The War and the Arts," *New York Times Magazine*, Mar. 31, 1985.

Material on the Iran-Contra affair is from *Nightingale*; Theodore Draper, *A Very Thin Line: The Iran-Contra Affairs* (New York: Hill and Wang, 1991); *Taking the Stand: The Testimony of Lieutenant Colonel Oliver L. North* (New York: Pocket Books, 1987).

Opinion poll data on support for the war by age group and educational level is from Levy, *Debate*, 103, and Charles DiBenedetti, *An American Ordeal: The Antiwar Movement of the Vietnam Era* (Syracuse, N.Y.: Syracuse University Press, 1990), 394. Phil Berrigan's attempted protest at the National Security Agency is described in the *Baltimore Sun*, July 5, 1996.

Additional Material

See Landon Y. Jones, *Great Expectations: America and the Baby Boom Generation* (New York: Coward, McCann & Geoghegan, 1980); Todd Gitlin, *The Sixties: Years of Hope, Days of Rage* (New York: Bantam, 1987) and *The Twilight of Common Dreams: Why America Is Wracked by Culture Wars* (New York: Metropolitan Books, 1995); also Nancy Zaroulis and Gerald Sullivan, *Who Spoke Up?: American Protest against the War in Vietnam, 1963–1975* (Garden City, N.Y.: Doubleday, 1984).

James Carroll, *An American Requiem: God, My Father, and the War That Came Between Us* (Boston: Houghton Mifflin, 1996) is a compelling memoir of how the war affected one American family.

For an analysis of public opinion on the war and the impact of the antiwar movement, see John Mueller, *War, Presidents and Public Opinion* (New York: Wiley, 1973); also Mueller's essay "A Summary of Public Opinion and the Vietnam War," in Peter Braestrup, ed., *Vietnam As History: Ten Years After the Paris Peace Accords* (Washington, D.C.: University Press of America, 1984).

Chapter 4: The Syndrome

Sources for discussion of the Vietnam syndrome and interpretations of the Vietnam failure include Fuller, "The War in Words"; Norman Podhoretz, *Why We Were in Vietnam* (New York: Simon & Schuster, 1982); Morton Keller, "Reflections on Politics and Generations in America," *Daedalus*, fall 1978; Richard Nixon, *No More Vietnams* (New York: Arbor House, 1985); Sheehan, *Bright Shining Lie*; Barbara W. Tuchman, *The March of Folly: From Troy to Vietnam* (New York: Knopf, 1984).

Pham Van Dong's comment on Munich is in Bernard Fall, *Last Reflections on a War* (Garden City, N.Y.: Doubleday, 1967), 161. President Nixon's regret on not bombing North Vietnam was reported in the *New York Times*, Apr. 11, 1988.

"Confounded, dismayed, and discouraged" is from Gen. Bruce Palmer Jr., *The 25-Year War: America's Military Role in Vietnam* (Lexington: University Press of Kentucky, 1984), 204. Other sources on the military's reactions to Vietnam include Melvin Gurtov and Konrad Kellen, "Vietnam: Lessons and Mislessons," (Santa Monica, Calif.: Rand Corporation, June 1969); Jim and Sybil Stockdale, *In Love & War* (New York: Harper & Row, 1984); Bob Woodward, *The Commanders* (New York: Simon & Schuster,

1991); Drew Middleton, "Vietnam and the Military Mind," *New York Times Magazine*, Jan. 10, 1982; Andrew F. Krepinevich Jr., *The Army and Vietnam* (Baltimore: Johns Hopkins University Press, 1986). The quote from Admiral Sir John Fisher is in Atkinson, *Long Gray Line*, 284.

Material on policy disputes in the Reagan administration is from Richard Halloran, *To Arm a Nation: Rebuilding America's Endangered Defenses* (New York: Macmillan, 1986) and George P. Shultz, *Turmoil and Triumph: My Years As Secretary of State* (New York: Scribner's, 1993).

On the Persian Gulf War: "Administration officials worried" is from Richard J. Barnet, "Reflections—The Use of Force," *New Yorker*, Apr. 29, 1991. Other sources include Woodward, *Commanders*; Michael R. Gordon and Gen. Bernard E . Trainor, *The Generals' War: The Inside Story of the Conflict in the Gulf* (Boston: Little, Brown, 1995); Jerry Lee Lembcke, "The Myth of the Sat-Upon Vietnam Veteran: The Rhetorical Construction of Soldiers As Means and Ends in the Persian Gulf War," *Viet Nam Generation*, 6, nos. 3–4, 1995; Marilyn B. Young, "Remembering Vietnam," unpublished paper, 1993 (in author's files); Rick Atkinson, *Crusade: The Untold Story of the Persian Gulf War* (Boston: Houghton Mifflin, 1993). Opinion polls following the Gulf War were reported in the *Baltimore Sun*, Jan. 16, 1994.

On Somalia, sources include Sidney Blumenthal, "Why Are We in Somalia?" *New Yorker*, Oct. 25, 1993, and Jonathan Stevenson, *Losing Mogadishu: Testing U.S. Policy in Somalia* (Annapolis, Md.: Naval Institute Press, 1995). The observation that Mogadishu "had a bigger effect than the Persian gulf war" is from the *New York Times*, Mar. 6, 1995.

On Bosnia and Haiti: Charles A. Kupchan's comments are from his article "Bosnia and the Decline of the West," *Baltimore Sun*, July 25, 1995; "maps and rhetoric and ignorance" is from James C. Thomson Jr., Peter W. Stanley, and John Curtis Perry, *Sentimental Imperialists: The American Experience in East Asia* (New York: Harper & Row, 1981), 258; Fareed Zakaria's observations are in Zakaria, "Bosnia Explodes 3 Myths," *New York Times*, Sept. 26, 1993. The opinion poll on Bosnia was reported in *Newsweek*, May 3, 1993. Comments to a reporter are from *New York Times*, May 2, 1993; comments on Haiti by McCain and members of the House of Representatives are from *Congressional Record*, 103rd Congress, 2nd session, S12753 and H9097–H9100; Madeleine Albright's statement is from *Washington Post*, Sept. 20, 1994. *Time*'s essay criticizing Clinton appeared in the issue of Oct. 3, 1994. Military leaders' "professional judgment" on Bosnia is in *Situation in Bosnia*, House International Relations Committee hearing, June 8, 1995, 36. Administration statements and congressional reactions on sending U.S. troops to Bosnia are in *U.S. Policy towards Bosnia*, House International Relations Committee hearing, Oct. 18 and Dec. 6, 1995, and *The Peace Process in the Former Yugoslavia*, Senate Foreign Relations Committee hearing, Oct. 17, 1995. The remark by a former U.S. diplomat was reported in *Time*, Sept. 16, 1995.

Chapter 5: The Myth

H. Bruce Franklin's well-researched *M.I.A., or Mythmaking in America* (New Brunswick, N.J.: Rutgers University Press, rev. ed., 1993) convincingly debunks the POW/MIA movement and its claims of American prisoners still held in Vietnam long after the war. Other principal sources for this chapter include U.S. Senate Select Committee on POW/MIA Affairs, *Final Report* (Washington, D.C.: Jan. 13, 1993); Douglas L. Clarke, *The Missing Man: Politics and the MIA* (Washington, D.C.: National Defense University Press, 1979). Monika Jensen-Stevenson and William Stevenson, *Kiss the Boys Goodbye: How the United States Betrayed Its Own POWs in Vietnam* (New York: Dutton, 1990) is an extreme example of the conspiracy-theory school. J. C. Pollock, *Mission M.I.A.* (New York: Crown, 1982) is the archetype for fictional treatment of the MIA issue.

Analysis of the true number of "discrepancy cases" is from Franklin, *M.I.A.*, 93–95. The Defense Department answer to Maj. Smith is from U.S. Defense Department, "Smith/McIntire Chronology" (Washington, D.C.: no date). Guidelines for KIA/BNR status are in Clarke, *Missing Man*, 14. The Pentagon's acknowledgment that 567 MIA remains cannot be recovered is in U.S. Department of Defense, *A Zero-Based Comprehensive Review of Cases Involving Unaccounted for Americans in Southeast Asia*, Nov. 13, 1995. "As though the North Vietnamese kidnapped four hundred Americans" is from Jonathan Schell, *The Time of Illusion* (New York: Knopf, 1976), 231. Quotes from POWs are from Craig Howes, *Voices of the Vietnam POWs* (New York: Oxford University Press, 1993), 13, 9.

Information on MIA fund-raising and fake MIA evidence is largely drawn from the Senate Select Committee's final report, chapter 6, "Private Efforts." Additional material (including appeals from Skyhook II and letters to President Reagan from attorney Mark Waple and Rep. Billy Hendon concerning the $4.2 million film) is in the author's files. Also see Paul D. Mather, *M.I.A.: Accounting for the Missing in Southeast Asia* (Washington, D.C.: National Defense University Press, 1994).

"Rambo-grams" are mentioned in Franklin, *M.I.A.*, 151. Gritz's record of falsifying evidence is in U.S. Department of Defense, "Smith-McIntire Chronology." The investigative article on H. Ross Perot appeared in the *Washington Post*, June 21, 1992.

Leo Cawley's comment is in Cawley, "The War about the War: Vietnam Films and American Myth," in Linda Dittmar and Gene Michaud, eds., *From Hanoi to Hollywood: The Vietnam War in American Film* (New Brunswick, N.J.: Rutgers University Press, 1990), 73.

Additional Material

Elliott Gruner, *Prisoners of Culture: Representing the Vietnam P.O.W.* (New Brunswick, N.J.: Rutgers University Press, 1993) relates the POW/MIA issue and its treatment in popular culture to other legends stretching far back into American history. Also see Susan Katz Keating, *Prisoners of Hope: Exploiting the POW/MIA Myth in America* (New York: Random House, 1994), and Garry L. Smith, *The Search for MIAs* (Spartanburg, S.C.: Honoribus Press, 1992). Smith, who served as an Army intelligence specialist during the war and was later assigned for three years to the Joint Casualty Resolution Center, denies that there is any evidence of POWs held captive after the war or that anyone could have silenced military investigators if they did have such evidence.

Chapter 6: Learning about the War ———————————

Principal sources for this chapter include Project on the Vietnam Generation, *Report on the Survey of Courses on Vietnam Era Events* (Washington, D.C.: Dec. 1985) and *Report on the Survey of Courses on Vietnam Era Events—1986 Update* (Washington, D.C.: Jan. 31, 1987); Ronald H. Spector, "'What Did You Do in the War, Professor?'—Reflections on Teaching about Vietnam," *American Heritage*, Dec. 1986; Fox Butterfield, "The New Vietnam Scholarship," *New York Times Magazine*, Feb. 13, 1983; Karen J. Winkler, "The Vietnam War Scores Well at the Box Office, but It Fails to Attract Many Researchers," *Chronicle of Higher Education*, Sept. 30, 1987; also the following articles from the Jan. 1988 issue of *Social Education*: Jerold M. Starr, "Teaching the Vietnam War"; Martha Matlaw, "Teaching the Vietnam War at Full Circle High School"; George Kirschner and Eric Weisberg, "Teaching and Learning about the Vietnam War"; Fred Wilcox, "Pedagogical Implications of Teaching 'Literature of the Vietnam War.'"

"Vietnam is one long blur" is in the *New York Times*, Oct. 19, 1984.

Contradictory opinion poll results are in Veterans Administration, *Myths and Realities*, 60. Perry Oldham's experience is from Oldham, "Some Further Thoughts on Teaching Vietnam Literature," *English Journal*, Dec. 1993.

Henry Kissinger's complaint about Vietnamese deviousness is in Kissinger, *White House Years* (Boston: Little, Brown, 1979), 259. "Our problem was us" is in Loren Baritz, *Backfire*, 22. "Usually we are talking about ourselves" is from Lelyveld, "Enduring Legacy."

Additional Material

See Marc Jason Gilbert, ed., *The Vietnam War: Teaching Approaches and Resources* (Westport, Conn.: Greenwood Press, 1991).

Chapter 7: The New Americans

Important sources for this chapter include James A. Freeman's oral history collection *Hearts of Sorrow: Vietnamese-American Lives* (Stanford, Calif.: Stanford University Press, 1989); Lady Borton's vivid account of the Pulau Bidong refugee camp, *Sensing the Enemy* (Garden City, N.Y.: Dial, 1984); also Bruce Grant, *The Boat People* (Blackburn, Victoria, Australia: Penguin, 1979); Joseph Cerquone, *Uncertain Harbors: The Plight of Vietnamese Boat People* (Washington, D.C.: U.S. Committee for Refugees, Oct. 1987).

Yearly refugee statistics and developments in U.S. policy are in the annual surveys published by the U.S. Committee for Refugees. See also U.S. State Department Refugee Bureau, *Report of the Indochinese Refugee Panel*, Apr. 1986, and hearings and staff reports published by the U.S. Senate Judiciary Committee's Subcommittee on Immigration and Refugee Policy.

The quote from Prime Minister Kriangsak is in William Shawcross, *The Quality of Mercy: Cambodia, Holocaust and Modern Conscience* (New York: Simon & Schuster, 1984), 88. The economic success of the first Vietnamese refugees is reported in Alison Landes, Betsie B. Caldwell, and Mark A. Siegel, eds., *Immigration and Illegal Aliens: Burden or Blessing?* (Wylie, Tex.: Information Plus, 1991), 107–108.

The Hmongs' difficulties in the United States are described in two articles by Marc Kaufman, "The Last Victims of Vietnam?" *Philadelphia Inquirer*, July 1, 1984, and "At the Mercy of America," *Philadelphia Inquirer Magazine*, Oct. 21, 1984. Cases of blindness among Cambodian women were reported by Alec Wilkinson, "A Changed Vision of God," *New Yorker*, Jan. 24, 1994. Material on South Vietnamese veterans in the United States, including interview with Phan Nhat Nam, is from Seth Mydans, "Preparing to Commemorate the Fall of Saigon," *New York Times*, May 1, 1995; see also Norman Boucher, "The Other Vietnam Vets," *Boston Globe Magazine*, Apr. 30, 1989.

Additional Material

Robert Olen Butler, *A Good Scent from a Strange Mountain* (New York: Holt, 1992) examines the Vietnamese American experience in a stunning collection of short stories. Butler, who learned to speak Vietnamese while serving in Army intelligence during the war, writes sensitively and imaginatively in the voices of various Vietnamese characters.

The Vietnamese experience has also been chronicled in a still small but growing collection of memoirs by Vietnamese American authors. Some titles are Yung Krall, *A Thousand Tears Falling: The True Story of a Vietnamese Family Torn Apart by War, Communism, and the CIA* (Atlanta: Longstreet, 1995); Nguyen Qui Duc, *Where the Ashes Are: The Odyssey of a Vietnamese Family* (Reading, Mass.: Addison-Wesley, 1994); Jade Ngoc Quang Huynh, *South Wind Changing* (St. Paul, Minn.: Graywolf, 1994).

Also see Linda Hitchcox, *Vietnamese Refugees in Southeast Asian Camps* (New York: St. Martin's, 1991); and Kali Tal, ed., *Southeast Asian-American Communities* (Woodbridge, Conn.: Vietnam Generation, 1990).

Chapter 8: Ghosts _____

Many details in this chapter were reported in *Indochina Digest* (Washington, D.C.: Indochina Project), a weekly summary of internal and international developments in Vietnam, Laos, and Cambodia, or in *Vietnam Update* (Washington, D.C.: Institute for Democracy in Vietnam), which first appeared in 1988 and had unusual access to Vietnamese dissident sources.*

Other sources include two thorough and thoughtful books by historian William J. Duiker, *Vietnam Since the Fall of Saigon*, Ohio University Monographs in International Studies, Southeast Asia Series, no. 56 (Athens: Ohio University Center for International Studies, rev. ed., 1985) and *Viet-*

*In 1996, *Indochina Digest* was reborn with a new name, *Mekong Digest*, and a new publisher, the International Center in Washington, D.C. Due to funding difficulties, *Vietnam Update* was no longer appearing regularly; the Institute for Democracy in Vietnam had relocated to Newport Beach, California.

nam: Revolution in Transition (Boulder, Colo.: Westview, 2nd ed., 1995). Also Neil Sheehan, *After the War Was Over: Hanoi and Saigon* (New York: Random House, 1992); Barbara Crossette, "All Vietnam Is Now a Stage; Its Players Are Mostly Angry," *New York Times*, Apr. 22, 1988.

Material on veterans' journeys back to Vietnam is from Broyles, *Brothers*; Gordon Livingston, "We Might as Well Forgive Ourselves," *Baltimore Sun*, May 29, 1995; George C. Wilson, "Vietnam Revisited: Veterans Go Back to Battlefields to Lay Their Nightmares to Rest," *Washington Post*, Feb. 6, 1990; Tim O'Brien, "The Vietnam in Me," *New York Times Magazine*, Oct. 2, 1994. John Phillip Baca's story is in the *Baltimore Sun*, May 30, 1993.

On Vietnam's economic crisis after liberation, sources include Stanley Karnow, *Vietnam: A History* (New York: Viking, 1983); Tiziano Terzani, "Vietnam Revisited: Sweet Tears Turned Sour," *Far Eastern Economic Review*, Sept. 19, 1985; Duiker, *Vietnam Since the Fall*; David Chanoff and Doan Van Toai, *Portrait of the Enemy* (New York: Random House, 1986); *Toward a Market Economy in Vietnam* (Rockville, Md.: Pacific Basin Research Institute, Dec. 1993); Ma Zongshi, "Perestroika in Vietnam: A Balance Sheet," *Indochina Report* (Singapore: Information and Resource Center, Oct.-Dec. 1988); Robert Shaplen, *Bitter Victory* (New York: Harper & Row, 1986); Tony Clifton and Ron Moreau, "A Wounded Land," *Newsweek*, Apr. 15, 1985; William Branigin's articles on Vietnam in the *Washington Post*, Apr. 21–26, 1985.

On U.S.-Vietnam relations: the best account of the 1977–78 negotiations and subsequent events is in Nayan Chanda, *Brother Enemy* (New York: Harcourt Brace Jovanovich, 1986). Also see U.S. General Accounting Office, *U.S.-Vietnam Relations: Issues and Implications*, Apr. 1995, and the weekly *Indochina Digest*. Mary McGrory's description of President Clinton's speech is in the *Washington Post*, July 13, 1995; John McCain's observations are in McCain, "Let's Normalize Relations with Vietnam," *Washington Post*, May 22, 1995; the Warren Christopher quote is from the *Washington Post*, Aug. 7, 1995.

Details of Nguyen Van Linh's background are from Sheehan, *After the War*, 74–81. Sources on Vietnam and doi moi also include *Yearbook on International Communist Affairs, 1986* (Stanford, Calif.: Hoover Institute Press, 1987); Murray Hiebert, "A Bridge to Reform," *Far Eastern Economic Review*, July 23, 1987; Nguyen Thi Lieu, "Artistic Freedom in Vietnam," *Vietnam Update*, winter/spring 1988.

Vignettes of Saigon and Hanoi are drawn from Tracy Dahlby, "The New Saigon," *National Geographic*, Apr. 1995; Duiker, *Revolution in Transition*, 190; numerous issues of *Indochina Digest*; James Grady, "Still in Saigon," *New Republic*, Mar. 9, 1992; Sys Trier Morch, "Surprising Vietnam," *Travel Holiday*, Nov. 1993; Anne Crittenden, "Discovering a Village in Vietnam," *New York Times*, Apr. 23, 1995; Paul Quinn-Judge, "Peace without Honor," *Boston Globe*, Dec. 6, 1992. The *New York Times Magazine*'s fashion layout appeared Nov. 21, 1993.

The exchange between Linh and the Vietnam Writers and Artists Association is in *Vietnam Update*, winter/spring 1988.

On political change in Vietnam, sources include Duiker, *Revolution in Transition*, 117–119; Human Rights Watch/Asia, *Vietnam: Human Rights in a Season of Transition* (Washington, D.C.: Human Rights Watch, 1995); Nguyen Huu Tho, "Democracy: A Struggle, Not a Gift," *Vietnam Update*, summer 1989. Hoang Minh Chinh's commentary is reported in *Indochina Digest*, May 3, 1991. Also see Philip Shenon, "Reaching for the Good Life in Vietnam," *New York Times Magazine*, Jan. 5, 1992.

Material on the aftermath of the war in Vietnam is from William Branigin, "Hanoi's Asylums: War Never Ends," *Washington Post*, Oct. 23, 1993; Tim Larimer, "Vietnam's Vets Feeling Forgotten," *Washington Post*, Dec. 28, 1994; Anh-Huong Thi Tu, "Apocalypse Then: Going Back to Vietnam, in Memory and Spirit," *Washington Post*, Feb. 13, 1994; Bao Ninh, *The Sorrow of War*, Phan Thanh Hao, trans. (New York: Pantheon, 1995); Duong Thu Huong, *Novel without a Name*, Phan Huy Duong and Nina McPherson, trans. (New York: William Morrow, 1995).

Additional Material

In addition to the authors cited in the opening segment of this chapter, a number of other U.S. veterans have written about returning to Vietnam. Two fine accounts are W. D. Ehrhart, *Going Back: An Ex-Marine Returns to Vietnam* (Jefferson, N.C.: McFarland, 1987) and Frederick Downs, *No Longer Enemies, Not Yet Friends: An American Soldier Returns to Vietnam* (New York: Norton, 1991).

A vivid portrayal of postwar Vietnamese and their memories is in Lady Borton, *After Sorrow: An American among the Vietnamese* (New York: Viking, 1995). The veteran *New York Times* correspondent Henry Kamm, whose coverage of Southeast Asia dates back to the 1960s, depicts the contemporary scene in *Dragon Ascending: Vietnam and the Vietnamese* (New York: Arcade, 1996). A collection of writings by Vietnamese dissidents is in *Vietnam: The Unheard Voices* (Newport Beach, Calif.: Institute for Democracy in Vietnam, 1996). For striking visual impressions, see Geoffrey Clifford's photographic collection, *Vietnam: The Land We Never Knew*, text by John Balaban (San Francisco: Chronicle Books, 1989); also, Rick Graetz, *Vietnam: Opening Doors to the World* (Helena, Mont.: American Geographic, 1988); and Lou Dematteis, *A Portrait of Vietnam* (New York: Norton, 1996).

Literature reflecting the Vietnamese experience during and since the war is slowly becoming more available to American readers. Some notable examples of contemporary Vietnamese writing are in Wayne Karlin, Le Minh Khue, and Truong Vu, eds., *The Other Side of Heaven: Post War Fiction by Vietnamese and American Writers* (Willimantic, Conn.: Curbstone, 1995). This collection is remarkable in that its editors and contributors represent both Vietnamese sides, as well as the United States. Also see John Balaban and Nguyen Qui Duc, eds., *Vietnam: A Traveler's Literary Companion* (San Francisco: Whereabouts Press, 1996), a collection of short stories translated from Vietnamese. The winter 1995 issue of *Manoa*, published at the University of Hawaii, includes a selection of new fiction, poetry, essays, and photographs from Vietnam.

The poems quoted at the end of Chapter 8 are Larry Rottmann, "A Farmer from Vinh," in Rottmann, *Voices from the Ho Chi Minh Trail* (Desert Hot Springs, Calif.: Event Horizon Press, 1993), and an excerpt from Tran Thi My Nhung, "A Vietnamese Bidding Farewell to the Remains of an American," adapted by W. D. Ehrhart from a translation by Phan Thao Chi. Here is the full text:

> *Was your plane on fire, or did you die*
> *of bullet wounds, or fall down exhausted?*
> *Just so you died in the forest, alone.*
>
> *Only the two of us, a woodcutter and his wife,*
> *dug this grave for you, burned joss sticks,*
> *prayed for you to rest in peace.*
>
> *How could we know there'd be such a meeting,*
> *you and I, once separated by an ocean,*
> *by the color of our skin, by language?*
>
> *But destiny bound our lives together.*
> *And today, by destiny's grace,*
> *you are finally going home.*

I believe your American sky
is as blue as the sky above this country
where you've rested twenty years.

Is it too late to love each other?
Between us now, the ocean seems so small.
How close are our two continents.

I wish a tranquil heaven for your soul,
Gemmed with twinkling stars and shining moon.
May you rest forever in the soil of your home. *

Author's Note

Some sharp-eyed readers may have noticed that the first and last pages of the text give conflicting numbers of names on the Vietnam Veterans Memorial. The discrepancy occurs because names are added from time to time as Vietnam casualty records continue to be updated and corrected. The total of 58,219, reported on the opening page of chapter 1, was correct as of September 1999. The figure 58,183, which appears on page 199, was the total in November 1993, the date of the scene described in the epilogue.

*©by W. D. Ehrhart. Reprinted by permission.

LIST OF SOURCES

Appy, Christian G. *Working-Class War.* Chapel Hill, N.C.: University of North Carolina Press, 1993.

Atkinson, Rick. *The Long Gray Line.* Boston: Houghton Mifflin, 1989.

———. *Crusade: The Untold Story of the Persian Gulf War.* Boston: Houghton Mifflin, 1993.

Balaban, John, and Nguyen Qui Duc, eds. *Vietnam: A Traveler's Literary Companion.* San Francisco: Whereabouts Press, 1996.

Bao Ninh. *The Sorrow of War.* Phan Thanh Hao, trans. New York: Pantheon Books, 1995.

Baritz, Loren. *Backfire: A History of How American Culture Led Us into Vietnam and Made Us Fight the Way We Did.* New York: William Morrow & Co., 1985.

Barnet, Richard J. "Reflections—The Use of Force," *New Yorker,* Apr. 29, 1991.

Baskir, Lawrence M., and William A. Strauss. *Chance and Circumstance: The Draft, The War, and the Vietnam Generation.* New York: Knopf, 1978.

Berman, David M. "Interviews with Two Vietnam Veterans: Welcome Home," *Vietnam Generation* (summer–fall 1989).

Bethell, John T. "Harvard and the Arts of War," *Harvard Magazine* (Sept.–Oct. 1995).

Blumenthal, Sidney. "Why Are We in Somalia?" *New Yorker,* Oct. 25, 1993.

Borton, Lady. *Sensing the Enemy.* Garden City, N.Y.: Dial Press, 1984.

———. *After Sorrow: An American among the Vietnamese.* New York: Viking, 1995.

Boucher, Norman. "The Other Vietnam Vets," *Boston Globe Magazine,* Apr. 30, 1989.

Braestrup, Peter, ed. *Vietnam As History: Ten Years After the Paris Peace Accords.* Washington, D.C.: University Press of America, 1984.

Branigin, William. "Hanoi's Asylums: War Never Ends," *Washington Post,* Oct. 23, 1993.

Broyles, William Jr. "A Ritual for Saying Goodbye," *U.S. News & World Report,* Nov. 10, 1986.

————. *Brothers in Arms: A Journey from War to Peace.* New York: Knopf, 1986.

Bryan, C.D.B. "Barely Suppressed Screams: Getting a Bead on Vietnam War Literature," *Harper's Magazine* (June, 1984).

Butler, Robert Olen. *A Good Scent from a Strange Mountain.* New York: Holt, 1992.

Butterfield, Fox. "The New Vietnam Scholarship," *New York Times Magazine,* Feb. 13, 1983.

Carroll, James. *An American Requiem: God, My Father, and the War That Came Between Us.* Boston: Houghton Mifflin, 1996.

Cawley, Leo. "The War about the War: Vietnam Films and American Myth," in Linda Dittmar and Gene Michaud, eds., *From Hanoi to Hollywood: The Vietnam War in American Film.* New Brunswick, N.J.: Rutgers University Press, 1990.

Cerquone, Joseph. *Uncertain Harbors: The Plight of Vietnamese Boat People.* Washington, D.C.: U.S. Committee for Refugees, October 1987.

Chanda, Nayan. *Brother Enemy.* New York: Harcourt Brace Jovanovich, 1986.

Chanoff, David, and Doan Van Toai. *Portrait of the Enemy.* New York: Random House, 1986.

Clarke, Douglas L. *The Missing Man: Politics and the MIA.* Washington, D.C.: National Defense University Press, 1979.

Clifford, Geoffrey. *Vietnam: The Land We Never Knew.* Text by John Balaban. San Francisco: Chronicle Books, 1989.

Clifton, Tony, and Ron Moreau. "A Wounded Land," *Newsweek,* Apr. 15, 1985.

Coleman, Horace. *In the Grass.* Woodbridge, Conn.: Viet Nam Generation and Burning Cities Press, 1995.

Coles, Robert. *The Middle Americans.* Boston: Little, Brown, 1971.

Crossette, Barbara. "All Vietnam Is Now a Stage; Its Players Are Mostly Angry," *New York Times,* Apr. 22, 1988.

Dahlby, Tracy. "The New Saigon," *National Geographic* (Apr. 1995).

Dematteis, Lou. *A Portrait of Viet Nam.* New York: Norton, 1996.

DiBenedetti, Charles. *An American Ordeal: The Antiwar Movement of the Vietnam Era.* Syracuse, N.Y.: Syracuse University Press, 1990.

Dittmar, Linda, and Gene Michaud, eds. *From Hanoi to Hollywood: The Vietnam War in American Film.* New Brunswick, N.J.: Rutgers University Press, 1990.

Downs, Frederick. *No Longer Enemies, Not Yet Friends: An American Soldier Returns to Vietnam.* New York: Norton, 1991.

———. *Aftermath: A Soldier's Return from Vietnam.* New York: Norton, 1984.

Duiker, William J. *Vietnam Since the Fall of Saigon.* Ohio University Monographs in International Studies, Southeast Asia Series, No. 56. Athens, Ohio: Ohio University Center for International Studies, rev. ed. 1985.

———. *Vietnam: Revolution in Transition.* Boulder, Colo.: Westview Press, 2nd ed., 1995.

Duong Thu Huong. *Novel Without a Name,* Phan Huy Duong and Nina McPherson, trans. New York: William Morrow, 1995.

Egendorf, Arthur. *Healing from the War: Trauma and Transformation After Vietnam.* Boston: Houghton Mifflin, 1985.

Egendorf, Arthur, et al. *Legacies of War: Comparative Adjustment of Veterans and Their Peers.* New York: Center for Policy Research, 1981.

Ehrhart, W. D. *Passing Time.* Jefferson, N.C.: McFarland, 1989.

———, ed. *Carrying the Darkness: The Poetry of the Vietnam War.* Lubbock, Tex.: Texas Tech University Press, 1989.

———, ed. *Unaccustomed Mercy: Soldier-Poets of the Vietnam War.* Lubbock, Tex.: Texas Tech University Press, 1989.

———. *Going Back: An Ex-Marine Returns to Vietnam.* Jefferson, N.C.: McFarland, 1987.

Fallows, James. *National Defense.* New York: Random House, 1981.

———. "What Did You Do in the Class War, Daddy?" *Washington Monthly* (Oct. 1975).

Franklin, H. Bruce. *M.I.A., or Mythmaking in America.* New Brunswick, N.J.: Rutgers University Press, rev. ed., 1993.

Freedman, Samuel G. "The War and the Arts," *New York Times Magazine,* Mar. 31, 1985.

Freeman, James A. *Hearts of Sorrow: Vietnamese-American Lives.* Stanford, Calif.: Stanford University Press, 1989.

Frey-Wouters, Ellen, and Robert Laufer. *The Legacy of a War: The American Soldier in Vietnam.* Armonk, N.Y.: M. E. Sharpe, 1986.

Fuller, Jack. "The War in Words," *Chicago Tribune Magazine,* Sept. 19, 1982.

Furey, Joan A. "Women Vietnam Veterans: A Comparison of Studies," *Journal of Psychosocial Nursing,* Mar. 1, 1991.

Gilbert, Marc Jason, ed. *The Vietnam War: Teaching Approaches and Resources.* Westport, Conn.: Greenwood Press, 1991.

Gitlin, Todd. *The Sixties: Years of Hope, Days of Rage.* New York: Bantam, 1987.

———. *The Twilight of Common Dreams: Why America is Wracked by Culture Wars.* New York: Metropolitan, 1995.

Glick, Allen. *Winters Coming, Winters Gone.* New York: Pinnacle, 1985.

Gordon, Michael R., and Gen. Bernard E. Trainor, *The Generals' War: The Inside Story of the Conflict in the Gulf.* Boston: Little, Brown, 1995.

Grady, James. "Still in Saigon," *New Republic,* Mar. 9, 1992.

Graetz, Rick. *Vietnam: Opening Doors to the World.* Helena, Mont.: American Geographic, 1988.

Grant, Bruce. *The Boat People.* Blackburn, Victoria, Australia: Penguin, 1979.

Greene, Bob. *Homecoming: When the Soldiers Returned from Vietnam.* New York: G. P. Putnam, 1989.

Greider, William. "The Rolling Stone Survey" and "Hell No, We Won't Go!" *Rolling Stone,* Apr. 7, 1988, in William Dudley and David Bender, eds., *The Vietnam War: Opposing Viewpoints.* San Diego, Calif.: Greenhaven, 2nd ed., 1990.

Gruner, Elliott. *Prisoners of Culture: Representing the Vietnam P.O.W.* New Brunswick, N.J.: Rutgers University Press, 1993.

Halloran, Richard. *To Arm a Nation: Rebuilding America's Endangered Defenses.* New York: Macmillan, 1986.

Hansel, Sarah, et al., eds. *Soldier's Heart.* Lutherville, Md.: Sidran Press, 1995.

Heinemann, Larry. "Syndrome: Making One's Way, Again, through Vietnam," *Harper's Magazine* (July 1991).

Hiebert, Murray. "A Bridge to Reform," *Far Eastern Economic Review,* July 23, 1987.

Hitchcox, Linda. *Vietnamese Refugees in Southeast Asian Camps.* New York: St. Martin's, 1991.

Howes, Craig. *Voices of the Vietnam POWs.* New York: Oxford University Press, 1993.

Human Rights Watch/Asia. *Vietnam: Human Rights in a Season of Transition.* Washington, D.C.: Human Rights Watch, 1995.

Huynh, Jade Ngoc Quang. *South Wind Changing.* St. Paul, Minn.: Graywolf, 1994.

Jensen-Stevenson, Monika, and William Stevenson. *Kiss the Boys Goodbye: How the United States Betrayed Its Own POWs in Vietnam.* New York: Dutton, 1990.

Jones, Landon Y. *Great Expectations: America and the Baby Boom Generation.* New York: Coward, McCann & Geoghegan, 1980.

Kakutani, Michiko. "Novelists and Vietnam: The War Goes On," *New York Times Book Review,* Apr. 15, 1984.

Kamm, Henry. *Dragon Ascending: Vietnam and the Vietnamese.* New York: Arcade, 1996.

Karlin, Wayne. *Lost Armies.* New York: Henry Holt, 1988.

Karlin, Wayne, Le Minh Khue, and Truong Vu, eds. *The Other Side of Heaven: Post War Fiction by Vietnamese and American Writers.* Willimantic, Conn.: Curbstone, 1995.

Karnow, Stanley. *Vietnam: A History.* New York: Viking, 1983.

Kaufman, Marc. "The Last Victims of Vietnam?" *Philadelphia Inquirer,* July 1, 1984.

———. "At the Mercy of America," *Philadelphia Inquirer Magazine,* Oct. 21, 1984.

Keating, Susan Katz. *Prisoners of Hope: Exploiting the POW/MIA Myth in America.* New York: Random House, 1994.

Keller, Morton. "Reflections on Politics and Generations in America," *Daedalus* (fall 1978).

Kirschner, George, and Eric Weisberg. "Teaching and Learning about the Vietnam War," *Social Education* (Jan. 1988).

Krall, Yung. *A Thousand Tears Falling: The True Story of a Vietnamese Family Torn Apart by War, Communism, and the CIA.* Atlanta: Longstreet, 1995.

Krepinevich, Andrew F. Jr. *The Army and Vietnam.* Baltimore: Johns Hopkins University Press, 1986.

Kulka, Richard A., et al. *Trauma and the Vietnam War Generation: Report of Findings from the National Vietnam Veterans Readjustment Study.* New York: Brunner/Mazel, 1990.

Landes, Alison, Betsie B. Caldwell, and Mark A. Siegel, eds. *Immigration and Illegal Aliens: Burden or Blessing?* Wylie, Tex.: Information Plus, 1991.

Larimer, Tim. "Vietnam's Vets Feeling Forgotten," *Washington Post,* Dec. 28, 1994.

Lelyveld, Joseph. "The Enduring Legacy," *The New York Times Magazine,* Mar. 31, 1985.

Lembcke, Jerry Lee. "The Myth of the Sat-Upon Vietnam Veteran and the Rhetorical Construction of Soldiers As Means and Ends in the Persian Gulf War," *Viet Nam Generation: A Journal of Recent History and Contemporary Culture* 6, nos. 3–4, 1995.

Levy, David W. *The Debate over Vietnam.* Baltimore: Johns Hopkins University Press, 1991.

Livingston, Gordon. "We Might as Well Forgive Ourselves," *Baltimore Sun,* May 29, 1995.

Lyons, Paul. *New Left, New Right and the Legacy of the Sixties.* Philadelphia: Temple University Press, 1996.

Ma Zongshi. "Perestroika in Vietnam: A Balance Sheet," *Indochina Report.* Singapore: Information and Resource Center (Oct.–Dec. 1988).

MacPherson, Myra. *Long Time Passing: Vietnam and the Haunted Generation.* Garden City, N.Y.: Doubleday, 1984.

Maraniss, David. *First in His Class: A Biography of Bill Clinton.* New York: Simon & Schuster, 1995.

Marshall, John Douglas. *Reconciliation Road.* Syracuse, N.Y.: Syracuse University Press, 1993.

Mason, Robert. *Chickenhawk: Back in the World.* New York: Viking, 1993.

Mather, Paul D. *M.I.A.: Accounting for the Missing in Southeast Asia.* Washington, D.C.: National Defense University Press, 1994.

Matlaw, Martha. "Teaching the Vietnam War at Full Circle High School," *Social Education* (Jan. 1988).

Merritt, William E. *Where the Rivers Ran Backward.* Athens, Ga.: University of Georgia Press, 1989.

Middleton, Drew. "Vietnam and the Military Mind," *New York Times Magazine,* Jan. 10, 1982.

Mithers, Carol Lynn. "Missing in Action: Women Warriors in Vietnam," in John Carlos Rowe and Rick Berg, eds., *The Vietnam War and American Culture.* New York: Columbia University Press, 1991.

Mueller, John. *War, Presidents and Public Opinion.* New York: Wiley, 1973.

———. "A Summary of Public Opinion and the Vietnam War," in Peter Braestrup, ed., *Vietnam As History: Ten Years After the Paris Peace Accords.* Washington, D.C.: University Press of America, 1984.

Mydans, Seth. "Preparing to Commemorate the Fall of Saigon," *New York Times,* May 1, 1995.

Nguyen Huu Tho. "Democracy: A Struggle, Not a Gift," *Vietnam Update* (summer 1989).

Nguyen Qui Duc. *Where the Ashes Are: The Odyssey of a Vietnamese Family.* Reading, Mass.: Addison Wesley, 1994.

Nguyen Thi Lieu. "Artistic Freedom in Vietnam," *Vietnam Update* (winter/spring 1988).

Nixon, Richard. *No More Vietnams.* New York: Arbor House, 1985.

Norman, Michael. Introduction in Sal Lopes, ed. *The Wall: Images and Offerings from the Vietnam Veterans Memorial.* New York: Collins, 1987.

O'Brien, Tim. "The Vietnam in Me," *New York Times Magazine,* Oct. 2, 1994.

———. *The Things They Carried.* Boston: Houghton Mifflin/Seymour Lawrence, 1990.

Oldham, Perry. "Some Further Thoughts on Teaching Vietnam Literature," *English Journal* (Dec. 1993).

Palmer, Bruce Jr. *The 25-Year War: America's Military Role in Vietnam.* Lexington, Ky.: University Press of Kentucky, 1984.

Palmer, Laura. *Shrapnel in the Heart: Letters and Remembrances from the Vietnam Veterans Memorial.* New York: Random House, 1987.

———. "The Nurses of Vietnam, Still Wounded," *New York Times Magazine,* Nov. 7, 1993.

Perl, Peter. "A Matter of Honor," *Washington Post Magazine,* Oct. 25, 1992.

Podhoretz, Norman. *Why We Were in Vietnam.* New York: Simon & Schuster, 1982.

Pollock, J. C. *Mission M.I.A.* New York: Crown, 1982.

Project on the Vietnam Generation. *Report on the Survey of Courses on Vietnam Era Events,* Washington, D.C.: Dec. 1985.

———. *Report on the Survey of Courses on Vietnam Era Events—1986 Update,* Washington, D.C.: Jan. 31, 1987.

Puller, Lewis B. *Fortunate Son.* New York: Grove Weidenfeld, 1991.

Quinn-Judge, Paul. "Peace without Honor," *Boston Globe,* Dec. 6, 1992.

Rottmann, Larry. *Voices from the Ho Chi Minh Trail.* Desert Hot Springs, Calif.: Event Horizon Press, 1993.

Rowe, John Carlos, and Rick Berg, eds. *The Vietnam War and American Culture.* New York: Columbia University Press, 1991.

Schroeder, Eric James. *Vietnam, We've All Been There: Interviews with American Writers.* Westport, Conn.: Praeger, 1992.

Scott, Wilbur J. *Politics of Readjustment: Vietnam Veterans Since the War.* New York: Aldine de Gruyter, 1993.

Shafer, D. Michael. "The Vietnam-Era Draft: Who Went, Who Didn't, and Why It Matters," in Shafer, ed., *The Legacy: The Vietnam War in the American Imagination.* Boston: Beacon, 1990.

Shaplen, Robert. *Bitter Victory.* New York: Harper & Row, 1986.

Shawcross, William. *The Quality of Mercy: Cambodia, Holocaust and Modern Conscience.* New York: Simon & Schuster, 1984.

Sheehan, Neil. *A Bright Shining Lie: John Paul Vann and America in Vietnam.* New York: Random House, 1988.

———. *After the War Was Over: Hanoi and Saigon.* New York: Random House, 1992.

Shenon, Philip. "Reaching for the Good Life in Vietnam," *New York Times Magazine,* Jan. 5, 1992.

Shultz, George P. *Turmoil and Triumph: My Years As Secretary of State.* New York: Scribner's, 1993.

Smith, Garry L. *The Search for MIAs.* Spartanburg, S.C.: Honoribus, 1992.

Spector, Ronald H. "'What Did You Do in the War, Professor?'—Reflections on Teaching About Vietnam," *American Heritage* (Dec. 1986).

Starr, Jerold M. "Teaching the Vietnam War," *Social Education* (Jan. 1988).

Stevenson, Jonathan. *Losing Mogadishu: Testing U.S. Policy in Somalia.* Annapolis, Md.: Naval Institute Press, 1995.

Stockdale, Jim and Sybil. *In Love & War.* New York: Harper & Row, 1984.

Taking the Stand: The Testimony of Lieutenant Colonel Oliver L. North. New York: Pocket, 1987.

Tal, Kali, ed. *Southeast Asian–American Communities.* Woodbridge, Conn.: Vietnam Generation, 1990.

Terry, Wallace. *Bloods: An Oral History of the War by Black Veterans.* New York: Ballantine, 1992.

Terzani, Tiziano. "Vietnam Revisited: Sweet Tears Turned Sour," *Far Eastern Economic Review,* Sept. 19, 1985.

Thomson, James C. Jr., Peter W. Stanley, and John Curtis Perry. *Sentimental Imperialists: The American Experience in East Asia.* New York: Harper & Row, 1981.

Timberg, Robert. *The Nightingale's Song.* New York: Simon & Schuster, 1995.

Toward a Market Economy in Vietnam. Rockville, Md.: Pacific Basin Research Institute, Dec. 1993.

Tu, Anh-Huong Thi. "Apocalypse Then: Going Back to Vietnam, in Memory and Spirit," *Washington Post,* Feb. 13, 1994.

Tuchman, Barbara W. *The March of Folly: From Troy to Vietnam.* New York: Knopf, 1984.

U.S. Department of Defense. *A Zero-Based Comprehensive Review of Cases Involving Unaccounted for Americans in Southeast Asia.* Nov. 13, 1995.

U.S. Department of Defense, Office of the Assistant Secretary for Force Management Policy. *Population Representation in the Military Services: Fiscal Year 1994.* Dec. 1995.

U.S. General Accounting Office. *U.S.–Vietnam Relations: Issues and Implications.* Washington, D.C.: April 1995.

U.S. House of Representatives, Committee on International Relations. *Situation in Bosnia,* hearing, June 8, 1995.

U.S. House of Representatives, Committee on International Relations. *U.S. Policy towards Bosnia,* hearing, Oct. 18 and Dec. 6, 1995.

U.S. Senate, Foreign Relations Committee. *The Peace Process in the Former Yugoslavia,* hearing, Oct. 17, 1995.

U.S. Senate Select Committee on POW/MIA Affairs. *Final Report.* Washington, D.C.: Jan. 13, 1993.

U.S. State Department, Refugee Bureau. *Report of the Indochinese Refugee Panel.* Apr. 1986.

U.S. Veterans Administration. *Myths and Realities: A Study of Attitudes toward Viet-*

nam Era Veterans. Washington, D.C.: Senate Veterans Affairs Committee, July 1980.

Van Devanter, Lynda. Home Before Morning. New York: Beaufort, 1983.

Vietnam: The Unheard Voices. Newport Beach, Calif.: Institute for Democracy in Vietnam, 1996.

Von Drehle, David. "McNamara's War over the War," Washington Post, Apr. 24, 1995.

Walker, Keith. A Piece of My Heart: The Stories of Twenty-Six American Women Who Served in Vietnam. Novato, Calif.: Presidio, 1985.

Wilcox, Fred. "Pedagogical Implications of Teaching 'Literature of the Vietnam War,'" Social Education (Jan. 1988).

Wilkinson, Alec. "A Changed Vision of God," New Yorker, Jan. 24, 1994.

Willenson, Kim. The Bad War: An Oral History of the Vietnam War. New York: New American Library, 1987.

Wilson, George. "Vietnam Revisited: Veterans Go Back to Battlefields to Lay Their Nightmares to Rest," Washington Post, Feb. 6, 1990.

Winkler, Karen J. "The Vietnam War Scores Well at the Box Office, but It Fails to Attract Many Researchers," Chronicle of Higher Education, Sept. 30, 1987.

Woodward, Bob. The Commanders. New York: Simon & Schuster, 1991.

Yearbook on International Communist Affairs, 1986. Stanford, Calif.: Hoover Institute Press, 1987.

Zaczek, Ron. Farewell, Darkness. Annapolis, Md.: Naval Institute Press, 1994.

Zaroulis, Nancy, and Gerald Sullivan. Who Spoke Up?: American Protest against the War in Vietnam, 1963–1975. Garden City, N.Y.: Doubleday, 1984.

INDEX

THE AMERICAN MOMENT
Stanley I. Kutler, Series Editor

The Library of Congress has cataloged the hardcover edition of
this book as follows:

Isaacs, Arnold R.
    Vietnam shadows : the war, its ghosts, and its legacy /
Arnold R. Isaacs.
    p.   cm.
    Includes bibliographical references and index.
    ISBN 0-8018-5605-1 (alk. paper)
    1. Vietnamese Conflict, 1961–1975—United States.
2. Vietnamese Conflict, 1961–1975—Influence.   3. United
States—History—1969–   I. Title.
DS558.I84   1997
959.7'3373—dc21   97-10823

ISBN 0-8018-6344-9 (pbk.)